THE
WILD
HORSE
CONSPIRACY

DEDICATION

To my dear family,
with me
during struggles and triumphs alike,
to comprehend,
and bring justice and freedom
to our noble horse and burro
companions on planet Earth:
mother Alice, father Robert,
brother Robert, sister Catharine,
and last but not least,
loyal friend and companion of my youth
braveheart horse Poco
—what memorable adventures we shared!
They have all stood
the true test of time,
steadfast through thick and thin.

And to all who appreciate
the spirit of freedom
that lives in the horse
and his cousin the burro.
May this spirit
more truly revive in the West
and throughout the world
as we humans
come to better comprehend
all of Life
and to share the Earth
with our fellow beings
dwelling with us here.

My sincere gratitude also to John Brian for his
support and encouragement for this book.

TABLE OF CONTENTS

INTRODUCTION

The year 2011 celebrates the fortieth anniversary of the Wild Free-Roaming Horses and Burros Act of 1971, but its true intent must be restored—as the wild herds themselves—before there can be any true celebration. My meditation upon America's last wild horses and burros appropriately recommenced on Independence Day 2007. My earlier book *Wild Horses: Living Symbols of Freedom* (Downer 1977) had been published exactly thirty years prior, as I began two years' service as a Peace Corps wildlife ecologist in western Colombia. Much water has flown under the bridge since those illustrious times, and the natural world now finds itself in more serious jeopardy, with such ominous clouds overhead as global warming, mega-extinction, and the general unraveling of the global ecosystem. Amidst this scenario, the cause of wild horses and burros and of their freedom remains as urgent as ever. Indeed, the entire horse family Equidae runs a great risk of extinction—zebras, asses, and caballine horses alike. And the preservation of wild horses and burros in the wild assumes a greater importance in light of this fact, since the true vigor of any life form is preserved *in the wild.*

These beautifully powerful and elegantly wise animals have much to offer, an important role to play in restoring planetary life, and many crucial lessons to teach us, but they are being squeezed off of their ancient North American homeland by insensitive and greedy, often vindictive and mendacious interests. Some of the more shameless even try to lay the burden of their own guilt for disrupting life on Earth upon the wild horses and burros, just as people have made them bear such physically backbreaking loads in the past. I call this "scapegoating" at its worst, and my friend and fellow activist Wild Horse Annie must surely be turning over in her grave because of this.

During the more peaceful 1970s, many of us derived inspiration from the free-living horses and burros and found comfort in our government's more evident commitment to them. The act for which we had fought so long and hard was in place. And we believed it guaranteed a viable place for the horses and burros still living upon a relatively small but significant portion of the western public lands and that this place, this freedom, would last far into the future. The disturbing fact is that this law, this sacred intent, has been grievously subverted, yet it is by no means beyond repair.

Along with the National Environmental Protection Act, the Wilderness Act, the Endangered Species Act, and the Clean Air and Clean Water Acts, the Wild Free-Roaming Horses and Burros Act helped form a wave of unprecedented, ecologically and species respectful laws that came into being during the 1960s and 1970s. These laws were our thinking and caring response as a nation to such alarms as Rachel Carson's 1962 book *Silent Spring* concerning the poisoning of our Earth by pesticides; Senator Gaylord Nelson's call for wilderness preservation and ecological responsibility; Ralph Nader's meticulous investigations and pleas for the reform of "consumerism;" and Wild Horse Annie's sympathetic and intelligent call for wild horse and burro protection and restoration, for a sharing of compassion and freedom with these wonderful presences. The serious mandate of such exemplars of conscience is to realize, inculcate, and implement a more sensitive, respectful, mindful, and responsive attitude toward the Rest of Life and the world we all share. Implicit here is the message that in preserving and restoring ecological health and integrity, people will enhance their very own quality of life by transcending human self-centeredness and thereby gaining a higher identification with life's greater whole.

During the 1960s and 1970s, there was more than just a hint of noble altruism in the air. There was a sense of farsighted valuing and humility in relation to life's greater whole. We sensed an immanence in all the vast and varied forms of life that mere material aggrandizement by humans ignored. No part of this powerful wave rose higher than the wild horse and burro movement, with its ideals concerning life's intrinsic freedom and the beauty of the natural life—both so magnificently embodied in free horses and burros. Here was a sense of higher mission unfolding over time among all ever-interrelated beings and kinds, a mission for which horses and burros living freely and naturally were indispensable. –But let us put this in the present, future-aspiring tense, for their role still unfolds today, both in North America, the horse family's evolutionary cradle, and worldwide.

We now celebrate the fortieth anniversary of the act, for the valiant spirit of this movement has never died. I know this because it has not died in me, not in my family, and not in many fellow Americans or citizens of the planet Earth. Though we advocates have witnessed the repeated and worsening betrayal of wild horses and burros by our elected representatives and public servants sworn to uphold the law, miraculously our vision has not been extinguished. Somehow we know that the horse's and the burro's—as ultimately all life's—blessed freedom will prevail and that a new enlightened age awaits all of life and soon.

In response to many unjust treatments that America's wild equids have received, I here humbly assert my testimony alongside that of many other fervid witnesses. Our aim is to shore up the wild horse and burro movement and to reinstate both species in their original, legal herd areas throughout the West, as well as in any other regions where they belong by natural and moral law. A whole mountain of grievous injustices toward our equid companions and their human supporters has simply become too burdensome. These are unique beings—amid two unique groups of beings—to whom we humans owe an enormous debt of gratitude for service rendered, even in many instances for love and loyalty unflinchingly given and to the very point of painful death. The abominable injustice to the equid spirit of freedom that is now being perpetrated can no longer be tolerated! And it is my burning hope and prayer that these horses and burros again may realize their natural place in the free order of a world that we humans—by the lofty grace of God—will most surely restore.

To this end, I have written this book; and I start with the compelling proof that wild horses and burros truly belong in North America.

1. WFHBA, aka Public Law 92-195, 16 U.S.C. 1331-1340, passed unanimously on December 15, 1971, and requires the "protection, management and control of wild free-roaming horses and burros on public lands."

2. Responsibility for implementing the act was delegated to the Bureau of Land Management through the Secretary of the Interior and the U.S. Forest Service through the Secretary of Agriculture (Section 2a).

3. In its preamble, WFHBA declares that: (a) wild horses and burros are living symbols of the historic and pioneer spirit of the West; (b) they contribute to the diversity of life forms within the nation and enrich the lives of the American people; (c) wild free-roaming horses and burros shall be protected from capture, branding, harassment or death; and (d) they are to be considered in the area where presently found [1971 as year-round habitat area] as an integral part of the natural system of public lands.

4. WFHBA (Section 8[6]) stipulates criminal penalties of up to $2,000 and/or a year in jail for violating the law. Penalties increased under the Sentencing Reform Act of 1984, and fines can now be as high as $100,000 and/or ten years in prison for violating WFHBA.

5. BLM and USFS must manage wild horses and burros so as "to achieve and maintain a thriving natural ecological balance on the public lands" and "at the minimum feasible level." (Section 3[a])

6. WFHBA (Section 2[c]) defines a wild horse/burro range, or legal area, as "the amount of land necessary to sustain an existing herd or herds of wild free-roaming horses and burros ... and which is devoted **principally** but not necessarily

exclusively to their welfare in keeping with the multiple use management concept for the public lands." [Emphasis added.]

7. The Federal Land Policy and Management Act of 1976 (FLPMA) amended WFHBA to allow for helicopter roundups. Earlier in 1959, the Wild Horse Annie Bill (Public Law 86-234) had prohibited the use of motor vehicles in rounding up or "hunting" wild horses and burros as well as the "pollution" or poisoning of their watering holes. FLPMA requires the development of land use plans that incorporate sustained yield and multiple use principles.

8. The Public Rangelands Improvement Act of 1978 (PRIA) also amended the WFHBA. It required a current inventory of wild horses and burros to determine appropriate management levels, or AMLs, meaning the number of wild horses/burros sustainable by the resources of the range. Under this law, AMLs are supposed to be adjusted according to resource availability. The law also involved the definition of "excess" wild horses or burros for any given legal area.

9. In 2004, the Burns Amendment to the WFHBA facilitated disposal of wild horses and burros to slaughter buyers for horses or burros who are either over ten years of age or who have been offered unsuccessfully for adoption three times.

10. The National Environmental Policy Act (NEPA) also governs how the wild horses and burros are treated, as this act requires environmental assessments/environmental impact statements of any action that might have a major impact on any and all aspects of our life and world, including wild horses and burros.

11. Code of Federal Regulations 4710.5 and 4710.6 specifically provide for the curtailment or cancellation of livestock grazing privileges on public lands in order to ensure thriving healthy herds of wild horses and burros in their legal areas.

12. Section 6 of WFHBA authorizes cooperative agreements with landowners and state and local governments to better

accomplish the goals of the act. This allows for providing complete and unimpeded habitats for long-term viable wild horse/burro populations.

13. Section 2 (b) of WFHBA defines "wild free-roaming horses and burros" as "all unbranded and unclaimed horses and burros on public lands of the United States," meaning BLM and USFS lands and possibly other agency lands as well.

14. Section 3 (a) of WFHBA authorizes the designation of specific ranges on public lands as sanctuaries for the protection and preservation of wild horses and burros upon consultation with state wildlife agencies.

15. Section 3 (d) prohibits selling any deceased wild horse or burro or part thereof, i.e., no commercialization.

16. Section 7 authorizes creation of the wild horse and burro advisory board.

17. Section 8 allows power of arrest by a federal employee of anyone violating WFHBA in his/her presence.

18. Section 10 mandates a report to Congress on the wild horse and burro program every two years and also authorizes studies of wild horses and burros.

19. Section 4 allows public officials to remove wild horses and burros that stray onto private property, but also allows private landowners to maintain wild free-roaming horses or burros on their private lands or on lands leased from the Government provided that they do so in a manner that protects them from harassment and that the animals were not willfully removed or enticed from the public lands. The latter must keep the federal government informed of the number of wild horses and burros so maintained. This is an outstanding opportunity for the public to help in preserving and protecting the wild horse and burro herds at healthy population levels, i.e., to complement federal herd areas and territories.

CHAPTER I

EVOLUTION & HISTORY OF WILD HORSES, BURROS & THEIR KIN IN NORTH AMERICA

Because the political establishment on public lands today is mainly supportive of livestock, big game, and other exploitive interests, it has targeted wild horses and burros for discrediting and removal, or at best minimization at overly reduced and restricted, non-viable population levels. As a consequence, the positive aspects of equid history and ecology upon this continent are being ignored. When brought up, these are often rudely denied; and, frequently, evidence in support of the horses/burros is sabotaged. As with the animals themselves, wild horse and burro advocates have been unfairly discriminated against and maligned. They find themselves passed over, transferred, or dismissed from professional positions affecting the equids even in spite of outstanding qualifications. Too often the valid message borne in the hearts and minds of wild equid supporters, which transmits their greater story, has been thoughtlessly squelched by a power-obsessed media beholden to rancher, hunter, and other big economic interests.

During the mid-1990s, horse remains were discovered by placer miners in the Yukon. They were well preserved in the permafrost and seemed to have died recently, yet proved to be approximately twenty-five thousand years old. Their rufous color, flaxen mane, and solid hooves had the aspect of a typical, small and wiry mustang of the West. Based on external morphology, the specimen was identified as the "Yukon horse," whose Latin name is *Equus lambei;* but, intrigued, the paleontologists conducted a genetic analysis of this specimen that showed it to be one and the same as the modern horse: *Equus caballus.* Further independent analysis conclusively proved this. With this substantiation came a more widespread recognition of wild horses as returned native species in North America (Kirkpatrick and Fazio 2008). According to Forsten (1992): "The early branching-off time indicated by *mtDNA* [mitochondrial DNA] supports an origin of the caballoids [the horse branch of the horse family: Equidae] in the New World, and the fossil record suggests an even rather late dispersal to [the] Old World."

The fact that the Yukon horse is genetically identical with the modern horse reveals the latter to be one of the most deeply rooted and justifiable natives in North America. This native status is additionally substantiated by its large geographic distribution upon this continent that is evident from the fossil record and the great variety of ecosystems in which it can adapt and live. The modern horse traces back ca. 2 million years in its present form, but actually should be regarded in the continuous context of equid evolution that dates back at least 58 million years in North America (MacFadden 1992, 304).

When contemplating the horse and its kindred, we should not limit ourselves to their historical association with man alone, as do many. We should consider this prodigious group within time's vaster dimension. Here is a revealing quote from MacFadden (1992, 300): "...the general community structure in which horses evolved has a longevity of over 200 myr [million years]....[E]arliest terrestrial communities... arose several times independently...in North America, Eurasia, South Africa. An important point here is that even though the taxonomic compositions...are quite different, there are many ecological similarities, most notably trophic specializations and the relative numbers of herbivores versus carnivores seen in this."

Spanning approximately seven thousand years, the history of equids as domestic species under man's control is a mere drop in the bucket when compared with these species' millions of years of evolution in the wild. While much the same can be said about any domesticated species, there is something very graphic and compelling about the horse's well-evidenced story as a symbol for all life's story. For the horse living unfettered, striving forth in the world of nature, eloquently expresses life's inalienable freedom and pursuit of higher end.

All branches of the horse family (Equidae) share an ancient evolutionary origin and long-standing duration *in North America*. Perhaps no other family can lay more claim to native status and belonging here. (Two other families to consider are the camel family and the pronghorn family, both rooted in North America.) From George Gaylord Simpson (1951) to Bruce MacFadden (1992), various scientists have described the horse family's fascinating story; and their works reveal the ascent of many distinctive yet interwoven equid genera and species over the eons. The horse family has naturally branched out to all continents except Australia (prior to the arrival of whites) and Antarctica. These animals have contributed positively to our planetary communities, and they continue to do so in many ways and on many levels today.

The rapid reoccupation of vacant niches in North America may be viewed as corroborating the equids' return to ancestral grounds. In the words of the Plains Indians: "The grass remembers the horses." Such does not occur with just any species. Also, North America has been greatly reduced in large herbivore and carnivore species since the last Ice Age when a massive die-off of large animals, predators as well as herbivores, occurred (Benton 1991). It is estimated that some three-quarters of large mammals (approximately thirty-three genera) died out, including all of the elephants, tapirs, peccaries, camels, ground sloths, as well as various predators and deer, according to Benton (page 135). Though this "great Pleistocene extinction" has been attributed to a combination of overkill by Amerindian hunters, climatic changes, and disease, it now appears that the strong impact of a large meteorite in the subarctic ice fields of northeastern North America may have triggered this process (University of Cincinnati 2008).

MORE RECENT DATES FOR HORSE PRESENCE IN NORTH AMERICA

Though obstinately resisted, a considerable body of evidence has surfaced concerning the more recent survival of the horse species in North America. Though the prevailing view maintains that the entire horse family died out around ten thousand years ago at the end of Earth's last major glaciation, evidence for horse presence from anywhere from a little over seven thousand YBP (years before present) to less than 1,000 YBP is too substantial to dismiss. Among other lines of evidence, this comes in the form of fossil bones that have been age-dated to more recent times, horse geoglyphs (ground drawings) dated to about one thousand years ago (Joseph 1999), and petroglyphs, or stone depictions (see Figure 1).

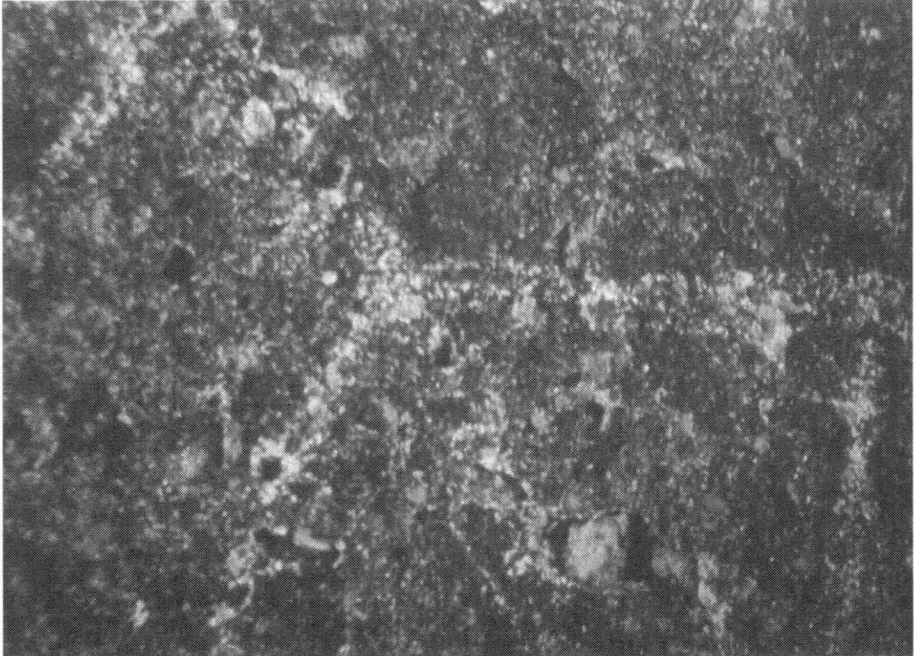

Figure 1. Horse petroglyph discovered in the summer of 2002 by author west of White Mountains, eastern California.

Carbon-14 datings of mitochondrial DNA (passed along the maternal line) have been meticulously analyzed by Dr. Ann Forsten (1992) and have substantiated the origin of the modern horse in North America at 1.7 MYA (million years ago). The full significance of this is still sinking in and should soon result in the horse being treated as a native wildlife species.

The *FaunMap* produced and published by the Illinois State Museum of Springfield, revealed a number of horse fossil datings within the post-Pleistocene and pre-Columbian period that occurred well after the time at which all members of the horse family are commonly believed to have disappeared from North America. Some of these are quite close to Columbus's discovery of America in 1492 (Illinois State Museum 2004).

SUPPRESSION OF EVIDENCE SUPPORTING WILD HORSES IN THE WILD

As concerns the *FaunMap*, the paleontologist in charge of this revealing compilation and who provided me with a copy now seems to have deleted all more recent fossil datings that disagreed with prevailing theory of horse die-off approximately ten thousand years ago. Such suppression of facts related to the horse's more recent presence in North, Central, and South America has repeatedly cropped up during my years of investigation. This is often traceable to high-handedness by established interests bent on discrediting the place of the horse or burro as native species in the Americas. Often at the root of this prejudice lie the livestock and big-game hunter establishments with their desire to secure the *status quo* and to even further monopolize public lands. The current Secretary of Interior Kenneth Salazar, a cattle rancher from Colorado who oversees the BLM, made a public statement prior to his appointment that wild horses do not belong on public lands. In North America, the Wild Free-Roaming Horses and Burros Act only gives legal right for wild horses and burros on about one-sixth of the public Bureau of Land Management (BLM) and U.S. Forest Service (USFS) lands according to these agencies' own recognition, and livestock already occupy ca. 95% of these lands and a similar percentage applies to big game animals. Yet in spite of this, greedy interests continue to egg for the further elimination of wild horses and burros in the wild (Appendix I Forever Wild and Free speech: available by request from author; Wuerthner and Matteson 2002).

According to the U.S. General Accounting Office (GAO) and contrary to BLM's claims: as of 1990 "wild horses consume much less than 40% of the available forage in areas where found. In the four Nevada resource areas [GAO] reviewed, wild horses consumed 19 percent of the available forage compared with 81 percent by domestic livestock" (U.S. General Accounting Office 1990, 55). It bears noting that present figures would be about half of the above, given the draconian wild horse roundups that have taken place since 1990, especially during the G. W. Bush administration and continuing into the Obama administration—both being virtual pawns of the public lands ranchers. "Bush & Company" removed approximately eighty thousand of these magnificent animals from their legal herd management areas and herd areas as well as territories. And the Obama administration has only stepped up roundups (Stampede to Oblivion 2009; also see www.wildhorsepreservation.org).

SIDEBAR: USEFUL DEFINITIONS: Herd areas are the original BLM areas where the wild horses and burros were found in 1971 at the passage of the act in their year-round occupied habitats. Here they have legal status to remain. Herd management areas are usually diminished though in some cases are equivalent areas where BLM has decided to manage for wild horse/burros. So, ironically, what is called a herd area has become synonymous with a zeroed-out, though still nominally legal, area for wild horses/burros. On USFS lands the designation is wild horse/burro territory.

With the one-track mind of a hunter, enemies have targeted wild horses and burros for discrediting in the public eye and for elimination, even from the minor portion of the public lands where they have a legal right to live. A large part of this conspiracy involves the subversion of honest scientific inquiry. Though, compelled by the overwhelming evidence, the latter persists in its attempts to reveal the greater story of the horse family, genus, and species, particularly within its evolutionary cradle and place of long-standing development: North America.

Recently an exhibit in Toronto's natural history museum highlighted the origin and long-standing evolution of the horse in North America. But according to reports I received, this was deliberately sabotaged by physically defacing and removing parts of the exhibit by those resenting both the proof of evolution and the native place of the horse in North America. Similar suppressive acts I have witnessed reveal a hysterical, knee-jerk campaign amongst anti-wild-horse segments. Chomping down on a beef steak or a hamburger or blasting some innocent animal appear to be their idea of the ultimate good, while anything that stands in the way of this they ferociously attack, for definitely at gut level! With wild horse enemies, we are dealing with visceral appetites and blindly followed habits and traditions that seek to press their advantage and force their way. But higher justice-seeking walks hand-in-hand with the objective pursuit of greater truth as concerns all living kinds and the realization of each kind's fitting place in the world.

PETROGLYPHS, HORSE FOSSILS, GEOGLYPHS, AND MORE CONCEALMENT

California Finds

During the summer of 2002, I visited the austere White Mountains east of the towering, snow-capped Sierra Nevada near Bishop, California. This ancient range rises to over thirteen thousand feet at Boundary Peak and contains one of the most ancient life forms on Earth: the majestic, die-hard Bristlecone Pine, one of which has been dated to near nine thousand years of age (Cohen 1998, 47). Intrigued by this atmospheric region on the edge of eastern California and western Nevada, I went on to explore the desert valley just to the west of these mountains. Here I came upon some fascinating petroglyphs dating from modern times to a few thousand years ago. These artful designs had been painstakingly chiseled with hard tools on granite to form hypnotizing spirals, geometrical checkerboards, arrowheads, lances, strange anthrozooic (man-animal) figures, eagles, bighorn sheep with large, curved horns, and then, much to my amazement, a definite horse figure, without apparent rider, bridle, rope, or saddle, rendered in simple rectilinear fashion—but with proportions unmistakably those of a horse (see Figure 1).

Judging from the brownish oxidation on the chiseling, this horse was not a recent addition to the ancient petroglyphs here. Scientific analysis of the patina of some of these petroglyphs has revealed ages in excess of three thousand years. By visually comparing patina hues, I estimated this horse could be well over one thousand years old.

Excited about this intriguing find but wary of those who might seek to remove or destroy it, I informed Dr. Steven Jones at Brigham Young University in Utah. Dr. Jones is an anthropologist interested in ancient horse fossils and Amerindian depictions of horses. He seemed quite intrigued and said he had funds to date both fossils and petroglyphs pertaining to a possible "pre-Columbian/post-Pleistocene" presence of horses in North America. He had earlier done some horse fossil datings that contradicted the established theory that horses had died out approximately ten thousand years ago and was collecting a wealth of supportive information such as that from the Little Box Elder Cave, located in Converse County, Wyoming. At his suggestion, I made some initial inquiries at the BLM office in Bishop, California, and spoke with their government archeologist. The latter indicated that a professional archeologist or anthropologist associated with a recognized research institute would have to be involved in any dating of the artifact. Here I was counting on Dr. Jones to follow through, but one year turned into two, and two years into four, etc., and still no professional action has resulted. Again, I perceive an underhanded manipulation by the anti-wild-horse establishment pulling the political strings at both academic and government land management levels. Recently I learned that Dr. Jones was dismissed from his position at Brigham Young University. The reason, I gathered, was political differences with the power establishment at this institution.

Regarding Dr. Jones's findings, a horse fossil that hails from the Little Box Elder Cave was age dated to ca. 700 YBP. Though this date is well before Columbus's arrival in America in 1492, but long after the commonly accepted extinction of horses in North America, this very newsworthy discovery has been ignored by establishment paleontology as by the news media in general.

Joseph (1999) revealed geoglyphs depicting horses in the Mojave desert near Blythe in southeast California. These were also featured in another scholarly work as an eight-meter horse geoglyph pictured alongside a twenty-five-meter human (White 2003, 206). There are two horses among these several geoglyphs, collectively known as the Blythe Giants and representing the Earth Figure Tradition, which overlaps with the Great Basin Tradition. They were formed by removing stones of desert pavement to reveal lighter substrata, a process called *intaglio*, often associated with trails and dance circles formed by the pounding of human feet. They indicate that horses were held in high regard by Amerindians and in relatively recent times. The figures have been expertly dated by geologists from the University of California-Berkeley at 900 AD +/- 100 years and were first discovered by pilots from the U.S. Army Air Corps flying between Hoover Dam and Los Angeles in 1932. They are presently under the care of the Bureau of Land Management, whose officials seem in no way anxious to advertise their significance. But as Joseph puts it: "This [figure] meant that someone in California knew enough about the horse to represent it on the desert floor...centuries before the Spaniards re-introduced the animal to North America" (Joseph 1999, 12). Though airline pilots and later observant investigators and writers have instantaneously recognized this figure as a horse, BLM officials claim it depicts a puma and have restricted the public from accessing the area and deciding for themselves (see Figure 2).

Figure 2. Horse geoglyph, Mojave Desert, southeast California, dated to about nine hundred years ago (Joseph 1999).

Could the Mojave Indians inhabiting this region have depicted a remnant native wild horse population, or was this horse brought over from the Old World by other peoples, such as the Scandinavians, Celts, or Chinese (Thompson 2006; M. A. Simonds 2008)? This is a subject for further research and should be linked to a professional age dating of the horse petroglyph I found, again on BLM land and not far to the north in central eastern California.

ARGENTINEAN FIND

Flying far to the south, another similar experience involved my visit to the national Natural Sciences Museum in Buenos Aires, Argentina, during November 2004. As one of the world's few in-depth investigators of the endangered mountain tapir (*Tapirus pinchaque*) (see www.andeantapirfund.com), I asked museum officials for permission to examine any tapir bones, teeth, or other fossilized or semi-fossilized remains. But I soon learned that their tapir specimens were meager. Undaunted,

I turned my attention to their abundant horse collection. I recalled that, similar to the case with tapirs, at least two genera in the horse family had entered South America from North America during the connection of North with South America via the Isthmus of Panama ca. 3 MYA (million years ago). These were *Hippidion*, whose presence in South America extended from the mid-Pliocene (ca. 3 MYA) to the mid-Pleistocene (ca. 1 MYA) and then again the modern genus *Equus* from the mid-Pleistocene (ca. 1 MYA) into the Recent epoch (our present time period).

While examining one well-preserved *Equus* mandible, I was surprised to find a tarry substance exuding from this semi-fossilized bone. I immediately brought this to the attention of my facilitator, Dr. Alejandro Kramartz. We discussed the possibility of a more recently surviving horse, perhaps persisting to the date of the European discovery of the Americas. Kramartz considered it possible that the horses and donkeys that Europeans had brought over could have interbred with native surviving equids thus masking the latter's original presence in South America. We both agreed that the *Equus* specimen should be age dated and that the program of Dr. Steven Jones in Utah should be contacted to support a state-of-the-art carbon-14 age dating.

As I was about to leave the museum to return to the lively streets of Buenos Aires on the afternoon in question, I noticed an older, gray-haired museum official perhaps in his seventies or eighties. To my surprise, he wore a scowl on his face, uttered a complaining moan, and conveyed a covert hostility through his body language after overhearing my conversation and plans with Dr. Kramartz. Though I gave his comportment little thought at the time, I later had reason to consider it significant.

When I informed Dr. Jones of my find, he seemed quite enthused, stating that he had funds for just such an age dating. (He was still working on the possibility of age dating the petroglyph I had discovered.) I immediately conveyed this good news to Dr. Kramartz and details of the specimen's ID number and substantiated provenance, etc., were obtained. However, again, as weeks turned into months, then months into years, I discovered that the bureaucracy at the museum was unwilling to have even a tiny sliver of this *Equus* bone express delivered to a car-bon-14 age-dating laboratory in Florida, whose charges, including ship-ping, Dr. Jones would have gladly assumed. Clearly someone had put the kibosh on our exciting find and for reasons I believe to be very much the same as those plaguing the North American establishment. No ex-cuse was ever offered to me, but as I have come to realize, the livestock culture is quite cosmopolitan and quickly closes ranks against any pos-sible competitor for grass and water. Its tentacles are far-reaching, and its minds are closed.[1]

Further investigations of South American paleontology revealed a nu-merous contingent of professionals who maintained that native wild horses *did* survive prior and right up to the arrival of modern-day Europeans with their European horses into South America ca. 1500 AD. These held that aboriginal South American horses mixed with the European horses and that their hybrid descendants carry on to this day among the famed wild horses of the Pampas of Argentina. Perhaps the old crouching man in the museum did not want to have entrenched theory, i.e., that of horse extinction in South America, exposed by the inconvenient but very substantial specimen Dr. Kramartz and I had no-ticed. This makes me wonder whether this specimen is still even there!

What hand might the gigantic cattle/sheep culture in Argentina be play-ing in suppressing evidence concerning the horse's native place in the Americas? Worldwide, livestock cultures tend to monopolize the land for purposes of increasing production and profits and to the exclusion of so many valuable and meritorious native species. Yet these species most definitely lend balance and greater ecological health to the land that is their ancient home. I also question why Simpson (1951, 198) in his classical and oft-cited work summarily dismisses as mere legend the possibility that "wild horses still lived in the Argentine when the Spaniards arrived there and that their blood is mingled with that of the *jinetas* (thoroughbred Spanish horses) in the feral pampas horses..." based solely on Dr. Angel Cabrera's very dated evaluation (Cabrera and

---

1 Perhaps no nation in the world is so dominated by the livestock culture as Argentina, unless it be

 neighboring Uruguay; and many of the gauchos suffer from protein poisoning because they eat too

 much meat.

Yepes 1940), one made without the advantage of modern fossil dating techniques. My encounter of the tar-exuding horse skull fossil in the *Museo Argentino de Ciencias Naturales* in Buenos Aires in October 2004, provides a tantalizing clue that should be pursued. Unfortunately certain obstructions posed by bureaucrats have thwarted the age dating for which I still hope. These very obstructions indicate there may be something substantial to this find.

HOLLAND HAGUE'S RESEARCH

Coming back to North America, I quote from a letter of December 11, 2007, written by Holland Hague and from a conversation with him on August 19, 2011. Holland is a lifelong, amateur researcher from Virginia now in his mid-sixties and advocate of a native surviving horse population at the time of the European "discovery" of America in 1492:

> The Wolf Spider Cave [Colorado] horse bone was accurately dated to 700 years before present by Dr. Steven Jones, but now both Dr. Jones and the whereabouts of the bone seem to have dropped out of sight.
>
> Here is a passage from Gunnar Thompson [2006]: "... [in] *Secret Voyages* on page 107 [is] described the "Inca" bronze horse pin that was identified in a publication by the New York Natural History Museum. Also the Utz-Oneata inscription [from Missouri] was dated by radiocarbon to 1300 A.D.—though the archeologist assumed it had to be a "deer"—but that was just because of the assumption of horse extinction which is unproven....keep in mind that the Icelandic Sagas report horses in [Estotiland]...in the 10th or 11th Century...the horses were here. In more recent developments, another contact of mine has done some DNA testing of West Coast mustangs and has found that the DNA is not consistent with a post-Columbus horse introduction."

One point is certain: not only anecdotal, but much factual evidence in North America exists to support the horse's presence on this continent at more recent times than current theory allows. Why is this evidence being ignored, suppressed, and in some cases even destroyed? Such evidence is widespread throughout the continent and is substantiated by radioactive carbon-14 (C-14) dating, among many other lines of evidence.

SHIELD TRAP FOSSIL SITE

One of the most convincing series of finds comes from the Shield Trap fossil site in Carbon County, Montana (Illinois State Museum 2004)[2].

Here four strata have been excavated. In Stratum I, part of the late Holocene period, carbon dating from bone collagen samples (collagen consisting of the fibrous albuminoid component of bone) from two different horses has yielded precise edge dates of 1745 and 1270 YBP (Years Before Present). In Stratum II, dating between 5490 and 2185 YBP, four different individual horse dates have been obtained. Three of these were again obtained from bone collagen, as well as from cartilage and other connective tissue types. These dated at 3190, 2675, and 2185 YBP. A fourth horse C-14 dating was done from charcoal associated with the fossil and produced the extraordinarily young date of 620 YBP, indicating the distinct possibility of horse presence in North America just over a century prior to Columbus's arrival in America. Though the latter was inconsistent with the date of the soil of Stratum II, it is not uncommon for earth movements or erosion to produce such mixing. If contamination can be ruled out, this fossil could go a long way toward proving the continuous occupation of North America from ancient times to the arrival of Europeans and the reintroduction of horses to North America.

In Stratum III of the Shield Trap fossil site, seven C-14 datings again revealed horse presence at later dates than is recognized by mainstream paleontology. Stratum III extends from 7540 to 5490 YBP and is in the Middle Holocene period. C-14 dates obtained from charcoal from five

2 This is located on the east Pryor Mountain quadrangle (7.5 minute map)

horses yielded dates of 7540, 7540, 7540, 7165, and 7165, while the two horse fossils that were C-14 age dated from bone collagen yielded 7245 and 5490 YBP. The age datings ca. 7000 YBP were more accepted by the establishment in past years than in recent years due to more recent refinements in C-14 age-dating techniques that yielded older dates. Nonetheless, the 5490 YBP age dating is remarkable and substantiates a later survival of the horse in North America. Recently surfaced DNA discoveries in soils in Alaska renew our credence in horse presence in North America that is less than eight thousand years ago (see Haile et al. 2009 and page 19 in Chapter I).

Covering between 9230 and 7165 YBP representing the early Middle Holocene, the deepest Stratum IV yielded only one horse C-14 dating at 9230 YBP from bone collagen. Still this date is substantially later than what has been given as the last extant horse in North America by several authorities.

The horse fossil series at Shield Trap gives solid evidence for a continuous horse lineage from the time of the "Great Die Out" at the close of the Pleistocene to modern times, i.e., after the advent of Columbus and the European colonization of the Americas. The area around the site should be explored for additional fossils to further substantiate these findings.

OTHER INTRIGUING FOSSIL SITES

Still another well confirmed series of dating for a horse fossil comes from the earlier mentioned Wolf Spider Cave in Colorado. These yield a date of 700 +/- 50 YBP and are clearly post-Pleistocene and pre-Columbian and, again, not far before the arrival of Columbus in 1492. The Wolf Spider horse was dated by Elaine Anderson, whose expertise is highly regarded by professionals in the field of paleontology. The Pratt Cave fossil site in Texas has a horse fossil that has been dated to about ten times that of Wolf Spider, or 7080 +/- 40 YBP; and another possible post-Pleistocene and pre-Columbian horse fossil is reported from Quintano Roo, Yucatan, Mexico. This has been C-14 dated at 1280 YBP.

However there is some question as to whether this is, indeed, a horse fossil. Further professional investigation is in order.

Many other sites yield horse fossils with scientific datings that indicate more recent horse survival (see Figure 3). These datings range from the High Holocene (HIHO) 0 to 450 YBP, the Late Holocene (LHOL) 450 to 4500 YBP, the Middle Holocene (MHOL) 3500 to 8500 YBP, and the more generalized catchall early Holocene/middle Holocene (EMHO) 3500 to 10,500 YBP. (See Sidebar.)

SIDEBAR: LIST OF HORSE FOSSIL SITES.
(SEE TEXT FOR MEANINGS OF ABBREVIATIONS.)

Some of the fossil sites are:

1. Ventana Cave, Arizona: two horses from LHOL, one from MHOL, one from HIHO

2. Awatovi, Arizona: one horse from HIHO

3. Fort Davy Crocket, Colorado: one horse from HIHO

4. Kin Tl'iish, Colorado: one horse from LHOL

5. Long House, Colorado: one horse from LHOL

6. Merina, Colorado: one horse from LHOL

7. Cemochechobee, Georgia: one horse from LHOL

8. Calf Island, Massachusetts: one horse from HIHO

9. Blacktail Cave, Montana: one horse from MHOL

10. Hoffer, Montana: one horse from LHOL, two horses from HIHO

11. Amahami, North Dakota: one horse from LHOL, one horse from HIHO

12. Navajo Reservoir Site LA 3430, New Mexico: two horses from LHOL

13. Fort Randall Historic Site, South Dakota: one horse from LHOL

14. H. P. Thomas, South Dakota: one horse from HIHO; one from LHOL

15. Lubbock Lake, Texas: one horse from EMHO, one from MHOL, one from LHOL

16. Site 45AS80, Washington: one horse from LHOL

17. Chief Joseph Dam Site 450K2, Washington: one horse from HIHO, one from LHOL

18. Chief Joseph Dam Site 450K258, Washington: one horse from LHOL, two horses from HIHO

19. Site 48UT370, Wyoming: one horse from MHOL

Two other sites for which evidence exists for more recently dated horse fossils are: one site near Rock Springs, Wyoming (post-Columbian but still with intriguing fossil horse skeleton), 429 YBP; and the Horsethief Cave fossil site also in Wyoming that has produced a horse femur dated by thermoluminescent means to 3124 YBP. Similar records have been reported from Canada and parts of Mexico, and Central and South America.

The dates of 1,000 YBP or less, such as from the Shield Trap fossil site and from Wolf Spider and Little Box Elder caves, lend particular weight to the hypothesis that remnant horses survived to the time of the colonization of the Americas by Europeans. These remnant survivors could have interbred with European-derived horses, especially those escaped to the wild, the denominated *mostrencos* (Spanish for "unclaimed"), or mustangs. This is an intriguing possibility that should be investigated using state-of-the-art genetic analysis—and soon. To sum up, we have at least fifty different horse fossils from twenty-three different sites including in the East, the West, the North, and the South of the United States and the Americas. The majority of these indicate a much wider horse distribution and at much later dates than is commonly accepted by mainstream paleontologists today (see Figure 3).

EVIDENCE	LOCATION	AGE DATING	METHOD	REFERENCE
Horse Geoglyph, Intaglio (Fig. 2)	Blythe Giant Figures, SE Cal.	900 A.D. +/- 100 years	Ground surface weathering	Joseph, 1999. White, 2003
Horse (Fig. 1) Petroglyph	BLM land, Central E. Cal.	Rough estimat. 1,000 - 3000 ybp	Associated figures, patina.	Downer, C.C., present work
Horse Fossil	Little Box Elder Cave, Converse County, Wyom.	700 years before present (ybp)	Carbon 14	Dan Walker, paleontological worker, Wyom.
Horse Fossil Skull w/ organic exudation	Argentina. In Nat. Hist. Mus. Buenos Aires	Rough Estim. Pre Colum./Post Pleistocene	Remains to be professionally dated	Downer, C.C., present work
2 different Horse Fossils from Stratum I	Shield Trap, Carbon County, Montana	1745 ybp & 1270 ybp	Carbon 14 from bond collagen	Illinois State Museum, Springfield
3 different Horse Fossils from Stratum II	Shield Trap, Carbon County, Montana	3190 ybp, 2675 ybp, 2185 ybp	Carbon 14 from bond collagen	Illinois State Museum, Springfield
1 Horse Fossil from Stratum II	Shield Trap, Carbon County, Montana	620 years before present	Carbon 14 from charcoal assoc. with fossil	Illinois State Museum, Springfield
5 Horse Fossils from Stratum III	Shield Trap, Carbon County, Montana	3 at 7540 ybp & 2 at 7165 ybp	Carbon 14 from charcoal assoc with fossil	Illinois State Museum, Springfield
2 Horse Fossils from Stratum III	Shield Trap, Carbon County, Montana	7245 ybp & 5490 ybp	Carbon 14 from bond collagen	Illinois State Museum, Springfield
1 Horse Fossil from Stratum IV	Shield Trap, Carbon County, Montana	9230 ybp	Carbon 14 from bond collagen	Illinois State Museum, Springfield
Horse Fossil	Wolf Spider Cave, Colorado	700 +/- 50 ybp	Carbon 14	Elaine Anderson paleontologist
Horse Fossil	Pratt Cave, Tex.	7080 +/- 40 ybp	Carbon 14	Dr. Steven Jones, Paleont. Utah.
Horse Fossil	Horsethief Cave, Wyoming	3124 ybp	Thermolumines-cent	Dan Walker, palenont. Wyom

Figure 3. Pre-Columbian and Post-Pleistocene Horse Fossils and Other Types of Evidence with Dating, Location, and Source.

In addition to the above, several horse fossils have been dated by association from the geological strata in which they were found and also fall within the post-Pleistocene and pre-Columbian period. They proceed from such disparate areas as: (1) the Spencer and Laatch Archeological Mound, Wisconsin; (2) Truman Reservoir, Missouri; (3) the Hopewell Burial Mound, Ohio; (4) prehistoric Indian kitchen middens of Arizona, ca. 3000 YBP (see Groves 1974; Downer 1977); and (5) reportedly from Winnemucca Lake Flats, just east of Pyramid Lake, Nevada. Apparently the fossils of Winnemucca Lake were discovered ca. 1978 and dated to ca. 1,000 YBP by the University of Nevada, though later all trace and record of this horse fossil appear to have vanished under suspect circumstances (Holland Hague, pers. comm. and documents in his possession).

The myth of the destructive, non-native horse is rapidly falling by the wayside, as people broaden their horizons in regard to the horse's deeply rooted North American presence and the many substantial contributions it makes to the native ecosystem. And, as earlier mentioned, an exciting analysis of the DNA contained in the soils of permafrost regions of Alaska has come to light proving that both horses and mammoths were present in North America thousands of years later than previously thought. This is a comeback to what was espoused for decades by paleontologists, i.e., horse presence upon this continent to approximately seven thousand years ago. An international team of scientists assembled at Camp Stevens, Alaska, conducted this study, and its results are most encouraging for those who sense the horse's true belonging in North America (Haile et al. 2009).

DISTINCTIVE RACES

Do distinctive races of both North and South American wild horses still survive? Could one be the Kiger mustang of southern Oregon (See Figures 37 & 38 in Additional Photos)? According to local reports, the animated horses of the intriguing Steens Mountains and adjacent Alvord Desert avoid breeding with other wild horses, as though instinctively seeking to preserve their own special character. Perhaps genetic analysis would reveal unique genetic markers if tissue samples could be taken from a few of the remaining Kiger mustangs and analyzed. Is it possible that a small remnant of aboriginal horses survived in this remote region, managing to escape the devastation brought by "civilized" humanity? Unfortunately, our "public servants," meaning the BLM officials in charge, have already nearly eliminated these unique and intriguing mustangs. They have overly managed these hardy survivors, toward whom a policy of either minimization or elimination has prevailed, as they cater to established livestock, hunter, or other interests who exclude the wild horses from their value system and are bound and determined to monopolize the public lands.

A young stallion from the Kiger herd became the model for the main character in the popular animated movie *Spirit: Stallion of the Cimarron*. I visited this stallion, also named "Spirit," in the Return to Freedom wild horse sanctuary near Lampoc, California, where Neda de Mayo oversees his care. Karen Sussman of the International Society for the Protection of Mustangs and Burros (ISPMB) also preserves unique blood lines, e.g., White Sands mustangs from New Mexico in her sanctuary in South Dakota.

As earlier indicated, South American reports of a distinctive type of wild horse still inhabiting the Pampas and Patagonian regions have come to my attention; and I briefly glimpsed a few of these fleeting bands during my travels there. These horses run free as the wind against the backdrop of the towering, snow-capped Andes to the west. Some display a unique purplish-pinkish coloration and a conformation found no where else. In fact, many reports of native surviving horses predating Columbus exist among the Amerindians of Patagonia. Comparative genetic, morphological, and paleontological studies along with historical investigations could yield enlightening finds, maybe even proof of a native surviving horse present to greet its cousins when the Spanish brought Andalusian horses across the Atlantic to this "land of the bigfoot".

TWO HYPOTHESES

In summary, much evidence exists for horse presence in the Americas, especially North America, during the post-Pleistocene and pre-Columbian period at dates scattered through the period beginning ca. 10,000 YBP and reaching very near to 1492 AD. Two hypotheses have been proposed to explain these apparent anomalies:

(1) A continuous lineage of horses survived in small remnants up until the reintroduction of European horses. When the latter escaped from or were released by the Spanish, other Europeans, or Amerindians, they thrived on the plains and southwestern deserts in the very land of their evolutionary origin as a species and reproductively intermingled with the already present, aboriginal horses. Populations of these aboriginal horses were absorbed by the greater influx of horses brought over by colonists, conquistadors, etc., many of whom derived from Spanish haciendas or Catholic missions. The distinctively American traits of certain wild horse populations lend support to this hypothesis as do depictions of un-mounted horses *au naturel* in geoglyphs and petroglyphs, some of which are dated hundreds of years before the arrival of Columbus (see Figures 1 and 2).

(2) Horses disappeared from North America during the late Pleistocene ca. 10,000–7,000 YBP, but were brought back to North America by other cultures in pre-Columbian times. Possible cultures for which evidence exists include: (i) Chinese immigrants in junk ships hugging the coasts of the Pacific Northwest; (ii) Scandinavians in long ships by way of Greenland and landing in Newfoundland or Nova Scotia, and (iii) other cultures, such as the Celts from Wales or Ireland, or people in boats from southern France who came clinging to the southernmost edges of northern ice caps that had extended far to the south. The latter left their distinctive form of spears in the New World.

Regardless of which of these two options is true or whether a combination of such or some other option, after the Spanish brought horses, beginning with Hernan Cortez in the early 1500s, escapees and horses stolen by the Indians began to repopulate the Americas to a large degree. These could have reproductively intermingled with horses that had been brought by other cultures in earlier times and/or that were in North America originally. These horses likely possessed a superiority over other races, a hybrid vigor giving them survival advantages in the wild. This is all the more reason for preserving the mustang herds *in the wild* today (Luis et al. 2006).

AMERINDIAN EVIDENCE FOR
SURVIVING NATIVE HORSES

Evidence for more recently surviving horses in North America is to be found in the cultural knowledge of native tribes that has been handed down from generation to generation. Many of these oral histories have their origin in pre-Columbian times. In her excellent book *In Plain Light: Old World Records in Ancient America*, Gloria Farley (1994) presents illustrations indicating post-Pleistocene, pre-Columbian horses in North America. These include petroglyphs similar to the one I discovered (Figure 1). According to my interview with prehistoric North American horse investigator Yuri Kuchinsky, many early people who arrived on this continent reported Indians with horses when they first struck ground; and the oral history of many tribes indicates that horses may have been present in North America since time immemorial. According to Kuchinsky, who is Canadian, horse petroglyphs have been found in western Oklahoma, California, Arizona, Arkansas, Kansas, southeastern Colorado, and Alberta, Canada, but the American government does not want this information to come to light and the academic establishment follows their authoritarian policy due to its dependency on the government as a major grant source.

Kuchinsky considers remnant native American horses to have been quite different from Spanish or English horses, with much more pinto coloration and a smaller, more compact and pony-like stature. He suggests a possible link with either Celtic inhabited Greenland, or China, or both, and has documented great similarities between Amerindian equestrian customs and those of Mongolians. As with other investigators, he signals the Kiger mustangs as especially unique, perhaps harboring pre-Columbian ancestral characteristics, and considers unconscionable the very low, non-viable population levels to which the Bureau of Land Management has reduced them.

Frank Gilbert Roe (1955) notes that early explorers of northwestern North America consistently found Indians to be accomplished horsemen when first encountered. This holds true for both northern and southern regions of North America, indicating a possible earlier association with horses than is consistent with their sole re-introduction upon the North American continent by the Spanish. Very large wild horse herds were repeatedly reported very early in the history of North American exploration, for example by Wissler in 1669 in Virginia. And many tribes had horses before 1600. Le Page du Pratz in 1719 noted that numerous wild horses in the southern United States were morphologically quite different from European horses, though they lived closer to the Mexican haciendas that were the main source of U.S. and Canadian mustangs. Though this may have been a phenotypic adaptation, the possibility exists that it was due to genotypic differences. In California's Sonora Valley in 1567, Sr. Francisco de Ibarra observed tribes that were expertly practiced horsemen (Denhardt 1937). Kuchinsky (2005) in his Internet article "Frank Gilbert Roe on Very Early Indian Horses" raises the percipient question: "How was it possible that the Natives close to Spanish areas could have horses so early, and a different kind of horse, the one that the Spanish were strongly prejudiced against and probably did not introduce?"

According to historian Claire Henderson (1991) of Laval University, Quebec, "Traditional Dakota/Lakota [Sioux] people firmly believe that the aboriginal North American horse did not become extinct after the last ice ages and that it was part of their pre-contact culture." Though established anthropological opinion has it that the Plains Indians acquired horses in the early 1500s, as escaped or stolen horses from Spaniards in Mexico and the southwestern United States, the Sioux claim that the North American horse survived the Ice Age and provided the mounts for their ancestors long before Columbus's discovery of America. They maintain that these distinctive native ponies, in fact, continued to thrive on the North American prairies until the first half of the 1800s "when the U.S. Government ordered them rounded up and destroyed to prevent Indians from leaving the newly created reservations." This massive slaughter is well documented (Ryden 1999); and the same negative view of wild horses continued throughout the twentieth and continues into the twenty-first century, as manifest both in the U.S. and Canada as bias, anti-wild-horse policies. Much of this negativity is attributable to domineering livestock and hunter segments of society that have long targeted wild horses for discrediting and elimination from the wild (Appendix I, Forever Wild and Free speech available by request from author).

Though much evidence backing the Sioux elders' claims was destroyed along with the horses, some remains. For example, the Dakota/Lakota possess different words for "horse," thus distinguishing between the *sunkdudan*, their own short-limbed horse, and the long-legged horse brought by Europeans. Sioux elders whom Henderson consulted said that the aboriginal pony stood about thirteen hands high (fifty-two inches) and had a straighter back, wider nostrils, and larger lungs than European horses. Accordingly, these ponies possessed even greater stamina and endurance than the nonetheless remarkable horses brought from Europe. Reports of shaggy hair and singed manes seem tarpan-like and were confirmed by Prince Frederick Wilhelm of Wurtemberg, Germany (South Dakota Historical Society 1938).

According to documented French accounts prior to the 1650s, remarkable equestrian riding and hunting skills, including spearing buffalo from horseback, were demonstrated by prairie-dwelling Indians. Henderson reasoned that the Amerindian had attained these skills with aboriginal horses, because insufficient time had passed between the European re-introduction of the horse in the early 1500s and 1650 in order for such consummate skills to be developed.

How long does it take a people to learn to ride on horseback in masterly fashion? Frank Trippett (1974) notes that "more than a century passed before the Assyrians, learning from more skilled horsemen like the Scythians, began to feel at home on horseback. Assyrian cavalrymen of the ninth century, BC, required aides to ride beside them and manage their mounts so that these cavalrymen would be free to use their weapons."

Henderson ended her plea with a call for the careful conservation of "the few remaining Indian ponies." I would add to this a call for a comparative genetic analysis among germane horse populations to determine if unique North American characteristics, including mitochondrial DNA markers, exist. In this connection, a search for possible remains of slaughtered Plains Indian horses should also be undertaken. Such remains, if not too degraded, could then be subject to modern DNA analysis in order to identify differences with European horses and to test the hypothesis that remnant native horses still survived in North America when Columbus and subsequent explorers such as the horse-toting Cortez "discovered" America. Care here should be taken to identify European horse lineages that have not been subject to interbreeding with American horse lineages since 1492 in order to realize this comparison.

CANADA

According to Dr. Robert M. Alison (2000): "...the complete extirpation of ancestral horse stock in Canada has yet to be completely confirmed and a bone found near Sutherland, Saskatchewan, at the Riddell archaeological site suggests some horses might have survived much later. The bone (Canadian Museum of Nature I-8581) has been tentatively dated at about 2900 years ago. Another *Equus* species bone found at Hemlock Park Farm, Frontenac County, Ontario, dates to about 900 years ago." [In his conclusion, Alison unequivocally states]: "...the main lineage originated on the North American continent. Horses are therefore indisputably native fauna, despite a multiplicity of genotypic variations." [In regard to the reintroduced horse from the Old World, he continues that] "...subsequent evolution elsewhere over a period of perhaps 8000 years [does not] make them non-indigenous." [He further observes that the] "inherent timidness of Canada's surviving free-ranging wild horses, and...genetic testing...confirm [that] these animals do not derive from escaped domestic Block farm/ranch stock" [and that] "their shy behaviour is consistent with a long history of sustained freedom...". He goes on to make a case for the predominantly Iberian genetic makeup of Canada's few hundred, legally unprotected, wild horses. Numbering in the millions, Canada's great mustang herds were present from the sixteenth to the nineteenth centuries and were compatible with bison, wolves, elk, bears, and other large, as well as small, wildlife species. Dr. Alison, a biologist, urges increased protection and resource provision for Canada's last remaining wild horses as contributors to the *native* North American biodiversity and warns of their imminent disappearance.

Unfortunately as of 2011, the Canadian government continues its antiquated, prejudiced policy that regards wild horses merely as escaped domestics, or "feral" equids, exotic to North America and unworthy of protection. Nor is any consideration given to their centuries of loyal and self-sacrificing service to mankind. Canada's intransigent policy reflects the bias of knee-jerk conservatives lacking a clear and refined, expanded view of horses and their deserved place in and contribution to the North American ecosystem. Unfortunately and as we have already revealed, this is all too typical of attitudes and policies in the United States as well. But the good news is that this can and will change.

In an e-mail communiqué of August 17, 2007, from P. Monteith, executive correspondence officer for the Canadian Prime Minister Stephen Harper, I was informed that the "feral" horses in Alberta are "governed under the Stray Animals Act and the Horse Capture Regulations." No mention of any wild horse protection in the wild was given, but only reference to humane regulations governing permits for capture issued to individuals. My protest of a proposed herd reduction and call for protective status were ignored. Undaunted, I again proposed that Canada's wild horses be given full protection as a returned native species rather than continue to be branded merely as "feral"—a label that does great injustice to their vast living history, and to the ecological and evolutionary role of these magnificent animals in wilderness North America.

THE BURRO

In similar fashion to the wild horse, the burro (*Equus asinus*) can trace its not-far-removed ancestry back to North America; and in many parts of this continent, wild ass fossils testify to a very similar species occupying a very similar niche as the one reoccupied by burros in recent centuries. It is a sad testimony that in blatant contravention of their rights under the Wild Free-Roaming Horses and Burros Act of 1971, wild burros have been almost entirely eliminated from their legal herd areas and territories throughout the West (MacDonald, C 2007; Appendix, Forever Wild and Free speech: available by request from author). Now only a few thousand remain.

MacFadden (1992) indicates that the ass branch of Equidae evolved in North America throughout the Hemphillian, Blancan, and Pleistocene periods, when one *Equus mexicanus* was clearly present. Though the modern burro, or donkey, is currently considered as having originated from African wild asses (*Equus africanus*) and can and does produce fertile offspring with such (Duncan 1992, 15), it is most probably not significantly different from its North American ancestors. Indeed, one respected paleontologist believes that the African Wild Ass originally arose in North America (Klingel 1979; University of Wyoming 1979). And until recently both burro and African Wild Ass were considered to be the same species, namely *Equus asinus*–which is still the case in many circles. Like the wild horse, when returned to North America, the burro readily adapts to an ecological niche which its not-so-distant ancestors filled for millions of years, particularly, I gather, in the dry Southwestern US and south into Mexico. The distinction between *E. asinus* and *E. africanus* seems more a political one than a sound biological one.

A BROADER PERSPECTIVE

Since shortly after the dawn of our present Cenozoic era, dating from the extinction of the dinosaurs ca. 65 MYA, the ascent of all three major branches of the horse family: zebras, asses, and caballine horses has taken place primarily in North America (MacFadden 1992).

During the course of their long co-evolution, members of the horse family developed many mutually beneficial relationships with plants and animals. Indeed, both asses and especially caballine horses can stake the claim to being among the very most ancient and long-standing members of the North American life community, more so than most other large mammals still surviving here. For example, among the bovid family both bighorn sheep (*Ovis canadensis*) and bison (*Bison bison*) had their origins in Eurasia before crossing over the "filter" Bering Land Bridge, or isthmus, during the Pleistocene epoch 2–3 MYA. This is when oceans receded with the tie-up of global moisture during the ice ages (Lindsay et al. 1980; Vaughn 1972, 246). Thus, the later two species are relative newcomers in North America when compared with the horse and other members of the horse family. Members of the deer family, Cervidae, including white-tailed and mule deer, elk and moose, arose in Asia during the Oligocene epoch 36–23 MYA and did not arrive in North America until the Miocene epoch 23–7 MYA. They crossed over the Bering Land Bridge to occupy North America. Though their origin is more in the Old World, few authorities would question their native status in North America. Yet, many of these same persons will question members of the horse family in this regard in spite of the fact that—to repeat—all three branches of the Equidae: zebras, asses, and caballine horses had their origin and long-standing evolution right here in North America, as an abundant fossil record proves (MacFadden 1992; Simpson 1951).

According to equid expert Dr. Hans Klingel (1979): "...there is...evidence that all the extant equids [members of the horse family] evolved as species on the North American continent, and that Grevy's Zebra and the African and Asiatic wild asses were the first to cross the Bering Bridge in the early Pleistocene, whereas the remaining species came to the Old World only during the late Pleistocene. This would explain the much wider range of Grevy's zebra in Africa during the Pleistocene, i.e., before their major competitors, plains and mountain zebra, had arrived. It is feasible that similar situations existed with respect to African and Asiatic Zebras."

REWILDING

Another line of attack used by wild horse enemies is to assert that horses have not been part of the North American life community since their die-out at the end of the Pleistocene epoch, i.e., the last ice age (Larry Johnson, pers. comm.). Even if they did die out, which seems untrue though a great subsidence in their numbers surely did occur, the relatively brief time period of their supposed absence of ca. 7,000–10,000 years (according to different sources) is not sufficient to undo the many mutualistic relationships horses established with native plants and animals. Furthermore, it is widely recognized that North America became species poor, or depauperate, in large mammals after the massive Pleistocene extinction that affected many other mammals, e.g., giant ground sloths, camels, rhinoceroses, saber-toothed tigers, dire wolves, tapirs, and mammoths. In light of the foregoing, the return of the horse and the burro can be viewed as a restoration of the North American ecosystem, a resuming of an age-old continuum, a repair in the anciently evolved web of life—in other words, a "rewilding" (Stolzenburg 2006; Donlow et al. 2005; Martin 2005).

It is also considered of vital importance that this rewilding take place today given the melting of the permafrost and so as to restore cool grasslands over extensive regions, including in Siberia (Zimov 2005). Horses undoubtedly played a crucial role in dispersing the seeds of many plant species composing the Pleistocene savannas of North America and should be greatly valued as returned natives here (Stolzenburg 2006, 34). They are a different type of herbivore, possessing a post-gastric, as opposed to the ruminant, digestion typical of the other major North American herbivores today. This will be discussed in greater detail in Chapter II.

THE ASIAN QUESTION

An intriguing line of evidence that horses were present in America over three thousand years before Columbus's arrival comes from Chinese writings. One manuscript dating from 2,200 BC indicates that the Chinese came to North America by sea at very early dates and described several animals occurring in "Fu Sang," or "the Land to the East." Their descriptions match certain North American animals, including bighorn sheep and—please note—*horses resembling the appaloosa*. Scholars question whether this involves horses that were earlier brought by the Chinese to North America and set loose, or horses that were already living here and subsequently captured and taken back to China. A distinctive gene has been identified in the patchy-rumped appaloosa breed of horse, and research is now underway to trace its origin. Perhaps this will substantiate a uniquely North American horse characteristic. The idea that the appaloosa originated in China is based on certain appaloosan traits, mainly to do with coloration, that are found in China; however, Chinese horses are generally chunkier in build than North American appaloosas.

Circa 627–656 AD in the middle of China's Golden Age (AD 581-907) during the reign of T'ang T'ai-tsung (AD 618-649) and his successors Ching-Kwan and Yung-Hwui, Chinese explorers traveled to Ta Han, or Da Han, meaning "the Land of the Great Giants" (Kuchinsky 2005). Again, the New Book of Tang reports this land as rich in sheep (perhaps referring to the bighorn, or Dall sheep) and horses. (See also Harris Rees 2011.)

North America, Europe, and North Asia share many faunal and floral elements, over both their more recent and more distant evolutionary histories. And equids, including horses and asses as well as zebras, figure prominently in this sharing (MacFadden 1992, Figure 7.7, 160-161). Though often separated by natural barriers, these three regions have experienced frequent faunal and floral interchanges during periods when barriers have either broken down, as through sea lowerings or freeze-overs, or been overcome by the versatile and persistent efforts of the animals themselves, including us humans. Again, this causes me to question the "destructive exotic" labeling of wild horses and burros by so many public land officials in North America, especially since the latter often are from ranching backgrounds, from a culture that views them as competing with livestock, or their agency's agenda itself is anti-wild-equid.

WILD HORSES AND BURROS AS TARGETS AND AS STIMULI TO REFORM

Vested livestock and hunter interests have long portrayed wild horses and burros in a negative light. This is due to their desire to monopolize the public lands and to impose their exclusive value systems. In my home state, the Nevada Departments of Wildlife (NDOW) and of Agriculture (NDOA) have repeatedly sought to eliminate wild horses and burros from the vast desert "basin and range" country (Trimble 1989) by challenging the constitutionality of the Wild Free-Roaming Horses and Burros Act, and in many other direct or indirect ways. In March 2011, Nevada Senate Joint Resolution 5 and Assembly Bill 329 sought to deny wild horses/burros any water in the state of Nevada by declaring them to be neither wildlife nor livestock. This runs very counter to the majority of Nevadans who value the wild horses and burros in their own right. Though these attempts have never been entirely successful, they have done much damage. The damage is seen in illegal killings encouraged by these agencies lack of support for wild equids and also in the influence of state agencies on policies of the federal government, since the BLM and USFS are mandated to consult with state departments of wildlife in carrying out the act's mandate. In Chapter V, 169-171, I describe what happened in such incidents as the St. Valentine's Day massacre of wild horses in northwest Nevada, a case that remains unsolved to this day.

The good news, however, is that a more enlightened attitude toward the free and naturally living horses and burros is emerging among the general public, as witness Nevadans' recent overwhelming vote for a wild horse scene on its official quarter. Attitudes may change in the twinkling of an eye, signifying in-depth reflection and sudden insight. As a fourth generation Nevadan and great grandson of nineteenth-century pioneers, I have witnessed this awakening and look forward to the wild-horse/burro-sharing society that will come because of it.

RECAP

Native status in North America is especially true for the modern horse species, *Equus caballus*, but applies generally to the entire family Equidae, genus *Equus*, and is generally true for the burro, *Equus asinus*. The caballine horse branch, the zebra branch, and the ass branch of the horse family originated in and evolved for many millions of years upon the North American continent, as attests an abundance of fossil and genetic evidence. Fossil asses closely resembling the burro are abundant in North America—indeed, the burro also probably arose in North America. The freedom of wild horses and burros here is also a moral question, when considering all that they have done for our kind over their seven thousand years of service to humanity.

The Ecology of Wild Horses & Burros in North America

Wild horses and burros complement North America's life community in many direct and obvious as well as more subtle ways. This they do when permitted their natural freedom to move and interrelate over a sufficiently extensive intact habitat and time period.

Dietary Benefits, Building Soils, Dispersing Viable Seeds

One obvious ecological relationship occurs between diet and habitat. Including today's extant zebras, asses, and horses, all equids possess a caecal, or post-gastric, digestive system. This is found in other perissodactyl families, including tapirs (Downer 2001) and rhinoceroses, as well as in other mammalian orders. Such a system enables equids to eat coarser, drier vegetation and, through symbiotic microbial activity, to break down cellulose cell walls to derive sufficient nutrients from the inner cell without overtaxing their metabolism. In drier regions, this often gives a distinct advantage over ruminant herbivores (those that have multiple stomach chambers and chew the cud) whose pre-gastric food processing requires expending considerably more metabolic energy and taking in more water. While it is true that equids must consume somewhat more vegetation, especially when dry and coarse, because of their less thorough extraction of nutrients from the food, this usually does not overly deprive ruminants, since much of what the equids consume would be of little or no value to them. As a matter of fact, the equids' consumption of this coarser, drier vegetation can greatly benefit sympatric, pre-gastric (ruminant) herbivores, and energize and enrich the ecosystem as a whole. By recycling chiefly the coarse, dry grasses as well as other dry, withered herbs, forbs, and bush foliage, the horses and burros expose the seedlings of many diverse species to more sun, water, and air, thus permitting them to flourish. The latter can then be consumed by ruminants (Bell 1970, 11–125).

Also of great importance is the contribution by wild equids of significant quantities of partially degraded vegetation in the form of feces deposited on the land. These droppings provide fodder for myriad soil microorganisms; the resulting fecal decomposition builds the humus component of soils, lending ecologically valuable texture and cohesiveness. As feces slowly decompose, they gradually release their nutrients over all seasons and, thus, feed the fungal garden that exists in soils, thereby increasing the soil's absorption of water—a vital limiting factor in semi-arid and arid regions. To reiterate: equid feces are much more valuable to the health of soils than ruminant feces (cattle, deer, sheep, goats, etc.) precisely because they are not as decomposed when exiting the body and, so, lend more sustenance to decomposers and food webs that involve mutually sustaining exchanges among all classes of organisms. The latter include many diverse insects, birds, rodents, reptiles, etc. And, similarly, the less degraded feces of equids contain many more seeds that are intact and capable of germination and from many more types/species of plants when compared with ruminant grazers, e.g. cows, sheep, deer, etc. Thus, the horses'/burros' wide ranging life styles greatly assist many plants in dispersing far and wide and, so, in filling their respective ecological niches.

IMPACT ON WATER, RELATION TO FIRE, AGENCY BETRAYAL

The increased ability of soils to retain water in equid-occupied eco-systems proves of crucial importance in restoring water sources in mountains and in elevating water tables in valleys, particularly in desert regions. The role that horses and burros play in this regard is very significant. Along with the major elimination of dry, flammable vegetation by equids, a healthier watershed works to reduce and prevent catastrophic fires, such as the West has experienced in recent years. This is in large degree due to mounting global climate change—a crisis caused by human-engendered neglect, particularly air pollution that threatens planetary life.

In an extensive desert region north of Las Vegas including the Spring Range and a spectacular area known as Red Rock, over thirty thousand acres were burned in a series of hard-to-control wildfires in recent years ("Stampede to Oblivion" 2009; "Wildfire Burns 2,000 Acres at Red Rock Canyon" 2007; Knapp 2007, pers. comm.). This occurred right after the BLM almost entirely eliminated the wild horses from their herd areas legally established by the 1971 act. In reducing the herd from several hundred to around twenty, BLM inadvertently caused the build-up of massive amounts of dry, flammable vegetation. All it then took was a spark to ignite this holocaust. Inevitable lightning storms or human negligence during recreational forays into the Red Rock provided this spark. This leads one to ask just how serious was BLM's Environmental Assessment required by NEPA for this major action.

Excessive wild horse and burro removal has been repeated through-out the West wherever BLM and USFS administer legal herd areas or territories and in other areas controlled by the National Park Service and the U.S. Fish and Wildlife Service. For example, the Sheldon-Hart Mountain National Wildlife Refuge in northeast Nevada and southern Oregon now plans to zero out all of its wild horses, even though scientific studies have proven the compatibility of wild horses with the pronghorn antelope, one of the major species managed in this refuge

(Meeker 1979). Since August 2011, USFWS has been proceeding with these helicopter roundups, thus betraying its promise as an agency made to Wild Horse Annie decades earlier.

In a prejudiced manner, these agencies have branded wild horses and burros as exotic misfits in North America, though nothing could be further from the truth! Resultant fires occurring in former wild-horse- or burro-occupied areas have left vast regions with scorched, steril- ized soils. This has occurred throughout the West in states such as California, Nevada, Idaho, Utah, Oregon, Arizona, and New Mexico— states where the wholesome contributions of the equids have disap- peared over many millions of acres. In spite of mounting evidence, our public servants remain oblivious to the serious damage their policies cause. Through their ignorance and/or perversity, they are setting back the sane work of the natural world and the wild equids in it, a work that has been accomplished over many generations. Through their in- different or downright hostile treatment of wild horses and burros in their free and natural state, they are displacing an indispensable healing agent, an ecological restorer and harmonizer of great significance here in North America.

TOPOGRAPHY ENHANCES HABITAT

Another germane point too often overlooked by authorities charged with protecting and managing wild horses and burros concerns the multiplication of ecological niche space that occurs in mountainous re- gions, with their accentuated topography. This creates greater oppor- tunities for plants and animals to derive a living when compared with flatter regions, because such terrain provides more surface area on which to live. And perfect examples of such occur in the Great Basin's hundreds of mountain ranges where most of America's remaining wild horses and burros have their legal areas. All this argues for higher gov- ernment assigned population levels, or Appropriate Management Levels (AMLs)! (As a student of the endangered Mountain Tapir of the northern Andes inhabiting from 6,000 to 16,000 feet elevation, I am well aware of the multiplication of niche space provided by steeper, mountainous terrain.)

BEHAVIORAL BENEFITS

Horses and burros aid myriad plant and animal species by their physical actions. As an example, breaking ice with their hooves during winter freezes allows other animals to access forage and water. Many of these would otherwise perish. Similarly, they open trails in heavy snow or through heavy brush, allowing smaller animals to move about in search of food, water, mineral salts, shelter, warmer areas, mates, etc. A little-recognized fact is that the wallowing habit of wild equids creates natural ponds whose impacted surfaces become catchments for scant precipitation or summer cloudbursts typical in the Great Basin. These provide a longer lasting source of water for a wide diversity of plants and animals. This can even help create an intermittent riparian habitat for desert amphibians (e.g., the remarkable spadefoot toad, which seals itself into a dry, muddy cocoon for many years, reanimating when moisture is again present) and many other desert species (Oxley and Downer 1994). Ephemeral plants that quickly flower and set seed, including many composites, also benefit from these catchments – especially valuable in regions with clayey soils. Wild equids locate water seeps through their keen sense of smell and enlarge these through pawing during critical dry periods of the year, even digging down to the sources at rocky fissures. This allows many other species to access water, species whose individual members would otherwise perish. For these and many other reasons, wild horses and burros should be treated as keystone species that contribute positively in a variety of ecological settings.

ROLE AS PREY

And let us not forget that wild horses and burros are the prey of native carnivores, including puma, wolves, and brown and to a lesser degree black bears. In geologically recent times, this included the famous saber-toothed tiger and dire wolf. Of course, these natural hunters have also been targeted for elimination by so-called "civilization," since people too often arrogate the near sole right to hunt the large prey mammals. These include deer, elk, moose, pronghorn, bison, and bighorn sheep, species upon which native predators have subsisted for thousands of generations and in a way that—unlike modern sports hunting—actually makes the prey populations more fit to survive over the long-term by taking the weak and infirm or those animals who have reached the end of their life cycle (Baker 1985).

The horse family is split into three main branches: zebras, asses, and caballine horses. And with practically no break unto the present, they have filled the ecological role of medium/large-sized prey mammals in North America for over 58 million years. This fact alone makes it ludicrous to deny wild equids' place in North America. The wild horse and burro are refilling their empty niches—only briefly unoccupied, paleontologically speaking, if at all (see Chapter 1). These have been formed over countless generations of coevolution with native plants and animals (Downer 2005; Oxley and Downer 1994).

It is a fact that equids are more anciently rooted in North America than the vast majority of big game species (including the white-tailed and mule deer, bighorn sheep, and bison) that are widely promoted by state and federal governments in the United States and Canada. Unlike the horses and burros, these species' origins are mainly in the Old World, and they have not been in America for nearly the time span of the horse family. North America is the evolutionary cradle of the horse species, genus, and entire family. Here all branches of this family (including ones now extinct) have experienced the vast majority of their evolutionary progression. To deny these uniquely beautiful and wise animals—the horses and the burros—their place in America epitomizes ignorance and is thoughtless in the extreme.

COEVOLUTION WITH HABITAT

To quote Dr. Patricia M. Fazio (2003): "[t]he Key element in describing an animal as a native species is: (1) where it originated; and (2) whether or not it coevolved with its habitat. Clearly, *E. caballus* did both, here in North America." Various Amerindian tribes of the Great Plains and Prairies have a saying concerning the wild horses: "The grass remembers them." In light of the more ample view of life's history provided by modern science, I respectfully stand in awe of their profound insight (Kirkpatrick and Fazio 2005; see also Henderson 1991).

Wild horses and burros are perfectly suited to life in the remote, semi-arid regions of the West. One reason is obvious: their great mobility. With their long limbs and sturdy, single-unit (soliped) hooves, they are made for movement. In such semi-arid or arid regions as they inhabit, this extensive movement is vital for survival. In order to obtain enough forage, a wild horse must often roam over several square miles each day, selecting appropriate plants to prune; reaching a water hole may involve traveling over one hundred miles round-trip in a grazing circuit of two or three days.

During very hot, dry spells, a wild horse band must stay close to water, tanking up every day with approximately twelve gallons for a mature horse. A spring can be shared by several bands. These form an orderly hierarchy for watering should more than one band arrive at a source at the same time, often late in the day. When melting snow or fresh cloudbursts paint the land with ephemeral water sources, wild horses can disperse into areas farther away from perennial lakes and streams and to ephemeral sources. Here they employ their keen sense of smell in detecting even very small and hidden water sources. They can also negotiate rougher, steeper and rockier terrain than domestic cattle.

Through a hammer-like hoof action upon the ground, wild horses and burros aid vegetation by pushing seeds firmly into the soil where they may successfully germinate. In October 2008 at the Wild Horse Summit in Las Vegas, Lakotan Sioux shaman Arvole Looking Horse of South Dakota described to me how wild horses are vital energizers that "pound Earth's drum" releasing energy from the inner planet and lending a musical rhythm that unifies diverse forms of life. Though criticized by their detractors for breaking the crusts, or desert pavement, of certain desert soils and, thus, accelerating wind erosion, when allowed adequate space and freedom, horses do not overwhelm an area. This is due to their sparse distribution and frequent movements and because, as most land-bound animals, they confine the majority of their long-distance displacements to trails. In certain areas, their compacting of soils helps these retain scant precipitation and dew. Especially in soils of higher clay content, this compaction can help retain moisture over long periods of time. However, such modification of soils, occurring naturally with nearly any hoofed animal, can become detrimental to an ecosystem with overcrowding. As with any activity, what is an ecological positive in moderation can become a serious problem when overdone. This is certainly the case with the severe overgrazing that humanity has imposed upon the West, as upon similar arid and semi-arid regions throughout the world, by forcing hordes of cattle, sheep, goats, deer, yaks, and, yes, even horses or burros, etc., in unnaturally high concentrations upon the land (Rifkin 1992; Downer 1987).

MAN'S IMPACT

In the latter 1800s, many millions of cattle and sheep were forced by their human possessors into the vast, unfenced western regions. While a graduate student at the University of Nevada-Reno, I viewed archival photographs from the late 1800s of interior regions of Nevada such as the Reese River or Humboldt River hydrographic basins. These revealed extensive valleys filled with exuberant tussock grasses that were soon to be replaced by unpalatable sage and rabbit brush due to livestock overgrazing, as more recent photos in these same places conclusively prove. In effect, we humans raped the West, greatly setting back this formerly healthy, though drier, life community (Jacobs 1991). We ignored the already established life communities that in many places included the returned native mustangs, and the possibility of harmonizing with such, while ignorantly imposing domesticated European species with a mind to maximizing production and profit in the short term. Today the arid land ecosystems our culture so invaded continue to be grazed by domestic livestock, though controls were imposed in the U.S. starting with the passage of the Taylor Grazing Act of 1934. Though somewhat alleviating the situation, this act assured that these lands would still be monopolized by livestock interests, thus, preventing the type of recovery that should have occurred.

DUST, GAS & EFFECTS OF LIVESTOCK, GLOBAL WARMING & PLACE OF WILD HORSES

Among the most insidious and globally harmful effects of domestic livestock hordes are the large quantities of dust blown into the air when the surface of soils are overly trampled and grazed. An article in *Nature* has revealed that "dust load levels have increased by 500% above the late Holocene [eleven thousand years ago] average following the increased western settlement of the United States during the nineteenth century." [This is largely attributed to] "... the expansion of livestock grazing in the early twentieth century" (Neff et al. 2008). The dust causes an increase in various chemicals affecting the pH of water, productivity, and nutrient cycles. Such fine particles can settle on plants and plug their tiny pores, or stomata, through which they breathe. They can also lodge in the interstitial lung tissues of many animals, including humans, where they cause pulmonary diseases, including cancer. Though insufficiently recognized, the "dust factor" is extremely damaging both to living organisms and the ecosystems they inhabit.

The enormous quantities of methane, nitrous oxides, and other gases that are emitted through the digestive processes of domestic livestock constitute one of the major accelerators of life-threatening global climate change (de Haan et al. 2006). Clearly, civilized man's so-called progress upon planet Earth has abysmally failed to consider the ecological balances that assure life's continuance. Urgently required is an all-out effort to restore the natural diversity of plant and animal species appropriate to each of the Earth's bio-regions, or ecological provinces. But this is going to involve a serious willingness on the part of us humans to modify our life-influencing values and priorities, both individually and collectively. This will permit us to live in a truly harmonious manner, to act as good neighbors toward our fellow species. Here the horses and burros come into play. Their post-gastric digestive system does not emit as much gas as is the case with pre-gastric ruminant grazers, and permits them to greatly reduce dry, fire-prone vegetation over vast areas of the West without overtaxing their metabolism. Thus, they help to prevent catastrophic fires that global warming, or more to the point, civilization's pollution of the atmosphere, is causing.

By drying out vegetation and provoking catastrophic fires—rampant in western and southern North America, Australia, and much of the world—the catchall global climate change threatens planetary life as we know it. This will especially be the case if global ocean currents

stop circulating due to ice cap melting. Annually a few to several million acres of forest, brush, and grassland have been going up in smoke
in the United States alone, especially in the West and South. Never in
historic times have we seen such destruction. But wild horses/burros
can greatly help to save the day if allowed to play their own special
role in reducing flammable vegetation, in building soils, in seed dispersal, and in preventing catastrophic, soil-sterilizing fires, etc. They stand
ready to counter imbalances brought on by human civilization and its
contamination of the atmosphere. Much of this contamination is caused
by hordes of domestic livestock that mow down vast vegetated areas, their over concentration and resultant destruction of soils, and
their production of flatulence and excrement in enormous proportions and intensities. Of course, these are imbalances brought on also
by automobile exhaust, factory fumes, forest burning, peat oxidation
in the Subarctic and Arctic, absorption of sunlight by darker seawater
where once reflective ice caps stood, etc. Millions of years of coevolution have made these equids best equipped to prevent the catastrophic fires we are experiencing and to restore many of the ecosystems
human civilization has either blindly or intentionally damaged. Let us
not take these magnificent animals and what they have to offer for
granted, for they are definitely a key part of the solution to all life's
problems.

Our individual and collective sacrifice of benighted, passé lifestyles is
necessary for the realization of better, more appropriate ways of living. (Has this not always been the case?) Among terrestrial ecosystems,
long-standing herbivore roles/niches have evolved. And in many regions,
particularly North America, equids, including today's wild horses and
burros, perfectly fill these roles. Such involve mutually beneficial relationships among the many diverse plant and animal species with which
equids have coevolved for millions of years. To narrow-mindedly ignore
these anciently rooted, yet ever newly evolving ecological relationships,
as modern man has been doing, is like throwing oneself in front of a
rapidly moving train with the momentum of many cars and a most
powerful engine to contend with as a result. And it is also like burning
up one's home in order to obtain just one night's warmth. Surely *Homo
sapiens*—the wise one—can do better.

OTHER FOES OF WILD HORSES

Add to livestock monopolization, the modern day onslaught of off-road vehicles (ORVs) and accelerating mining activities, which include oil and gas development and open-pit and heap-leach, low-grade extraction of metals such as copper, molybdenum, and gold, and you will see why the perpetrators of ecological crimes are so anxious to blame wild horses and burros for damages they themselves have caused. They need a scapegoat desperately.

Of relevance here, oil and gas drilling and transport are being used as an excuse to either zero out or extremely reduce herds from their legal herd areas throughout the West and particularly in states such as Colorado (West Douglas Herd Area) and Wyoming (Red Desert). Again specifically, the Ruby Pipeline, running from Opal, Utah through northern Nevada and southern Oregon, has been used to justify drastic wild horse roundups. Such occurred during the first two months of 2010 in the Calico Mountain Complex and involved five wild horse herd management areas. Though nearly 1,922 wild horses were removed, incredibly BLM roundups are again resuming, as per news releases of the Winnemucca District Office from June 15 through December, 2011 (for further information, conduct an Internet search for "Calico wild horse BLM roundup"). A drastic helicopter roundup has been occurring in the Triple B complex of four wild horse herd management areas in eastern Nevada, where the Mount Bald open-pit mine is sucking a significant portion of the aquifer dry. Coincidence? I think not. As of September 1, 2011, a federal district judge at least temporarily shut down the Triple B roundups due to the inhumane treatment of wild horses—at least twelve deaths—by the BLM-contracted Sun J company.

CHEAT GRASS AND FURTHER RUMINATIONS

A commonly eaten food of wild horses in northern Nevada's Granite Range is *Bromus tectorum*, aka the infamous "cheat grass" that is taking over the West (Berger 1986, table on 276–77). The measured percentage frequency of this invasive species from Central Asia in the Granite Range habitat was 89.9%, while the percentage cover was 12% and the percentage use by wild horses was a full 27.3%. Since cheat grass is a major contributor to fires in the West, perhaps wild horses could be a major agent for reducing this flammable vegetation. Equids could prevent its reproduction by consuming this grass before it is able to set seed, in spring or early summer, depending on elevation. Most of the other species in Berger's table also become dry and flammable and are eaten by horses, thus reducing the "fire fuel load" in their occupied habitat. Wild horses and burros, as well as zebras, are very effective fire hazard reducers. They are more effective in eliminating cheat grass and other dry, flammable grasses, and forbs than many ruminant grazers, spreading their grazing over larger areas, provided fences and other barriers do not overly confine them. They eat during 60% to 80% of the twenty-four-hour day (ca. 15 hours), keeping constantly on the move and not camping on moist riparian or lacustrine meadow habitats, as do domesticated cattle put out to graze on the same land. They are born to move. Their droppings also build the humus content of soil to a substantial degree. This humus allows soil to gain more texture and re-tain more water, which dampens out fires; humus promotes more pro-ductive and bio-diverse plant and animal communities (Ricklefs 1979, 51–65). Because their feces are not as thoroughly degraded in the gut as those of ruminant grazers, e.g., cow, sheep, deer, elk, moose, etc., they contribute more to food chains/webs, e.g., dung beetles to birds and lizards to higher trophic predators such as bobcats, etc. Equid feces aid the watershed by creating damper conditions, because the soil particles to which they reduce (*micelles*) retain more moisture, i.e., more water adheres to the surface area of these particles. Hence, ground water tables are replenished, feeding more seeps and springs more continu-ously. And upon these springs and seeps, many species of plants and animals depend. Of course, some fire is of benefit to an ecosystem, but fires that over-consume, overextend, and over-intensify can set the evolution of a terrestrial life community way back and result in a very sterile environment.

THE STOREY COUNTY STORY

In northern Nevada, including the historic Virginia Range (famous for the Comstock silver lode of the last half of the 19th Century and where Virginia City, Storey County, is located), families have long recognized wild horses to be effective reducers of flammable vegetation and fire. As in the Granite Range, a large percentage of their diet has been observed to be the dry, quickly ignited cheat grass, a fire hazard that horses could help to eliminate if their foraging patterns were properly timed to the seeding cycles. The fire-reducing value of wild horses was one of the main reasons why, back in the 1950s, citizens of this county became our nation's first government to pass a law protecting its wild horses in the wild (Henry 1966). Ironically, in recent years, the seizing of control of wild horses by the State of Nevada from the county led to a declaration by the Department of Agriculture that all the horses be removed. Fortunately, this met with vociferous protest by locals and people from all over America, causing officials to pull in their horns, at least for the time being (though in October 2010, this threat was again brandished).

UPPER INCISORS AND FURTHER INSIGHTS

Insight can stem from the most basic of observations. For example, wild horses and burros possess both upper and lower incisors that permit them to selectively nip pieces of vegetation, such as grass or the leaves of bushes or trees. Major ruminant grazers as for example cattle and sheep do not have upper incisors and consequently can and do rip up plants by their roots more frequently with the shearing action of their lower teeth against their upper hard palates. This often exposes soils to destructive wind and rain erosion, especially when too many of the ruminants are placed upon any given area of land. When over-crowded upon dry rangelands or marginal western brush or forest lands, livestock have and continue to cause enormous ecological degradation. Yet, the problem lies not so much with the animals themselves but with the humans who force them into habitats where they did not evolve and, more to the point, *where they are not even allowed to harmoniously evolve and adapt to prevailing conditions through the time-honored process of natural selection and ecological balancing.* About three-fourths of the U.S. public lands are in seriously degraded condition due to overgrazing by domesticated livestock. But, to reiterate, the root of the problem lies not with the animals themselves but with we people who unnaturally manipulate and force them upon the land. We should assume responsibility for what has gone so dreadfully wrong and respond, i.e., *change,* to correct this. Since we are the *problem*, by the same token, we are the *solution* to the problem.

MUTUALIST EQUIDS HELPING TO PROVIDE ECOLOGICAL STABILITY

Though domesticated for a relatively short evolutionary time, horses and burros actually restore the wild "equid element" in North America. Here they refill herbivore niches that have been millions of years in the making. This restored diversification lends greater stability and balance to the ecosystem by increasing the complexity of the web of life. Such is analogous to a circle of people all holding hands and leaning backwards from the top of a vertical pinnacle where they stand in a tight circle. If just one person lets go, all the people may fall to their deaths. This interdependence involving equids has been documented in the Serengeti of Africa by Bell (1970). Bell observed how zebras eat coarser, drier grasses, etc., to expose to sunlight finer, more delicate grasses, forbs, and other types of mature plants or their seedlings, thus, permitting their growth. The latter are more appropriate forage for wildebeest, Thomson's gazelle, topi, etc., that come in later seasons. A migratory sequencing of grazing pressures by these different species evolved over thousands of generations that is mutually beneficial to these species.

A similar complementarity to that of the Serengeti evolved in North America and involves members of the horse family, including *Equus caballus*, a species that originated and evolved upon this continent during the past few million years, as did its preceding ancestry dating clear back to the Dawn Horse, *Hyracotherium*, aka *Eohippus*, of 58-million-year antiquity. The plains and prairies of North America were home to a dynamically balanced community of prairie dogs, bison (commonly called buffalo), rabbits, pronghorn, deer, wolves, bear, foxes, coyotes, puma, diverse rodents, reptiles and amphibians, raptor and song birds, recycling microorganisms, etc. Over the many generations of their co-evolution and in their complex feeding, decomposing, photosynthesizing, pollinating, seed dispersing, warning, and other interactions, these have fashioned a life community that is highly adaptable to the vagaries of climate, volcanic activity, unexpected oscillations in the sun's radiation, etc. In other words, the complex web of species—as any true web—has provided a beautiful resilience involving cyclings up and down for all species. With this greater variety of species, the natural vagaries that pose ever new and different survival challenges can be ridden out by the whole of life. In this respect, any individual, family, race, or species of life is like a rider of a bucking bronco, entered into the greater arena of evolving time and circumstance, in a rodeo whose rules are set according to natural and universal law. Understanding this allows us to understand the changing proportions of species present in North America over time as a response to changing conditions, both living and so-called non-living (Simpson 1965, Figure 24). I say "so-called" because life written large encompasses our whole world, for such is imbued with spirit—alive!

One example of harmonious coexistence occurs between deer, either white-tailed or mule, and wild horses. Deer mainly browse the leaves of trees or bushes while horses eat mainly grasses when available. In a healthy habitat, these deer and horses hardly compete because of utilizing different resources, and their interactions are often of mutual benefit. These benefits may be obvious or more subtle, direct or indirect. And a similar harmony exists between mustangs and pronghorn—an ancient and singular species that originated in North America just as did the horse. The latter two have had a long time to learn to get along. Incidentally, the pronghorn seems never to have left North America (Meeker 1979).

Wild horses particularly thrive in North America's plains and prairies, but can adapt well further west of the Rockies in the Great Basin and west of the Sierra Nevada mountains in California, as they did so well in earlier centuries. Burros adapt well in drier areas of North America particularly in the arid Southwest. Both equid species diversify and strengthen the community they inhabit in a variety of ways when allowed to achieve population stability over time and when not over-imposed upon by humanity. The process of natural selection must be allowed to operate sufficiently long for this to be the case. Then these equids create a greater variety of environmental conditions that make possible a greater variety of niches that can by occupied by the species that have coevolved with them and continue to evolve here on planet

Earth. Being large, powerful animals, equids can push their way through thickets of brush to form trails. Specifically, they open thick vegetative understories to light and air, and the more diverse exposures resulting from the equids' activities create conditions intermediary to the extremes of wind, temperature and various soil conditions. This physically defines a greater variety of niches fillable by a more diverse array of species.

When allowed to integrate into wilderness, the individual life histories of wild equids come to reflect natural oscillations, such as annual seasons and more long-term cycles. This they do along with the plants and animals who share their habitat. They harmoniously blend over time. As large animals who eat relatively large quantities and disperse their grazing and browsing activity over broad areas as semi-nomads, equids become the harvesters and the renewers over vast ecosystems true to their *keystone* role. Their cropping of vegetation, often dry and coarse, reduces the possibility for major, soil-sterilizing fires (though ecologically healthy, minor ones still occur). This cropping sparks vegetative renewal, the re-budding of new and tender shoots of greater nutritional value, especially to ruminants whose digestive and metabolic systems are over-taxed by the coarse, dry vegetation that horses and burros can better handle. And, thus, the overall productivity of the land is increased annually (Fahnestock et al. 1999 [both]). Also, as earlier noted, these equids disperse the seeds for successful germination of many of the plants they eat as well as fertilize the soils with their droppings. For their neighbors including the ruminant grazers, their presence is truly "win-win."

IDENTIFYING THE PROBLEM AND ITS SOLUTION—US!

Livestock currently graze Western public lands in the equivalent of over a million year-round cattle, and big game interests promote unnaturally numerous deer herds for hunter harvest (Baker 1985). Combined with other pressures such as subdivisions, mining and energy development, this has created an unbalanced situation in which ecological recovery is not possible. On top of this, global climate change is exacerbating the whole situation. The solution to our predicament lies, above all, in our becoming more sensitive toward and more knowledgeable about the ecosystems we inhabit and the more optimal potentials that both people and ecosystems can realize in unison. "We the people" must learn to identify with and to care for all diverse individuals, unique species, and enthralling ecosystems to which we all, in turn, belong. We are all members of the club and must learn to inhabit our shared home in a respectful way. Learning to identify with the Rest of Life is key. Change is possible. And it can happen in the twinkling of an eye...the twinkling of enlightenment that will afford us a vision concerning where next to direct our steps.

OVERVIEW

Over the vast immensity of time—whose greater consideration ever proves enlightening—many relationships have evolved between and among diverse individuals and species. Over the greater span of time, these come to fashion what ecologists term *mutual symbioses*, or mutually beneficial ways of living together. The implicit logic here is that since equids have been in North America for nearly 60 million years, they are an integral part of the harmony that has evolved between and among the many species here. Had they not been in some important fashion harmonious, including as part of the food chain, they simply would not have fit in and would have died out.

CHAPTER III

INJUSTICE TOWARD AMERICA'S WILD HORSES & BURROS & WHAT MUST HAPPEN

The relative proportions of wild horses and burros, and livestock and big game on the public lands reveal a gross inequity; and the sad fact is that this applies even within the relatively minor portion that was legally set aside for the wild equids in the ten Western states, in alphabetical order: Arizona, California, Colorado, Idaho, Montana, Nevada, New Mexico, Oregon, Utah, and Washington. As officially indicated in Department of Interior annual reports called Public Lands Statistics (USDI, various years), the latter represent about one-sixth of those monopolized by livestock. As discussed earlier, according to very conservative official admission, there are 53.4 million acres of original wild equid herd areas on BLM lands. This compares to very close to 300 million acres—three Californias!—of public lands managed by BLM, USFS, and other government agencies for livestock (Wuerthner and Matteson 2002).

In spite of government efforts to conceal the gross inequity involved, "one hundred to one" more accurately describes the resource allocation of livestock and big game in relation to wild equids on the public lands. The grossly unfair ratios that favor livestock *even within* the original 1971 legal herd areas/territories and reduced herd management areas alone should be cause for immediate judicial as well as congressional rectification. That this is not happening in spite of major suits that have been brought and bills proposed reveals the extent to which our federal system is turning a blind eye to wild horses and burros, their legal right to live freely in fair numbers, and to the general public who support them. In herd management areas I have examined, livestock consume several times the resources that wild equids do. Even more egregiously, a large portion of our legal herd areas (ca. 40% by official estimation) have been totally "zeroed out" by our supposed public servants (see Figures 4, 5 and 6). These figures are even more alarming given subsequent roundups documented in Bureau of Land Management FY 2008–10 statistics (USDI, various years).

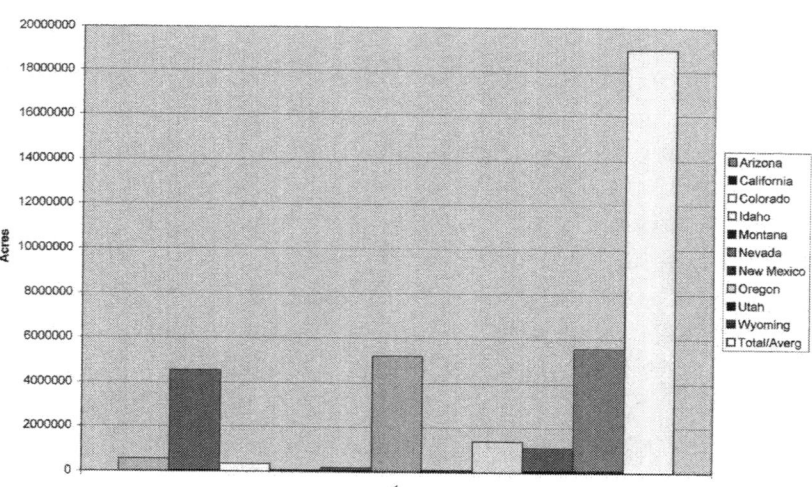

Figure 4: Original 1971 legal wild equid Herd Area acres that have been zeroed out by the federal government so as to contain no wild horses or burros, by state and as total.

Figure 5. % 1971 Herd Areas Zeroed Out

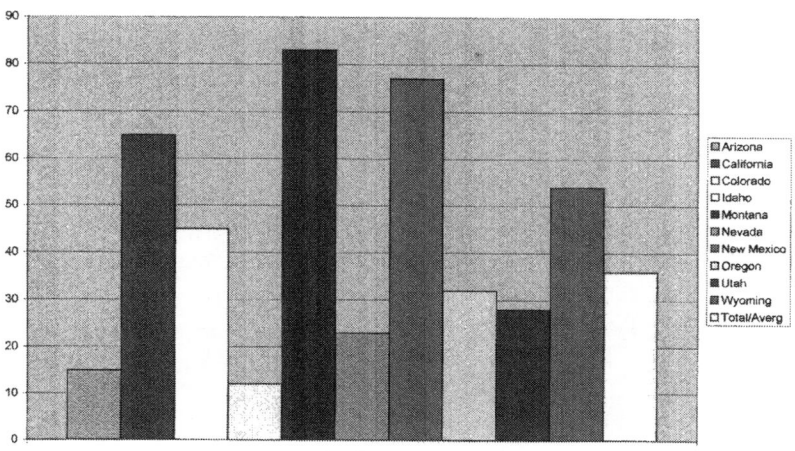

Figure 5: Percent of original 1971 legal wild equid Herd Area acres that have been zeroed out by the federal government, by state and as total.
Source for Figures 4 and 5: http://www.wildhorseandburro.blm.gov/statistics/2007/FY2007_Stats.pdf

Acres Per Remaining Individual Wild Equid (Horse and Burro) as of 2009

State	Original 1971 Herd Area	Reduced Herd Mgmt. Area 2009
Arizona	2120	1797
California	2237	777
Colorado	953	525
Idaho	595	521
Montana	1452	241
Nevada	1745	1345
New Mexico	1422	321
Oregon	2062	1406
Utah	1434	1036
Wyoming	2533	1171
US Average	1871	1206

Figure 6. Original 1971 Herd Area Acres per Remaining Wild Equid and Reduced Herd Management Area Acres per Remaining Wild Equid as of year 2009.

These figures in themselves should be enough to convince a federal judge to order that BLM exercise its authority under sections 4710.5 and 4710.6 of the Code of Federal Regulations so as to either temporarily or permanently remove livestock grazing in order to protect healthy population levels of wild horses and burros in the wild. This noble assertiveness would topple the livestock monopoly in the legal herd areas; but our federal judges and elected U.S. senators have been poor at requiring this of our public servants in the BLM and USFS. Thus revealed in all three branches of our government (congressional, judicial and administrative) is a deplorable apathy, complicity, prejudice, or even hostility toward free-roaming wild horses and burros and the general public who supports them. I must laud, however, the U.S. House of Representatives for passing in early 2009 the Restore Our American Mustangs (ROAM) bill, however imperfect, to restore the wild horses and burros, though the Senate killed this by refusing to bring it out of the Committee on Energy and Natural Resources and to a vote at the close of the 111th Congress in December 2010.

Whether elected or appointed, officials have been extremely recalcitrant when it comes to following the act's mandate to treat wild horses and burros as *integral* components of a *thriving natural ecological balance* on the public lands. This means we humans should not overly interfere with their natural place and role. Because this is at odds with ingrained traditions of domination over life and nature, BLM and USFS bureaucracies have ignored the strong and well-founded ecological mandate of the act. Ingrained views of horses and burros as mere escaped livestock, i.e. "feral," stubbornly persist and are officially promoted, e.g., the public information panel at BLM's Litchfield wild horse holding facility sports a graphic demonstration of why we should no longer call wild horses wild but refer to them only as feral horses (pers. obs. 9/2010) . So much of this attitude has to do with human egotism, but, as with so much in life, what demands our sacrifice is what is most needed. With great percipience the late Nancy Whittaker (wild horse advocate who worked for the Sacramento-based Animal Protection Institute) pointed out that a "thriving *natural* ecological balance" (emphasis added) does not include artificially imposed livestock upon the public lands. Yet this very valid point remains virtually ignored by authorities to this day (Whittaker 1999).

INFRINGEMENT ON SPACE TO ROAM, CHECKERBOARD LANDS

Central to the failure of America's wild horse and burro program has been an unwillingness by officials to truly fend for the legal and natural rights of these animals. Upon repeated occasions, when presented with opportunities to secure favorable water and other habitat requirements, including their very crucial *space to roam*, officials have simply refused to act, thus allowing wild horse and burro enemies to eliminate their targets. One aspect of this problem involves over-fencing within the legal herd areas in direct contradiction of the act. This occurs in nearly every legal territory, herd area (HA) or reduced herd management area (HMA) and has caused much mal-adjustment, suffering, and death to the horses and burros. These fences impede ecological integration through seasonal migrations and rest rotation of food sources and watering sites. One extreme example I observed in the Granite Range HMA of northwest Nevada as early as 1980 when I worked for the Animal Protection Institute.

A great abrogation of responsibility has occurred in the alternating federal and private sections, known as "checkerboard" lands. These were given by the federal government to companies such as Central Pacific or Union Pacific in exchange for their building the transcontinental railroad (Stillman 2008). Even in times much more politically favorable for wild horses and burros than the George W. Bush or the Barack Obama years, BLM has simply relinquished the rights of the wild equids to live in these largely unfenced, half public lands, though this agency is in a clear position to negotiate for a compromise that would permit both private and public interests to coexist, as is greatly encouraged by Section 6 of the act. As a consequence, today on millions of acres lying along railroads, we find livestock operators hogging nearly all of the natural resources and either no or only very few accidental wild horses and burros, in spite of their legal right to live there. In fact even within HA/HMAs that barely dip into the checkerboard, BLM has used this land status as a pretext to eliminate many entire herds, e.g., those that occurred in the corridor that bisects northern Nevada often near to Interstate Highway 80 and continuing into Utah.

THE BLM SQUEEZE PLAN

The BLM rounded up 4,960 wild horses between October 2007 and July 2008, of which 3,990 horses were permanently removed from the wilds. While during FY2010, BLM completed the roundup of over ten thousand wild equids—nearly all permanently removed (see p. 85). Roundups are generally suspended during the peak foaling season March 1 to July 1—basically the spring—unless justified as emergencies, though such are often not such. For FY2011, BLM asked and received from Congress another record budget to roundup a slightly lesser number of wild horses and burros (about eight thousand), all the while increasing privately owned livestock as well as catering to giant mining and energy companies with giant open pit mines that consume, disrupt, and toxify natural aquifers, e.g., the Bald Mountain Mine in the Triple B HMA in eastern Nevada. Such interests have a literal stranglehold upon our public lands. Little wonder: Interior Secretary Kenneth Salazar pro-claimed that on his watch he will accomplish "the industrialization of the public lands" and chief among his targets have been "nuisance" wild horses and burros. Many of the herds have been entirely zeroed out. Even his current ecosanctuary proposal must be met with suspicion if it displaces reproducing herds with non-reproducing herds within their legal areas.

BLM's justifications for roundups are packed full of unchecked, negatively slanted claims and assumptions concerning the horses' ecological effects and their ability to survive. Also, the large jumps in individual herd popu-lation numbers BLM reports are very suspect.[3] In many BLM districts, reduced herd management areas are intentionally selected to be the poorest in resources, then the horses/burros are rounded up when they go elsewhere to survive *even when this is within their original herd areas.* Such was clearly the case in the Black Rock East wild horse HMA, as attests biologist Katie Fite of Western Watershed Project in her article (Fite 2010). The HMA designation by BLM deliberately excluded vital win-tering areas that were within the original HA by placing the new bound-ary way up on a mountain side and setting the herd up for failure, thus "justifying" their miserably low AML of just 93 horses and their gutting as part of the draconian Calico Complex helicopter roundups of early 2010.

---

3 Assiduous wild horse/burro investigator Cindy MacDonald has assembled a table of unbelievable population jumps from one year to the next in 38 HMAs involving five states between 2004-2008. Some indicate a near tripling of the population, e.g., High Rock HMA (CA) with 124 horses in 2007 but 356 in 2008; or Maverick-Medicine HMA (NV) with 335 horses in 2005 but 875 in 2006; or Salt Wells Creek HMA (WY) with 480 horses in 2005 but 1,133 in 2006. Such rates of increase are biologically impossible, so one must either question the census accuracy or realize that the wild horses are doing what wild horses do naturally as semi-nomads, i.e., healthily shifting their grazing pressure—beware of double counting! (See www.americanherds.blogspot.com).

Sidebar: Triple B Suit, Butchering of Original Herd Areas:

Along with The Cloud Foundation and Lorna Moffat and as represented by Rachael Fazio and a Nevada lawyer, I have recently (July 2011) become a plaintiff before the Nevada Federal Court in Reno to stop the gutting of a remnant wild horse herd on four legal areas north of Ely that comprise nearly 1.7 million acres. These are the Triple B, Maverick-Medicine, and Antelope Valley HMAs and the Cherry Spring Wild Horse Territory, known collectively as the Triple B Complex. By rounding up over 2,000 wild horses, the BLM plans to leave less than 500 in this enormous area. The ones re-released would be PZPed and skewed as to their sex ratios (60% male: 40% female). This would leave the herd with traumatized individuals and dysfunctional societies. Less than 10% of the forage has been allocated to wild horses, in spite of the "principally" clause of the act. Yet, the past two years have seen record precipitation in this region, as I witnessed in my snowy field trip in April 2011, and again in a field trip between June 30 and July 5, when I observed knee-high grasses and other horse-edible plants springing up with unusual vigor. I have presented my field report as part of my declaration to the court, which strongly denounces the BLM's plan. Though an injunction against the roundup was initially granted then lifted permitting the gathering of over 1,200, the roundup has now been halted by court order due to inhumane occurrences involving the wild horses. This was denounced through an independent suit brought by Laura Leigh, who had been observing and filming the roundups. As concerns our Triple B suit, we remain confident that in the long run victory shall be ours and that we can even have the wild horses restored at higher population levels. Our appeal for a judicial review of BLM's decision to set such low AMLs and to deprive the horses of their "principal" proportion of resources, etc., will be based on its merits and probably heard in early 2012. But if the Ely BLM District gets its way and proceeds with the roundup, only one badly violated wild horse per 3,566 acres of legal HMA land will remain, while livestock and other bully interests will increase their strangulating grip on the public lands.

Wild equids throughout the West are being set up—betrayed by those officials who should be their protectors. I observed another dismal roundup in the Paymaster HMA on September 16, 2010. The Tonopah Field Office Manager (Battle Mountain BLM District) Tom Seley seemed very confident in his claims that there were not enough resources for the wild horses, yet on this public observation day, all of the fifty-five wild horses whom we observed being helicopter driven into the corrals were in excellent health, finely muscled, and energetic. The main reason Mr. Seley later gave for their near elimination was that they were outside their HMA. But as with the Black Rock East herd, the original HA gave them their wintering grounds which the HMA did not.

When I worked for the Animal Protection Institute in 1980-1981, I protested Nevada BLM's decision to greatly reduce the Pine Nut HA by 60% and its AML to 385. I was promised by officials it would never again be reduced, yet today the AML is only 179 wild horses.

ACCESS TO WATER

A major failure of legal duty by federal officials concerns wild equids' access to water in the West. The number one legal point to bear in mind here is that when all the wild horse and burro herd areas (BLM) and territories (USFS) were declared and their boundaries determined on the ground, these areas automatically acquired *Implied Federal Water Rights* for the wild horses and burros. These are the same as for any Indian reservation, National Wildlife Refuge, or National Monument, no different. The only difference is that the federal authorities have refused to exercise these rights of the wild horses and burros. Basically, their heart has neither been in protecting them nor in heeding the will of the general public (see Chapter IV: Sidebar: Interview with ... John Phillips, page 119-121). Since livestock grazing is a cancelable privilege and not a legal right upon the public lands, BLM and USFS officials are in a perfect position to assure access to water for the wild horses and burros, even when the rights to this water are "owned" by ranchers and other interests. However, what we too often observe is that the rancher simply shuts down his wells when his cattle or sheep are removed after their permitted grazing season, and BLM simply throws in the towel when it comes to fending for the wild horses or burros. The bargaining chip is simple: if the rancher refuses to share his water within a reasonable limit with the wild horses or burros, the government can cancel his livestock grazing privileges.

One case with which I am familiar is in the Diamond Mountain legal wild horse HAs just north of Eureka, in north central Nevada. This approximately thirty-mile-long range was once home to a healthy and long-term-viable herd of about one thousand wild horses. However, since the livestock operator grazing cattle here owned the major water source and refused to share it with the wild horses, the BLM greatly reduced the permitted wild horse population or AML to fifty-nine animals, clearly a sub-viable population subject to inbreeding and chance die out. The AML for Diamond Hills North is thirty-seven wild horses while the AML for Diamond Hills South is twenty-two. At the time of my visit in the summer of 1998, I found two dead wild horses with bullet holes through their skulls. (A similar find presented itself in January 2010 just south of the Black Rock West HMA during the infamous Calico wild horse roundups.) According to the *qui bene* (Latin for "who benefits") legal principle, the logical suspect was the local rancher who refused to share his water. Though I filed an official report and complaint with BLM's Ely District Office and was promised a thorough investigation, I have heard nothing further. As Bob Dylan's song "Just Like Tom Thumb's Blues" goes, "Because the cops don't need you / And man they expect the same."

EXTREME BIAS IN NEVADA & ELSEWHERE & EFFORTS TO OBTAIN RELIEF

In partial connection with oil/gas drilling leases and projected solar developments in eastern Nevada, BLM's Ely District put out an unfair Resource Management Plan (RMP) in December 2007. This aimed to eliminate wild horses from many of their legal herd areas. Alongside similar agency plans, it flew in the face of the Wild Free-Roaming Horses and Burros Act, the Multiple Use and Sustainability Act, the National Environment Protection Act, the Federal Land Policy and Management

Act, and the Public Rangelands Improvement Act. It also violated federal acts to preserve wildlife (e.g., the Endangered Species Act and the Wilderness Act) by setting as a major goal the wholesale elimination of pinyon-juniper woodland and sagebrush communities in many areas. The trees and bushes that this plan targets for elimination and replacement by grass and other more favored plants for livestock, in fact, act as very important barriers against wind erosion of the Great Basin's delicate soils. The deer, rabbits, returned native wild horses, golden eagles, troupes of distinctive pinyon jays (known for their unique "rolling ball" flight pattern), burrowing owls, sage hen, and a wide variety of other animals find essential shelter and food sources in these trees and bushes, which also filter particles from the air to help form soils (Oxley and Downer 1994). And the nut of the pinyon pine, which bears on a two-year cycle, was a major staple for Native Americans and could be again for many people today, if harvested with moderation and a mind to share with the rest of life in this biome.

Ely BLM's outrageous and now completed (as of December 2009) plan included the zeroing out of all wild horses from the Caliente Complex. This complex consisted of the following HMAs: Delamar Mountain, Clover Mountain, Clover Creek, Apple White, Blue Nose, Mormon Mountain, Meadow Valley Mountains, Little Mountain, Miller Flat, Highland Peak, Rattlesnake, Moriah, Jake's Wash, White River, Golden Gate, and Seaman's Range with further eliminations also in portions of the Buck and Bald HMA. Here in their formative stages solar energy development projects involving evaporation and requiring enormous quantities of water blanket the now zeroed-out HMAs. Coincidence? I think not.

Totaling 1.4 million acres, this zeroing out flew in the face of the very federal laws that BLM officials are sworn to uphold. Guising itself as a "multiple use plan," it was, in fact, a wild horse enemy's pipe dream. To quote from my letter of protest, which was also sent to Washington: "This [plan] makes you the worst enemies of the wild horse, for you have become their betrayers, people in positions of authority and with the power and duty to defend their [the wild horses'] basic rights to life and freedom [yet] who are doing all the opposite and, adding insult to injury, further denigrating their character and contribution to life [as a] whole!"

At a meeting of the Nevada State Commission for the Preservation of Wild Horses held on January 11, 2008, it was revealed that the elimination of the above mentioned Caliente/Ely District herds also had to do with water rights holders, mainly ranchers, and their refusal to share water. I have already indicated what BLM could do about this.

Again, two codes of Federal Regulations: (1) 4710.5, commonly known as "Closure to Livestock Grazing" and (2) 4710.6, "Removal of unauthorized livestock in or near areas occupied by wild horses and burros" could be applied to allow viable populations of wild equids. These codes have seldom been applied in the past; and the federal agencies have even been ignoring their own regulations that plainly state: "… wild horses and burros shall be considered comparably with other resource values in the formulation of [Land Use Plans]" (43 CRF 4700.0-6[b]). Though livestock out-consume natural resources by a ratio of one hundred-to-one on all U.S. public lands when compared to the wild equids and though public lands domestic livestock produce only 2% to 3% of the meat in the U.S., our public servants—whose salaries, retirement and insurance are generously paid for by the U.S. taxpayer—still refuse to provide for viable, naturally integrated wild horse and burro populations in their own legal herd areas, as the law requires.

And once again, this egregious injustice should have been checked by our legislative and judicial branches, but these have shown little or no interest. Instead they have allowed Obama's executive branch to eliminate wild horses and burros from the Caliente Complex, as elsewhere. Several wild horse advocates, including myself, had their appeal to the Interior Board of Land Appeals perfunctorily denied concerning this.

Similarly, as of May 2011, the Little Colorado wild horse herd in Wyoming was being undermined to favor oil and gas extraction. BLM's plan was and remains to zero out this small herd in a legal area of over half-a-million acres. One hundred as AML was not low enough. This too is being legally challenged.

Given these and many parallel outrages, will President Obama ever order a moratorium on roundups before all herds are similarly victimized?

This would be in conformance with the request signed by over two hundred U.S. congressmen and organizations and hundreds of thousands of citizens that have contacted him from all states. What will it take to make authorities listen to the majority of the people? In April 2011, Madeleine Pickens presented over 70,000 signatures in Washington calling upon the president to halt the wild horse and burro roundups, but this didn't even make the national news on any of the major networks.

SAME OLD, SAME OLD

To quote from an updated version of Hope Ryden's influential *America's Last Wild Horses* (1999, 305) and to show how little the situation has changed:

> [f]rom 1981 to 1988 more than 4,350,000 domestic
> livestock grazed annually on the 41.5 million acres
> of public lands in the ten Western states where wild
> horses and burros are found. In addition, approximately
> 2,000,000 antelope, deer, elk and other large wild
> animals inhabited this public domain. Yet, 60,000 [now
> less than half of this, 9/2011] wild horses and burros
> were held to be responsible for the overgrazing of
> the nation's rangelands. To put these numbers into
> perspective, wild horses and burros did not even
> represent 1% of the large grazing animals on a vast
> public domain that, in aggregate, is equal in size to all
> of France. By contrast, privately owned livestock added
> up to 68% of the grazing animals found there. And
> game animals, whose numbers were being promoted by
> every means know to wildlife biologists, made up the
> remaining 31% of the pie.

Ryden perceptively continues in her footnote: "While 60,000 wild horses were being cut by more than half, 50,000 desert bighorn sheep were listed as endangered and every effort was made to bolster their numbers." The gross unfairness being displayed toward the wild horses and burros sticks out like a sore thumb.

Herd Size

Concerning what they consider to be a minimally viable population (MVP), or herd size, BLM officials usually refer to Kentucky veterinarian Gus Cothran's recommendation of 150 (Cothran and Singer 2000). But 150 individuals actually falls far short of what is recommended for viability in the wild for other similar mammal species as well as for the eight species and twenty-two subspecies within the horse family Equidae that still barely manage to survive in the world today. And this includes the modern horse, *Equus caballus*, returned to the wild.

According to the IUCN, Species Survival Commission, Equid Specialist Group: "[f]or captive populations, we recommend a minimum population size (N) of 500 individuals, a studbook, and careful genetic management....for wild populations we recommend a minimum size of 2,500 individuals." These levels are stipulated "to prevent extinction and conserve the genetic diversity of equids" (Duncan 1992, 5). In light of the foregoing, it seems that both BLM and USFS are setting up the ca. 200 wild horse and burro populations that remain (out of ca. 350 original) for extinction by adopting a standard (i.e., 150 individuals) that is sixteen times less than what a truly viable population should be according to recognized world authorities on equids. And even this very substandard standard is not being applied.

Were the earlier mentioned Diamond Mountain wild horse herd with its combined AML of 59 an isolated anomaly, though perturbed, I would not be so alarmed. But having witnessed this prejudicial pattern again and again throughout the West, I am forced to conclude that a general hostility exists among responsible government officials. This *conspiracy*—for I can think of no better term—is aimed at the horses' and burros' eventual elimination from the wild in any true and meaningful sense.[4] And this hostility is also directed toward the human supporters of wild horses and burros in the wild, as I testify in Chapter V.

According to the U. S. General Accounting Office (1990, 3):

> Despite the lack of data, BLM has proceeded with horse removals using targets based on perceived population levels dating back to 1971 and/or recommendations from BLM advisory groups comprised largely of livestock permittees. ... [Furthermore,] BLM could not provide...any information demonstrating that federal rangeland conditions have significantly improved because of wild horse removals. This lack of impact has occurred largely because BLM has not reduced authorized grazing by domestic livestock, which because of their vastly larger numbers consume 20 times more forage than wild horses. ...In some areas...BLM increased authorized livestock grazing levels after it had removed wild horses...

Unfortunately a more recent report by GAO[5] (U.S. Government Accountability Office 2008) has pusillanimously betrayed this agency's tradition of critical, independent evaluation to become a rubber stamp

---

4 On page four of Colorado BLM's 1997 *White River Resource Area Wild Horse Program Analysis and Operational Plan*, this conspiracy becomes explicit in the following published statement: "[w]e may employ fertility control in West Douglas and North Piceance as part of our **closeout strategy** for these areas [emphasis added]." True to form as of August 2011, Colorado BLM's proposal remained to simply zero-out the West Douglas Creek Herd Area's remarkable herd, again using oil and gas development as its excuse. At last count there were 120 of these mustangs on 128,000 legal acres, over a thousand acres per mustang. This irresponsible position by the BLM has repeatedly been protested in the courts by the Colorado Wild Horse Coalition and The Cloud Foundation; and in 2010 Judge Rosemary Collyer of the D.C. Federal Court declared the move to eliminate the herd illegal. But as indicated, BLM officials persist in their attempts to zero-out this herd using a newly crafted environmental assessment to do the same as its earlier version, but with tighter language.

5 In 2004, the GAO's legal name was changed from the General Accounting Office to the Government Accountability Office.

for the continued elimination of our nation's very small and non-viable wild horse and burro herds (Animal Welfare Institute 2008).

TESTIMONY FROM A BLM VETERAN REGARDING SABOTAGE OF WILD HORSE PROGRAM

On the evening of April 19, 2011, I was telephoned by Mr. Lloyd Eisenhauer of Cheyenne, Wyoming. He is a retired biologist who had worked for thirty years with the BLM, including in the wild horse and burro program during its incipient years in the 1970s and early 1980s when a much more positive program was in place. He is heartsick about what has happened to the wild equids and the subversion of the act that has resulted. He had been a team leader for a BLM program known as Soil-Vegetation Inventory Method, or SVIM. This was meticulously establishing a sound database upon which to determine fair allocations of forage for wild horses and burros. Much of his work was done in Wyoming. The program took a positive approach to the wild horses and burros and envisioned certain range improvements for establishing viable population levels, while maintaining other grazing species.

Mr. Eisenhauer was especially upset by the current drastic reduction of over two thousand wild horses from the 479,078-acre Adobe Town and Salt Wells Creek Herd Management Areas in the Red Desert and the disproportionate levels of livestock there. BLM announced in March 2011, the planned removal of an additional five hundred to six hundred wild horses from the Red Desert Complex composed of five HMAs next to Adobe Town and Salt Wells. Additionally Wyoming's Rock Springs BLM Field Office plans to take off 696 more wild horses. This is a serious undermining of Wyoming's last herds and was scheduled to begin on July 20, 2011, when many foals and pregnant mares would again have been subject to the mayhem of helicopter stampedes in the soaring heat of summer, as they have recently been in Nevada where many deaths and injuries have occurred in the Triple B Complex roundups until they were stopped by court order. Fortunately some of the Wyoming roundups (Adobe Town HMA) have also been stalled due to legal suits brought against them by the American Wild Horse Protection Campaign and Carol Walker, wild horse photographer (as of 8/22/2011). However, as of 8/21/2011, another massive roundup is going ahead in the White Mountain and Little Colorado HMAs in which ca. 875 wild horses will be removed, thus, setting back the natural adaptive process and harmonization of these healers of the land ("BLM has roundup set for Saturday 8/21/11" Associated Press).

Eisenhauer emphasized that "the wild horse program needs to get back on track with a new inventory of resources and a truly fair resource allocation for wild horses and burros." In short it needs to take up where it left off. SVIM had been abruptly shut down when Ronald Reagan was elected as president. Eisenhauer regards this shut down as having been a deliberately violent act that was aimed at destroying the wild horse and burro program as well as the herds through the suppression of objective resource inventories. Undone was a fair-minded resource allocation and the promotion of suitable habitats for the wild equids. —But it is our adamant resolution that this nefarious act itself will be undone!

After his retirement, Eisenhauer and a partner conducted Backcountry Tours in Wyoming over a period of eight years. He exclaimed how wild horses were an absolute highlight of these tours, thrilling to public observers. In his remaining years, Eisenhauer would like to vigorously restore America's wild horse and burro program by implementing urgently needed reforms. His call was a breath of fresh air for me; and it would be great if he and others like him could testify before Congress and help draw up a new and better version of the ROAM bill that incorporates a mandate for SVIM's renewal and is aimed at restoring the herds. You can bet we have not heard the last from Mr. Lloyd Eisenhauer.

THE STATE OF NEVADA'S STANCE ON WILD EQUIDS, OFFICIAL VS. PUBLIC

In my native Nevada, where I am fourth generation, the political establishment has become particularly anti-wild horse and burro. As a prime example, Nevada's long-time Senator and current majority leader of the U.S. Senate Harry Reid (D-NV) has been an insidious and powerful enemy of America's last remaining wild horses and burros. According to many political insiders, rather than former Senator Conrad Burns (R-MT), it was Reid who really instigated the sneaky Burns' Amendment to the act in December 2004, permitting the sale of 10+ year-old horses and three-adoption-strikes-you're-out younger horses to go to sadistic killer buyers (www.americanherds.blogspot.com). He has also effectively blocked the ROAM bill and other progressive bills aimed at reinstating wild horses and burros to their rightful freedom and increasing the humane treatment of horses and preventing their slaughter. He is a prime example of how—in spite of wild horse advocates very cogent and lengthy pleas to rectify egregious injustice toward America's wild horses and burros (e.g. March for Mustangs [2010], Horses on the Hill [9/2009])—the wild horse conspiracy has permeated both major parties of our nation, Democrat and Republican, though the latter is by far the worst in relation to wild horses.

I think the political establishment today is jealous of the magnificence of these animals in their free and natural state and wants to hog all of the attention for themselves or vainglorious ranchers—as though they didn't already get their fair share! As in other western states, Nevada has been dominated by livestock interests. Yet, this situation is changing with the greater influx of Americans from other states. In 2006, a desert scene containing wild horses was publicly voted to appear on the official Nevada quarter, which subsequently won an international award for best coin. The quarter's dedication by Governor Kenny Guinn was the most publicly attended dedication in the history of the state, with approximately ten thousand people showing up including me. Another similar scene was adopted for a Nevada automobile license plate thanks to the persistent efforts of Sally Summers and her organization Horse Power. This license plate is now one of the most popular in the state, and its proceeds go to helping wild horses and burros here.

But entering the enemy side of the wild horse picture has long been the state's hunting establishment, represented by the Nevada Department of Wildlife (NDOW). Since the act's inception, this agency has repeatedly knifed wild horses and burros in the back, doing everything within its power to discredit and eliminate them from the wild. Using NDOW as its legal spearhead, the State of Nevada has repeatedly challenged the federal law protecting wild horses and burros on federal land. NDOW officials have consistently issued negative statements about these animals that over-magnify their ecological impacts and always interpret them negatively. Contrary to scientific finding, NDOW and similar agencies in other western states frequently deny horses' evolutionary origins in North America, instead describing them as destructive exotics.[6] The Nevada state government's blindness toward the horse family's proven evolution and ecological integration in North America is abysmal, and anyone possessing an ounce of appreciation for this august lineage should be highly offended.

Some of the most flagrant perversions of the Wild Horse Act have been committed through the *aegis* of the recently discontinued Nevada Commission for the Preservation of Wild Horses, whose last executive director of many years standing was Ms. Cathy Barcomb. This commission was set up in 1985 by the Nevada legislature with funds deriving from the last will and testament of the honorable Mr. Leo Heil. He had earlier bequeathed his substantial wealth of ca. .5 million dollars to the State of Nevada expressly "for the preservation of the wild horses in the state of Nevada." Yet, since the early 1970s, when he passed on, and for well over a decade, Nevada merely sat on this money, allowing it to accrue with interest to over one million dollars. During this time, the state did absolutely nothing to help wild horses in the wild with the funds. In the early 1980s, surviving family members of Leo Heil became alarmed that the bequest was being ignored and threatened to sue for the return of all funds. Finally prompted at the prospect of losing substantial money, state officials took steps to establish the commission in order to carry out—at least ostensibly—the stipulation of Leo Heil.

---

6 NDOW's stance is in line with skewed and biased reports on wild horses and burros issued by the national NGO The Wildlife Society. Its latest report of August 21, 2011, counts among the most flagrant examples of distortion and selective filtering of facts that has yet been published. The biologist Michael Hutchins is largely responsible for this report. Basically, The Wildlife Society is a pro-hunter organization that cannot be counted upon for objectivity or fairness toward all species in America.

Beginning in 1985, Ms. Terry Jay from Las Vegas was appointed as executive director and moved to Carson City. Known for her work as a healing therapist whose patients rode on horseback, Ms. Jay knew little about the actual horses in their wild and free state, but was a quick learner and seemed to take her role seriously as executor of the Leo Heil Will. During her tenure, she met with a barrage of inducements and attempts to brainwash her with the negative premises and goals of the anti-wild-horse establishment, largely controlled by ranchers and hunters who resented any infringement upon their political power.[7]

Once, Ms. Jay was given a guided tour out of Tonopah in south central Nevada. This tour aimed to convince her of how wild horses were ruining the range, water sources, and driving ranching families out of business. The state officials and ranchers, including long-time, virulent wild horse enemy Joe Fallini, Jr., took her to areas where hordes of cattle had been overgrazing the land for nearly a century. Acting conveniently to their interests, they proceeded to lay the blame for dusty, eroded, de-vegetated conditions upon the mustangs. At first Ms. Jay seemed a bit swayed, but some time later, perceiving the cowboy hyperbole, she grew suspect. She gave input to state and federal agencies more in the role of wild horse advocate than her successor Ms. Barcomb did; and this most likely led to Jay's ouster in the late 1980s. I recall that during one visit to her office, she complained that the commission was being set up for ineffectualness and that the teaming of her office with another office was a ploy to spy on and control her activities, thus effectively thwarting true compliance with Leo Heil's will.

One positive gain that Ms. Jay helped make possible for the wild horses was the creation of a public educational film through Heil legacy funds.

---

7 Indeed, they sought to take control over nearly all public lands, especially those held by BLM and USFS as part of the notorious "Sagebrush Rebellion." These rebels, including long-time state senators Dean Rhoades and John Carpenter, conveniently overlooked their culture's own dismal history of livestock overgrazing on Nevada's deserts, valleys, and mountain chains dating from the mid-1800s, as well as their wholesale predator extermination and the promotion of an unnaturally large population of game animals, particularly deer. For example, in 2010 NDOW, obeying this ilk, expanded hunting licenses for the couple thousand puma that still inhabit the state and now (2011) for the black bear so that more deer, elk, etc., would be available to hunt. (Baker 1985.)

This was entitled *Wild Horses of the Nevada Desert* by Sacramento film maker Peter Dallas (1987). I guided Dallas to several ranges, but especially the Pine Nut Range just east from Carson Valley, my home, to search out and film the wiry, wild mustangs. He particularly favored back-lighted scenes of the horses and took some stunning footage. The idea behind this film was to achieve a greater appreciation of and respect for the wild horses in the wild among the general public. This well-balanced, scientifically-based film had been the fruit of five years of painstaking labor, yet it was no longer used by the commission during its last years of operation during the first decade of the twenty-first century, and recent attempts to obtain a copy from the commission by the Carson Valley Museum for a mustang exhibit were in vain. (Fortunately, I had one copy to lend this museum.) In place of this fine film, showing at the Reno-Tahoe International Airport was a very biased film about wild horses placed by the commission and tailor-made to suit wild equid enemies, full of cleverly crafted distortions concerning their history and value in the wild, arbitrarily and non-objectively stressing their domestic as opposed to natural origins as well as "overpopulation" while failing to mention their North American roots and the proportions of livestock and big game versus remaining wild equids that truly dwarf the latter.

An official commission letter from the spring of 2007 was signed by Ms. Barcomb and directed to the U.S. Congress (Appendix II: Letter from Barcomb to Congress available by request from author). It painted an unrealistic picture of wild horses in Nevada and claimed they were overpopulated, destroying the ecosystem, and driving ranchers to bankruptcy, when the exact opposite was true. Of course, we should have a likely idea as to why Barcomb wrote this misleading letter. If she did not, she would be fired and replaced with some more willing pawn of Nevada's official though not popular anti-wild-horse establishment.

Additionally, we should know why the livestock establishment as well as the hunting establishment gets its way. They use violent means of obtaining what they want, including implied or direct threats, and the all-out delivery of harmful blows in a great variety of ways: economically, socially, politically, and, yes, even physically and all very much contrary to America's declared democratic way of life. The anti-wild-equid establishment does not complain, however, when it comes to receiving enormous subsidies from the federal government and the U.S. taxpayer in order to prop up their ecologically damaging and economically losing way of life. This is blind tradition at its worst, yet major media, including television, radio, magazine, and newspaper, too often continue to kowtow to these ruthless types, parroting the same lopsided stories that heap blame on our nation's scant remaining wild horses or burros while glorifying the puffed-up "cowboy" rancher, as though he could do no wrong. All this has more to do with bullying teamed with moral cowardice, dishonesty, and unwholesome attachment to blind tradition than with what is true and fair—as well as truly free (Stillman 2008, Part III).

SIDEBAR: A TYPICAL NEVADA STATE WILD HORSE MEETING AS AN EXAMPLE OF GOVERNMENT SUBTERFUGE

On Friday, January 11, 2008, a meeting of the Nevada Commission for the Preservation of Wild Horses took place in Carson City. Here I had the opportunity to hear extensive presentations from BLM and state officials concerning the wild horse program and give public testimony (Appendix III: Statement of C.C. Downer to the Nevada Commission for the Preservation of Wild Horses available by request from author). While perhaps convincing to those with little knowledge or much bias, the otherwise polished presentations by the officials were, in fact, quite tendentious. They ignored the major causes of ecological deterioration while fixing blame upon the relatively few wild horses still remaining free-living, though in a natural world terribly tampered with by humans. One very misleading statement came from the commission's executive director Cathy Barcomb. She stated that BLM-designated herd management areas (HMAs) were unchangeable since they had been established at the passage of the Wild Free-Roaming Horses and Burros Act in 1971. To correct this, I immediately made it known that HMAs were in most cases significantly reduced from the original herd areas (HAs) that had been established by the act. She immediately conceded this, but briefly and in a low tone. (How quickly our government officials can forget the rights of wild horses on their legal lands!)

At the meeting, Power Point imaged shows by BLM officials sought to justify continued, large-scale wild horse roundups, citing drought conditions and the necessity of bringing the herds within the ecological carrying capacity. Springs and riparian areas were shown appearing trampled and degraded. What was sorely omitted, however, was the greater picture as to why these conditions had been allowed to develop and what species were their major causes..

Intentionally omitted were the proportions of livestock to wild horses in the BLM districts in question, and, more tellingly, within each specific HMA, not to mention the greater original HA. Also un-emphasized were the manipulation and monopolization of public waters by local ranchers, game departments, miners, developers, and other exploitive interests, as well as over-fencing of these public lands to accommodate the rest rotation schemes of the livestock operators (Coffey 2010 a & b; Kathleen Gregg, pers. comm. 8/22/11 in relation to Twin Peaks, California, HMA).

To be fair, however, BLM's Suzie Stokke spoke up that in her agency's Ely District (eastern Nevada) in the region of several wild horse HMAs under question, local ranchers owned many of the water sources (possessed water rights). She said that these waters were, in all but a few cases, being denied to the wild horses, i.e., shut off when the ranchers' cattle or sheep were seasonally removed from the public lands. Nonetheless, this begged the question as to why BLM officials chose not to negotiate for the use of these waters, especially since they held the trump card: *grazing on public lands is a cancelable privilege* as well as the Implied Federal Water Rights that came with the act.

In the fall of 2007, by executive decree approving its Resource Management Plan, BLM's Ely District zeroed out an enormous 1.6 million acres of legal wild horse herd areas. In our meeting, several wild horse advocates accused the BLM of failing to exercise its authority to defend Ely's wild horses. We asked why BLM had failed to ensure adequate water for viable wild horse herds, since they could do this by working out a just compromise with local ranchers as above stated. Also BLM had clearly not exercised the Codes of Federal Regulations 4710.5 and 4710.6 to remove livestock in order to safeguard the rights and long-term viability of wild horses and burros in their legal areas. Though Ely's wild horse clearances met with vigorous public and legal protest, such have been largely ignored by authorities; and in the fall and early winter of 2009, BLM contractors, indeed, proceeded to zero out 12 wild horse HMAs from the vast area they had targeted and where only ca. 620 healthy but nervous wild horses had remained.

Since this meeting, BLM has proceeded with more massive roundups in many other areas, citing, as if by rote, conflicting uses. These include oil and gas drilling and pipelines, livestock, big game, massive, water-consuming mining and solar energy projects, drought conditions, and/or wild horses in excess of established appropriate management levels—set at outrageously low levels, I might add. According to the Public Rangelands Improvement Act (PRIA) of 1978, AMLs are not supposed to be set in concrete but should vary according to monitoring of resource condition and be set *fairly and comparably* in relation to the other grazing animals. And the wild horse/burro act clearly states that the wild equids are to be treated as the *principal* presences within their legal areas. However, BLM has allocated minimal resources to wild equids, abandoning its duty to protect and preserve them in the wild, including through "closure to livestock."

Though advocates were allowed to call attention to flagrant blind spots in current wild horse policy at both federal and state levels, I got the feeling of an exclusive "good old boys' club" operating at the commission meeting to achieve wild horse minimization on and where possible elimination from the public lands. All the while, the flagrant issue of traditional public lands monopolization by ranching, big game, and other interests was perversely ignored by the "members of the club." Other very pertinent questions that were ignored concerned the major deleterious effects of rampant open-pit mining on water tables and, hence, on spring sources in the arid valleys and ranges of Nevada, as well as southern Nevada's, i.e., Las Vegas's, attempt to siphon off massive amounts of water from eastern Nevada (Kunzig 2008). My experience of the meeting brought to mind the Biblical verse: 'one cannot serve two masters.'

SPRING RANGE, SOUTHERN NEVADA

Most of the legal wild equid herds throughout the West have danger-ously low populations and the ratios of wild equids to livestock/big game animals are ridiculously low. For example, in the Spring Mountain Complex of wild horse and burro herd areas, the Las Vegas BLM District and Humboldt-Toiyabe National Forest plans to allow only one wild equid per seven thousand-plus legal acres. Here big game and to a less-er extent livestock outnumber and out-consume the wild equids many times over (Appendix IX: Letter of Craig C. Downer [12/03/2006] re: Spring Mountain Complex of HMAs and BLM's preliminary man-agement plan, available by request from author). And here most of the Spring Mountain public waters have been fenced off so that wild horses cannot access them, but game animals, such as trophy bighorn sheep, can. Though this state of affairs directly violates the Wild Free-Roaming Horses and Burros Act, the National Environment Protection Act (NEPA), the Federal Land Policy and Management Act (FLPMA), the Public Rangelands Improvement Act (PRIA), as well as the Multiple Use and Sustainability Act, for the past approximately two decades most federal judges have blindly dismissed legal suits, including from dam-aged locals (e.g., National Wild Horse Association vs. BLM 2007; The Cloud Foundation, Downer and Moffat vs. Salazar et al. July 2011. Judge McKibben, Reno Federal Court re: Triple B roundup injunction appeal).

IBLA RENEGES

Though the Interior Board of Land Appeals is supposed to police the BLM, when it comes to the wild horses and burros for the past twen-ty years it has mainly rubber stamped the atrocious decisions and actions of this our nation's largest public lands agency. One of the most egregious cases concerns the above-mentioned zeroing out of the Caliente Complex of twelve HMAs in southeastern Nevada. A list and rundown of all the cases that have been decided by IBLA may be obtained by calling up www.oha.doi.gov/IBLA/finding IBLA.html then clicking on Search Decisions and typing in "wild horses burros". Here will be listed many cases such as those brought by Animal Protection Institute of America, WHOA!, Michael Blake, as well as my own. Many wild horse advocates with inside experience realize that the act's subversion has been on direct order from uncaring politicians in the "highest" of positions, which is to say, in bed with the wild horses' and burros' worst enemies.

WILD BURROS, THE WORST TREATED

The official treatment of our nation's last wild burros in their legal herd areas/territories has been even more unjust than that of the wild horses. Though small to begin with and occupying some of the most arid and harsh desert habitats, these remnant herds have been almost entirely eliminated from the wild. Most of the legal burro areas remain in name only, still legal but devoid of wild burros, thus making a mockery of the act.

In Nevada, only sixteen burro herd areas still have any surviving burros, eleven of which have AMLs of less than fifty, and in twelve of these, present populations are actually lower than the AMLs, suggesting some other nefarious factors are at work against them like illegal shootings or barricading of water sources. The Stonewall HMA has only twenty burros, yet its AML is only eight. That's right: eight burros in nearly 24,000 legal acres! The Lava Beds herd also has only twenty survivors, while its AML is set at sixteen individuals in nearly 233,000 original legal acres. Many of these burro herds have gone into a tailspin due to inbreeding and chance die out—all consequence of being set up by their supposed government caretakers. In cahoots with the burros' enemies, officials implement ever more hostile policies, further tightening restrictions on their freedom, so that the prejudiced claims they issue about these animals that they are inbred turn into self-fulfilling prophecies (see Chapter V).

A proposal by BLM's Las Vegas office would cripple one of the few remaining viable herds by reducing it from about six hundred burros to a non-viable level of twenty-two. This concerns the Gold Butte herd near Tonopah. A smear campaign against burros has been made to appear "scientific" but is nothing more than a pseudo-justification for their elimination (MacDonald, C. 2007; John Phillips, former BLM WH/B official, pers. comm., 8/2011).

As of summer 2008, in California, wild burros were practically gone. The last terrible blow was the elimination of the Clark Mountain herd in southeast California, a very distinctive and hardily adapted population of long-standing in these hot deserts that included the very rare, large, and long-haired Poitou burros. The official description of these admirable survivors was negatively cast, their positive aspects ignored, or, if brought up, speedily denied. A suit was brought to prevent their elimination, but the judges gave short shrift to the well-grounded complaints of the wild burro advocates. They sided *in toto* with the BLM officials, as did bighorn hunter organizations, the California Fish and Game Department, and certain chapters of the Sierra Club, maintaining that the burro has no place in the wilderness West. But in so doing, they ignored the fact that the ass branch of the horse family had its origin and long-standing evolution in North America and that fossils indicate equids very similar to burros inhabited much of the U.S. and Mexico for millions of years and until about ten thousand years ago (MacFadden 1992, 112, Figure 5.12 from Bennett 1980).

Top equine authority Dr. Hans Klingel argues that the African wild ass originated in North America since there is no substantial evidence that it has changed enough in the relatively short time since it came from North America to the Old World to warrant being declared a separate species (Klingel 1979). The African wild ass is the same species as the burro, or donkey, regardless of recent naming changes (*Equus africanus*), as attests such authoritative works as *Walker's Mammals of the World,* which refers to them as *Equus asinus,* their original and long standing name (Walker 1999, 1011–13).

Another important point: since the true vigor and ability to survive of any race or species is preserved in the wild and since the African Wild Ass is classified as in Critical Danger of Extinction by the IUCN Species Survival Commission (of which I am a member) and as Endangered with extinction by the United States Department of Interior, we should do all in our power to assure that the wild burros of America are restored to truly viable levels, for they could well have a better chance of surviving than those of their same species that remain under very beleaguered conditions in Africa (ibid, p. 1013). I find it atrocious that there are people who call themselves biologists

and conservationists as well as humans yet who are willing to absolutely trash the wild burros as well as the wild horses, just because
some of their lineage has been under domestication. Don't they see
that when they return to living free in the world of nature they are
returning to their own truer nature, taking up where they left off an
ever so short time ago when we consider the vastness of life's history
on Earth?

A Refresher on AML, MVP, Reduction of Herd Areas & Related Topics

According to its 2007 published statistics, BLM's nationwide Appropriate
Management Level (AML) for wild horses and burros was set at only
27,492 of which 2,695 were burros and the rest horses. This amounts
to leaving only one remaining wild equid for every 1,253 acres of reduced herd management areas, or for every 1,871 acres of original
herd areas created by the act (according to BLM's recognized acreages).
These token designations are outrageous (see Figure 6 on page 53 of
present chapter). The FY2009 nationwide AML was 26,578 for both
species, nearly a thousand less than that of 2007, and this still seems to
be in place as of 2011.

Out of thirty herd areas still with a few wild burros in Arizona, Oregon,
California, Nevada, and Utah, only six have AMLs that could even ques-
tionably be considered as genetically viable in the long term—all in
Arizona. In other words, twenty-four, or 80%, are mere token preserves
with a few to several thousand legal acres per remaining individual. The
sparse distribution of these hardy desert survivors represents a treach-
erous setup for their demise.

As earlier described, BLM's use of the low population figure of 150
individuals for minimum genetic viability (MVP) of horses or burros is
very questionable. As already indicated, its sole cited source is Dr. Gus
Cothran, a veterinarian specialized in horse genetics from Kentucky; and
even he cautions against overemphasizing this figure (Animal Welfare
Institute 2008, 23). Remember that 2,500 was recommended for the
viability of equid species in general by the IUCN SSC Equid Specialist

Group (Duncan 1992). For many other species, the MVP is often much higher, e.g., 5,000 adults for the desert tortoise.

GROSSLY UNFAIR AML AND HMA NUMBERS NATIONWIDE

Though possessing a legal right to live in their year-round 1971 occupied habitats throughout the West, burros have been totally eliminated from over 5 million acres and reduced to non-viable populations in nearly all the areas where they still live. According to the Animal Welfare Institute's analysis, 130 of the 199 wild horse/ burro HMAs, or 65 percent, have established AMLs that are less than 150 individuals, i.e., are even by BLM standards genetically non-viable (Animal Welfare Institute 2007, 22). According to BLM's 2008 statistics, of the original 319 herd areas, only 199 are still managed for wild equids in reduced herd management areas. These statistics list 2,745 as the nationwide AML for burros and 25,068 as the nationwide AML for both wild horses and burros. This translates to 22,323 as the nationwide AML for wild horses, spread throughout the West in many fragmented HMAs, certainly a lower population than occurred in 1971 at the passage of the act. But stop press! As of September 2010 only 180 HMAs are still to be managed for wild horses and burros by the BLM. Surprise? You've got to be kidding!

THE KIGER MUSTANGS

In southern Oregon survives a group of distinctive wild horses known as the Kiger mustangs. Centered around the fascinating Steens Mountain and the Alvord Desert, only a few hundred of these still survive, yet the appropriate management level for these herds has been repeatedly slashed by BLM officials. These have buckled under to the clamoring demands of wild horse enemies loathe to share freedom and the land or to give the wild horses one bit of credit. For example, a pathetic appropriate management level of eighty-two has been set for the aptly named Kiger Herd Area, thus assuring its decline. The estimated population here was fifty-one wild horses on approximately thirty thousand legal acres as of 2008 (U.S. Department of the Interior 2008). As is often the case, the relative proportions vis-a-vis livestock and big game remain unrevealed by our public servants, and the desires of the general public are again ignored. During the second week of July 2011, the Kiger and Riddle Mountain HMAs were again gutted by a BLM-contracted helicopter roundup that gathered all of the ca. 210 wild horses here in southeastern Oregon. Of these, 113 are planned for permanent removal, while 84 mustangs are to be returned based on color and other traits desired by Kiger mustang breeders, thus disregarding natural selection by this unique ecosystem or social selection by the wild horses themselves. The AML for these two areas is only 84 to 138 on 55,000 acres. Here the BLM permits 688 privately owned cattle to graze. One half of the stallions are to be gelded and returned. Thus created is a true set up for inbreeding and a socially dysfunctional herd. The policy for these herds is more a private breeding program than one that values and perpetuates these unique horses in all their wild vigor. Though I asked the Federal District Court in Pendleton for a Temporary Restraining Order, it was not granted. Together with The Cloud Foundation, I am now legally asking that these gathered Kiger mustangs be returned intact (The Cloud Foundation and Downer vs. Salazar et al. July 2011).

According to long-time observers to whom I have spoken, Kiger mustangs intentionally avoid out-breeding with other wild horse populations. When presented with such an opportunity, they instinctively stick to their own kind. Could it be they are seeking to preserve their own distinctive character and unique adaptiveness where God though fate has placed them? Could this be an incipient speciation? Some, such as behavioral biologist Mary Ann Simonds, doubt this and claim that the Kiger mustang image was created as a publicity ploy by BLM to more readily adopt this over-gathered herd (Simonds 2008). Still many maintain that these horses are quite special.

Possessing a trim, wiry build and energetic demeanor, Kiger mustangs seem most affiliated with pure Arabians, yet differ in significant ways from them. Our public servants should restore this unique lineage to viable population levels in the thousands rather than allowing them to become inbred, or so out-bred that their unique lineage becomes lost. Whether in the BLM or Forest Service, our federal officials should fend for their rights to adequate, year-round water, forage, and space appropriate for a truly long-term viable population, e.g., 2,500, not 150 (Duncan 1992).

Do Kiger mustangs represent a remnant of continuously surviving native American horses? Though many may consider this far-fetched, we should remain open-minded and do a DNA analysis to test this hypothesis. According to Alexandra Fuller (2009) writing in *National Geographic*, "[s]ome scientists argue that the Spanish Conquistadors' horses encountered and bred with a remnant native population...." Perhaps some remote populations still retain this native strain. It is believed that many of the Indian ponies who were massacred by Whites were composed of such autochthonous strains, and that some of these may still remain on reservations, e.g., of the Sioux (Henderson 1991; see Chapter 1). Regardless how such distinctive breeds originated, they are valuable and deserve much better protection and fairer numbers in the wild. Some equid students even consider the Kiger herd and a few others to preserve dwindling strains of the Spanish Sorraia (Oelke 1997). Regardless, the Kigers deserve respect in their own right and greater freedom upon all the land that was legally set aside for them.[8]

OTHER RARE MUSTANG POPULATIONS IN THE SOUTHWEST

Along with the Kigers, many other distinctive herds have received unjust treatment from the BLM and Forest Service. One inhabits Arizona's Cerbat Mountain. Though it represents a very pure and distinctive Spanish mustang lineage, its AML has been set at just ninety horses. In New Mexico, the only two herd areas still with any wild horses living in them have been assigned ridiculously low AMLs

---

8 The animated wild stallion of the Oscar-nominated movie *Spirit: Wild Stallion of the Cimarron* (2002) was modeled after a once wild and free Kiger stallion from these parts. Steven Spielberg purchased "Spirit" for fifty thousand dollars at a post-gather auction put on by the BLM. This magnificent stallion now resides at the Return to Freedom sanctuary near Lampoc, California, and can be visited, as author did in 6/2009.

entirely incongruous with their historical importance or the public's interest in them. These occur in the Atravesado and the Carracas Mesas HMAs and have been assigned AMLs of sixty and twenty-three horses respectively. Since the majority (77%) of New Mexico's legal herd areas have already been zeroed out, it would seem that these two remaining herds would be allowed much larger populations to preserve their long-term viability. This would be a start at compensating for the wild horses' extravagant elimination elsewhere. But this is not happening, as the purse nets of greed draw tighter on America's last wild ones. One recent and hopeful development from this state, however, was Governor Bill Richardson's support for a small wild horse sanctuary to contain approximately one hundred wild horses on about ten thousand acres.

In southern California the very distinctive, pure Spanish mustang race of the Coyote Canyon HMA was entirely zeroed out on March 17, 2003, as a result of a thoughtless agreement by the BLM with the California State Parks. This transferred the HMA to the state supposedly in order to protect a rare race of Peninsula Bighorn and in spite of a big niche separation between the two species. This herd of largely orange-brown mustangs is believed to trace back to the 1600s when the Jesuit Padre Eusebio Kino made missionary entrees into this region. Many of these mustangs are being kept by private individuals in the hope that they may be restored to their rightful freedom in the Beauty Mountain region on BLM land near Coyote Canyon. But so far this virtuous vision has been met only with rebuffs from BLM offices in southern California (Kathleen Hayden 2008, pers. comm.; Bergeron 2003).

SABOTAGE OF THE WILD HORSE ACT IN ARIZONA

In Arizona, long-time wild horse and burro supporter Terry Watt has gathered alarming proof of official and local sabotage of wild horse rights. This comes in the form of testimony from numerous witnesses and many dated photographs concerning wild horse populations occurring in this state. According to the gathered evidence, wild horses were systematically removed all along the Colorado River between the late

1960s until the early 1980s—even after the act's passage in 1971—and the horses were, thus, deprived of their legal areas. Watt has pictures of these illegal captures taken in 1980 between the Black Mountains and the Colorado River near Bullhead City. In Arizona, several thousand wild horses were estimated to survive, perhaps even over ten thousand on public and Indian lands in 1971, but they were removed *en masse* as part of a collusion among official and unofficial state and local enemies and in blatant disregard of the law.

A wild horse/burro roundup contractor revealed that well after the act's passage he participated in large-scale wild horse removals occurring north along Interstate Highway 40 to Bullhead City, along the Colorado River in the Mohave Valley. Bait traps were placed on the horses' watering trails to the river, and many wild horse deaths resulted. These were lingering deaths from dehydration, since the traps were checked only once every several days, and the desert heat here soars over 100°F, often exceeding 120°F in the summer. Watt insists that Arizona "did a lot of 'wild horse clean up' both before and after the passage of the act, to rid the state of as many as they could, leaving us a mostly burro state" (Terry Watt 2008, pers. comm.).

THE GILA MUSTANG HERD

Another distinctive example of Spanish mustangs from Arizona is to be found in the Gila herd. This population had inhabited the White Sands military testing area for generations, until it was decided to unceremoniously eliminate them all. Since military areas are not covered by the act and in spite of strenuous objection and section 6 of the act that encourages cooperative agreements with other agencies to preserve wild horses/burros, these horses were preemptively slated for trapping and possible slaughter. While most of these distinctive mustangs dwell no more on our earthly plane, owing to the valiant efforts of Karen Sussman of the International Society for the Protection of Mustangs and Burros (ISPMB), a small remnant of this once great herd was rescued and transported to the society's wild horse sanctuary near Lantry, South Dakota. A true heroine, Ms. Sussman had become disillusioned with government broken promises and chose to work with the Lakota

Sioux to assure the Gila herd, among other distinctive herds, a place in relative freedom, a place of sanctuary that in a brighter future will serve to restore populations where they have adapted and evolved, thus picking up the ancient threads. Among her most faith-restoring activities is simply wandering among and communing with these spirited horses (Brungardt 2006).

WILD HORSE ABUSE LINKED TO FAVORING OF RICH, TELLING STATISTICS, CALL FOR REFORM

Though the GAO had a fairly good track record for exposing the continued overgrazing and other abuses of our public lands ecosystems, its recommendations have been seldom heeded. Its 1992 report found that out of about twenty-three thousand public lands grazing permittees on BLM land, a mere five hundred held 47% of the privileges, and that the top twenty held 9.3% of allocated forage on BLM lands. This latter represents the use and abuse of 20.7 million public acres. Many of the permittees are wealthy individuals used to getting their way and include bankers, lawyers, and doctors. Many are hobby ranchers who receive enormous federal subsidies to impose livestock on our public lands (Hudak 2007).

As of November 2008, and as a bend-over-backwards favor by the Bush administration to public lands ranchers, the applied fee again became the minimum allowed under the Taylor Grazing Act of 1934. This is $1.35 for one Animal Unit Month (AUM = one cow and calf or five sheep grazing for one month, or one horse) and represents about one-twelfth of the fair market value. This minimum fee was again reinstated in March 2011 by the federal government. One major beneficiary is the estate of the late Idaho "potato king" billionaire J. R. Simplot, whose livestock grazing leases cover over two million acres of public lands throughout the West. Other examples are Conrad Hilton's corporation and the Anheuser-Busch beer empire.

Though livestock grazing is allowed on ca. 290 million acres of public lands of which 257 million acres are federal lands and 33-million acres are state controlled lands, such accounts for only 2.4% of beef produced in the seventeen western states; public-lands-raised sheep only represent a very minor 3.54% of all sheep raised in the United States. Livestock's tradition of despoliation is a lamentable "tragedy of the commons" dating back five centuries in the Americas and thousands of years worldwide (Rifkin 1992; Downer 1987). But mere duration of this insensitive and shortsighted plunder in no way justifies its continuance. Now is high time that we humans learn from our past mistakes, identify a more ecologically harmonious lifestyle, and make the necessary sacrifices in order to truly realize this positive change—before our predicament becomes irreversible and even our most sober efforts are too late.

According to the monumental documentation of livestock abuse and favoring on U.S. public lands *Welfare Ranching: The Subsidized Destruction of the American West* (Wuerthner and Matteson 2002), BLM permittees currently graze their livestock on 214 million acres of public land. Adding the U.S. Forest Service, U.S. Fish & Wildlife Service and other land jurisdictions (state, county, municipal) brings this figure to ca. 300 million public acres. The major share of grazing resources on this land is given primarily to livestock. But within USFS and BLM lands, at least 53.5 million acres (one-sixth of livestock grazed public lands) are actually legal wild horse and burro areas, where the wild equids by law have "principal" status among the multiple uses present. Why is it then that they have been entirely eliminated from 23 million (ca. 40%) of these legal acres, and now are to occupy only 26.6 million acres but in very sparse and greatly diminished, reproductively compromised numbers? (See figures 4, 5 and 7 [Figure 7 on p. 113]). Taking all the public lands into consideration, wild horses and burros may be outnumbered by private livestock and big game animals to the tune of two hundred-to-one in terms of relative consumption of resources (Brungardt 2006, 233). To add insult to injury, within their reduced legal herd management areas, the wild equids are greatly marginalized, unfairly and illegally outnumbered by livestock and, in many areas, big game grazers (Appendix I: Forever Wild and Free Speech of 10/12/2008 available by request from author).

As of February 29, 2008, 29,644 wild horses and 3,461 wild burros remained on the public lands for a total of 33,105 wild equids, though independent wild equid investigator Cindy MacDonald put the true number at about half this (www.americanherds.blogspot.com). In FY2009, and as of February 28, 2009, BLM reported 33,102 wild horses and 3,838 wild burros for a total of 36,940 wild equids. The nationwide Appropriate Management Level, however, decreased from 27, 219 to 26,578 wild equids. As of February 28, 2010, BLM reported 33,692 wild horses and 4,673 wild burros for a total of 38,365 wild equids. In FY 2010, animals removed were 9,715 wild horses and 540 wild burros, while only 2,742 horses and 332 burros were adopted (USDI Public Land Statistics 2010, Volume 195, BLM/OC/ST-11/001+1165. Pp. 247-248). Meanwhile the number of cattle permitted on western lands amounts to ca. 7.5 million (ibid, p. 90-91). And the number of sheep permitted to graze on these same lands amounts to several million more (ibid, p. 90-91). Though the season of use of livestock is not always year-round, this is still an enormous quantity of domestic livestock grazing, a sum that dwarfs resource consumption by wild equids. Public lands livestock permittees are given priority treatment and usually allowed to graze their livestock during advantageous seasons when plants have a greater nutrient value, while leaving what remains for wildlife grazers, including the returned native equids, to subsist on year-round.

The federal land livestock program constitutes an enormous subsidy to people who like to "play cowboy." When both financial and ecological costs are summed up, this subsidy amounts to at least a half-billion dollars of annual loss to Americans, though the ecological loss, superficially estimated at $150 million (Center for Biological Diversity 2002), is much more serious than mere money can express, for this is involved with such life-threatening issues as global species extinction and global climate change/warming (de Haan et al. 2006).

According to a recent report by the Department of Interior, recreation creates 19 percent of jobs associated with the public lands (388,127) and greater than $47 billion in economic benefits and activity. On the other hand, it was determined that public lands grazing was responsible for only two tenths of one percent (4,914) of all jobs generated by

Department of Interior, and produced only $0.64 billion in economic impact annually (USDI. 2010 [June 21]).

Of ca. 1 million livestock producers in the U.S., only about twenty-three thousand, or 2.3%, graze their livestock on federal lands as permittees. But a full 70% of western cattle producers own all of the land where their cattle are raised. It has been estimated that livestock producers on the public lands and the approximate eighteen thousand low-paying jobs directly related to the livestock industry could be replaced within a score of days by sound jobs given customary expansion of the U.S. economy (Handwerg 1980). In subsidizing these outfits, U.S. taxpayers loose at least $115 million per year according to Handwerg. In spite of these incontrovertible facts, the public lands livestock association has remained extremely powerful relative to the millions of non-vested but nevertheless public-lands-interested and benefiting people. The livestock association exerts great control over politics in the United States and abroad—much of this due to the Hollywood-promoted myth of the cowboy (Stillman 2008). Much of their power is also due to the livestock industry's "by hook or by crook" approach to getting their way, to maintaining and expanding their possession of the public lands and resources. This is in keeping with the historical tradition of occupying wild lands, supplanting their wild plants and animals, and, in general, plundering ecosystems with little thought of what the past has prepared for the future of life here or anywhere on Earth. The emphasis has clearly been on present advantage only.

In spite of all its ostentation, do you think this is so admirable and actually such a great model to emulate? This intolerable situation must and will soon change, when "we the people" not only discover, but actually implement a better way of life. The dare to change today in an ecologically benign way is a most urgent one. And each one of us must answer this in his/her own special way.

MORE ON MONOPOLIZATION OF PUBLIC LANDS AGENCIES CONTRASTED

To understand the extent of livestock grazing on the public lands, we should convert allocated Animal Unit Months (AUMs) to year-round cow-with-calf equivalents. This is simply done by dividing the AUMs by twelve. According to *BLM Public Lands Statistics 2002*, as of December 17, 2002, grazing privileges allocated to livestock totaled 7,872,819 AUMs on 163,311,163 acres. This number of AUMs is equivalent to 656,068 cows with their calves grazing year-round on BLM public lands. Given only about thirty thousand wild horses or burros remaining on BLM lands (U.S. Department of the Interior 2008 and subsequent years to 2011), this yields a ratio of twenty-two-to-one (4.5%) as concerns livestock vis-a-vis wild horse/burro grazing. Imagine a lemon-meringue pie cut into 22 equal pieces. Only one of these pieces is for the wild horses and burros. And please remember that this is on BLM lands alone.

On the lands of the U.S. Forest Service, the other agency charged with protecting and preserving our nation's wild horses and burros, there are even more livestock permitted to graze on about half as much land as BLM possesses. This may come as a surprise, since typically we like to think of the Forest Service as preserving our nation's last remaining forests, yet they are the nation's biggest promoters of public-lands-grazing livestock, even more so than the BLM. According to the *Grazing Statistical Summary Fiscal Year 2000 USDA-Forest Service*, there were 7,963,233 AUMs of livestock grazing permitted on 89,550,382 acres of land, many of which are in vital headwaters areas where livestock damage springs and streams feeding major rivers (with their fish spawning grounds), lakes, reservoirs, drinking and irrigation supplies, etc., located downstream. This figure works out to 663,603 cow-with-calf year-round equivalent units. Relatively—and quite suspiciously—very few wild horses or burros have been allowed to remain in their legal territories on USFS lands, the number being ca. 3,500. Again we witness the dirty politics that has operated against the wild equids. Given the figure of 3,500 wild horses or burros still on USFS land, the ratio of livestock to wild equids would be 189-to-1 (0.53%). As with the BLM, only to a more exacerbating degree, the disproportion of livestock to wild equids applies even within the legal wild equid territories. This is entirely at odds with the clear mandate of the 1971 act earmarking the wild horses and burros as the "principal" presence to be protected and managed "where found at the passage of the Act" along with other appropriate and harmonious uses, values, services, and species.

Two other agencies permitting livestock grazing on their lands are the National Park Service (NPS) and the U.S. Fish and Wildlife Service

(USFWS), although this seems inconsistent with their legal mandate to provide nature-oriented recreation that does not disrupt the eco-system and to preserve wildlife and wildlife habitat (Wuerthner and Matteson 2002). The NPS allows 81,752 AUMs of livestock grazing on a bit less than 3 million acres, while the USFWS allows 258,166 AUMs on 1,416,005 acres. This is the annual equivalent of 6,813 year-round cow-with-calf units (or 34,063 sheep) on National Park Service land and of 21,514 cow-and-calf units (or 107,569 sheep) on USFWS refuges. In spite of their large allowance for livestock, the current policy of these two agencies is to eliminate all (NPS) or nearly all (USFWS) wild horses and burros from their lands. Their officials conveniently brand these animals as ecologically destructive exotics, all the while entirely ignoring their positive contribution to the native North American ecosystem as returned natives (see Chapter I & II).

Concerning the Sheldon-Hart National Wildlife Refuge (USFWS), al-though an agreement with Wild Horse Annie's organization WHOA! had promised to allow for wild horses in perpetuity as harmonious co-dwellers with pronghorn, in July, 2010, officials here decided to elimi-nate all wild horses from their refuge. And another nearby refuge, the Ruby Lake NWR of northeast Nevada, while permitting nearly all of its solid ground to be grazed by ranchers, strictly forbids adjoining legal wild horse herds from even taking a drink at the edge of their ref-uge. These are the Triple B and Maverick-Medicine herds that have just been extremely reduced by helicopter round ups to the tune of over 1,200 wild horses (August 2011), supposedly because they lack water, though for the past two years this region has received abundant even record-breaking precipitation (The Cloud Foundation, Downer, Moffat vs. Salazar et al. 2011). Both USFWS and BLM clearly eschew Section 6 of the act permitting a cooperative agreement that would allow the wild horses to get a drink—for goodness' sake!

The total for grazing AUMs on the lands governed by the four federal agencies—BLM, USFS, NPS, and USFWS—equals 16,175,970 AUMs on 257,277,550 acres (USDI 2007; Jacobs 1991; Wuerthner and Matteson, 2002). This signifies that wild equids at their current population level of approximately thirty thousand animals, or three hundred and sixty thousand AUMs per year, are out-consumed on the public lands by a ratio of forty-five livestock forage consumption to every one wild equid forage consumption, i.e., 45:1. And this does not bring grazing by big game animals into the equation. Wild equids represent ca. 2.2% of federal land grazing pressure when combined with livestock alone but only ca. 1.0% of same when combined with both livestock and big game. This is one in a hundred—hardly a fair deal! Considering all that our national heritage wild horses and burros mean to the public-at-large both nationally and worldwide (over forty-five thousand books and hundreds of films on them) and the major evolutionary and ecological role wild equids have played in North America, tracing back nearly 60 million years, this situation is simply unacceptable.

STATES CONTRASTED

In the eleven western states, the considerable state lands where livestock grazing is permitted sum to 33,358,000 acres (USDI 2007; Jacobs 1991; Wuerthner and Matteson 2002). Here wild horses and burros should also be permitted at viable population levels within areas to be legally designated. Often these appropriate areas are adjacent to federal herd areas/territories and, so, provide more suitable habitat for viable populations (think Section 6 of the act). This is the situation of the famous Virginia Range wild horse herd of Storey County, Nevada, east of Reno, but BLM arbitrarily decided to zero out the wild horses on its portion of this natural mustang region in spite of their great popularity.

Examples of state land livestock grazing pressure and corresponding acreage are:

State	AUMs	Acres
Arizona	1,185,030	8,400,000
Montana	1,090,000	4,100,000
Wyoming	ca. 900,000	3,600,000
Colorado	598,980	2,600,000
Idaho	240,000	1,900,000
Utah	198,000	3,150,000
New Mexico	135,937	ca. 8,000,000
Oregon	68,844	550,000

I was unable to obtain AUM statistics for California, Nevada, and Washington, but state lands grazed in these three states are 75,000 acres for California, 110,000 acres for Nevada, and 873,000 acres for Washington, representing considerable livestock "privilege" indeed.

OVERVIEW OF SITUATION

The most glaring omission by officials concerns the Relative Proportions among the various classes of large mammalian grazers within their legal herd areas, particularly livestock, big game and wild horses/burros. This comparison should also include other exploitive industries such as mining and farming; these consume water, affect soils, pollute air, etc. In most legal herd areas/territories, livestock and/or other interests such as big game animals and mining activities are being given the preponderant share of resources relative to the wild horses and burros.

SOME ADDITIONAL SPECIFIC EXAMPLES OF INJUSTICE FROM STATES

CALIFORNIA

In California, according to BLM, all but ca. 700 of the 798,000-acre Twin Peaks HMA's ca. 2,300 wild horses were rounded up by helicopter in August and September 2010. Yet according to my straight line transect by over-flight, only an estimated 265 wild horses remain, and hardly any burros. Livestock are allocated 82% of the forage in this scenic high desert HMA that lies just to the east of the Cascade Mountains. In more concrete terms, according to the officially set appropriate management levels, wild horses and burros are allowed to number only 448 and 72 respectively for 5,808 total AUMs annually, while cattle and sheep are allowed to number 3,730 and 10,000 for 27,175 total AUMs annually (J. Johnston, 2011 pers. comm.). (Also see Elyse Gardner's www.humaneobserver.blogspot.com for reports on Twin Peaks and other areas.)

OREGON

Discussed earlier, Oregon's Kiger mustangs have been reduced from a barely minimally viable 154 (according to BLM's very questionable standards) to the sub-viable level of 41 horses and this in spite of an AML set at 82. Though BLM officials euphemistically call this a "maintenance gather," in truth it is a gutting of this unique herd. As with Montana's Pryor Mountain herd, this is yet another case of managing for the extinction of a rare and valued sub-population of authentic old mustangs.

Yet the story gets worse. Even more draconian is the total elimination of mustangs by BLM from Oregon's Riddle HMA, all eighty of which were permanently removed in October of 2007 and in spite of BLM's still listing an AML of fifty-six horses and a current estimated population of thirty-three (U.S. Department of the Interior 2008). Two other wild horse roundups in Oregon followed between December 1 and 14, 2007, removing practically the entire wild horse population in the USFS and BLM sectors of Murders Creek HMA. In the USFS sector, the horse population was reduced from 208 to a tiny remnant of 20, while in the BLM sector, the population was reduced from 82 again to a mere 20 horses. Even if these two tiny remnants are able to interbreed, in combination their total of 40 wild horses is far below even the minimally genetically viable level of 150 horses supposedly recommended by Dr. Gus Cothran, about the only genetic authority the BLM ever cites. Because of such blatantly insensitive reductions or "zeroings out," Oregon has been left with mere token, overly fragmented wild horse populations subject to inbreeding and chance die-out. In July 2011, the author sued the BLM before the Federal Court in Pendleton, Oregon, in order first to halt the roundup and then—after his injunction request was denied—to restore the Kiger and Riddle herds. So another drastic reduction coupled with PZP treatment of the few released mares has been allowed. Nonetheless our suit is still viable and asks for the return of the horses.

UTAH

Between January 17-19, 2008, Utah's Milford Flat wild horse herd was totally gathered; the reason given by BLM was simply "fire." I am suspect of this justification, since wild horses are capable of adapting to fire by shifting to new grazing areas. Also, BLM has a record of seizing any available excuse to reduce or eliminate remaining wild horses/burros. (All twenty-five horses were then shipped off to BLM holding facilities to await uncertain fates.) In Utah, between July 11-13, 2008, BLM plans were to totally remove the forty hardy horses surviving in the Paradise HMA. Again BLM conveniently cited "fire" with no independent evaluation. In Utah, the wild horses' worst enemies seem to be getting their way, while our democratically elected or appointed representatives and judges—as well as the president himself—turn a blind eye.

WYOMING

In Wyoming, between November 1-24, 2007, two wild horse herds were severely reduced. In White Mountain HMA, 612 wild horses were removed from a herd of 694, leaving only 82 in this vast area consisting of 207,981 BLM acres and 185,092 other agency acres (U.S. Department of the Interior 2008). "AML maintenance" was the only reason given, and, as usual, there was no mention of the relative proportions of resource consumption among the various users, including livestock. Neither was the number of legal acres per wild horse in the wild before and after the roundup even broached.

Also in Wyoming and during the same dates, BLM reduced the vast, six-hundred-thousand plus-acre Little Colorado HMA from 208 wild horses to 113, cutting it to a genetically non-viable level even by BLM's standards. In 2010, the Adobe Town wild horse herd was greatly reduced by helicopter roundup, leaving a tiny, crippled population in a vast area and causing some gruesome deaths, as was documented by photographer Carol Walker (www.wildhoofbeats.com).

NEVADA

In Nevada, using fire and/or drought as pretext, BLM has been on a real rampage, with no one to independently check its draconian wild horse reductions. For example, in the 260,000-acre New Pass/Ravenswood HMA, wild horses were recently reduced from 672 to 170, though the AML is 566 horses. This is the heart of the old Shoshone Indian herd known for its breath-taking paints and pintos. I am familiar with this herd and deplore its gutting. These animals should be allowed to naturally shift their grazing pressure to other areas of the vast BLM public domain where adequate forage exists for them. This would be part of a natural rest rotation that each herd instinctively performs. Members of the horse family are pre-adapted to survive by consuming parched, dry vegetation; and they are equally capable of re-seeding the burned-over areas through their feces during their extensive perambulations. Their feces are not as degraded in the digestive process as are ruminants' (see Chapter II). But this type of objectivity is being ignored by our land management officials.

Quite speciously, Nevada's BLM has recently eliminated all wild horses from the Augusta Mountains HMA. This 177,000-acre reserve was reduced from an original HA of 316,000 acres (BLM, 2008). BLM's helicopter gather for July 2008, in the 338,000-acre Owyhee HMA in the northern part of the state took one of America's few sizeable and viable populations of 546 wild horses down to a mere 145, just below Dr. Cothran's minimally viable population level, leaving one wild horse for every 2,331 acres. Again, though drought is BLM's announced excuse, no independent authority verified this, nor did BLM consider any alternatives that might allow these magnificent animals to remain both alive and free as a naturally self-stabilizing population, or herd. One point is certain, during my over-flights of this area I observed plenty of water at the ranches, which sported lush green meadows and overflowing ponds. Water that should have been shared was siphoned off the public lands to the wild horses' detriment.

One of the first roundups conducted in the fall of 2009 (fiscal year 2010) was of the previously mentioned Caliente Complex in southeast Nevada, named for its location near the old railway town of this name. This was composed of twelve wild horse HMAs totaling 1.4 million acres in southeast Nevada. The decision that came down was for the total elimination of all wild horses here. Though only 620 remained in this vast area, claims in official BLM documents (resource management plans, environmental assessments) of wild horse overpopulation, habitat destruction, and starvation were made.

These were proven false, however, when Dr. Donald Molde, a long-time animal defender from Reno, and I visited the HMAs during August 2009. Though we inspected hundreds of square miles in the core HMA areas, we were able to directly observe only five wild horses and very scant mustang spore. These five were in excellent condition, though very wary of humans, no doubt with good reason. Again belying BLM's claims, we found adequate grass for them as well as sufficient water sources. However, we did repeatedly notice a large degree of overgrazing and habitat destruction by livestock, including trespass cattle grazing out of season, particularly at and around water sources. Within the Delamar HMA, a muscular, red-and-white Hereford bull of great size ran frantically off, crashing through a pinyon-pine-juniper thicket with great momentum after we surprised him near a spring. Also along the Meadow Valley Wash, we observed numerous cattle camping among the willows and cottonwood trees in prime wildlife habitat and making a terrible mess. There has been a marked increase in the size of and forage consumption by public lands grazed cattle in recent years due to genetic engineering, yet the minimum fee of $1.35 per bull or cow and/or calf for a month remains the same year after year. This is an enormous subsidy at the U.S. taxpayer's expense that benefits those excessively favored Americans: the public lands ranchers.

While we visited this wild horse complex, Dr. Molde entered the Caliente BLM Field Office on his own to inquire about how the area's wildlife was doing. He received a glowing report from one of the officials that was totally opposite to BLM's environmental assessment that justified the clearance of the herds. And though Ms. Christine Jubic, a legal worker from New York, and several others (including myself) filed well-substantiated legal protests before the Interior Board of Land Appeals (IBLA) in Washington and against the outrageous Caliente decision to zero out by BLM's Ely district manager, the judge merely rubber stamped BLM's decision. IBLA's job, however, is to act as an internal policing agency. This judicial body must see that the Department of Interior and all of its agencies adhere to the laws that Congress has passed and the president has signed, and they must do so in a fair and judicious manner. Their beat includes, of course, the unanimously passed Wild Free-Roaming Horses and Burros Act of 1971 (P.L. 92-195). These judges should have questioned and corrected the BLM rather than ignoring our painstakingly founded complaints. Other factors also suspect here include massive solar energy projects planned for the very areas where the wild horses were zeroed out. These projects use an evaporative process that would require enormous amounts of water, very scarce in a desert. The original Ely district manager (John Harrington) seemed to recognize the justification of our complaints, indicating in a letter that the zeroing out would be reconsidered. Soon after he issued this letter, however, he was abruptly replaced by another BLM employee willing to do this agency's dirty work and with no qualms whatsoever.

The sabotage of Nevada's mustangs reaches very close to home when considering the Pine Nut Range just east of where I live. This 26-mile-long range could easily support two thousand mustangs, but most of its original herd area (ca. 60%) has been declared "horse free" by the Carson City BLM office and approved by the state office. Back in 1981 when I worked as director of research services for the Animal Protection Institute, I asked the BLM for a reason to justify this decision, but all I was able to obtain from them was a terse letter from the Bureau of Indian Affairs agent Robert Hunter. Here I quote this letter of March 2, 1981, directed to BLM Carson City district manager. "There are a large number of wild horses presently running on the Pine Nut allotments, Pine Nut Mountain Range." [Without offering any proofs or taking into account the large numbers of cattle and sheep grazing the Pine Nut Range, Mr. Hunter went on to state} "These horses are depleting the range and are causing a serious hardship on the Indian owners. As trustee for these Indians I am requesting that you remove these horses under provisions of the Wildhorse [sic] and Burro Act." Later when I asked the chief of the Washoe Indian Tribe whether it was true that the wild horses were causing problems, he simply denied this and said that his tribe was "being used" to accomplish others' agendas. Many of the Pine Nut resident Indians valued and still value the wild horses and hated to see them removed. They clearly should have protested under the Dawes Act of 1887, which gives Indians the right to retain wild horses on their legal lands throughout America, and specifically mentions the Pine Nut Range in this regard. Clearly the Pine Nut wild horses should be reinstated throughout this magnificent range, as

Doctor of Divinity and Native American religious scholar Christopher Sprulle agrees. In a conversation with him on September 3rd, 2011, he warned me that too many tribes today are being taken over by corporate interests and that their authentic native values and religion especially in regard to the Rest of Life, i.e., world of Mother Nature, are being sabotaged because of greedy agendas.

In September 2011, BLM's Carson City field office announced its plans to gut the wild horse populations in the Dogskin Mountains, Flanigan, and Granite Peak HMAs just north of Reno, declaring they were over-populated when it truth they were very under-populated. This they did by declaring such miserably low AMLs as 15 horses for the Dogskin (ca. 6,500 suspiciously low acres), 18 horses for Granite Peak (ca. 4,000 suspiciously low acres); and still miserable 125 for the Flanigan (ca. 17,000 suspiciously low acres). Here I quote from a alert of 9/14/11 from the American Wild Horse Preservation Campaign:"The ... BLM is accepting public comment on its plan to roundup and remove 287 wild horses from the Flanigan, Dogskin Mountain, and Granite Peak Herd Management Areas ... The action will leave behind just 10 horses in the Dogskin HMA and 10 horses in Granite Peak, while the equivalent of 872 cattle will be allowed to continue to graze these same public lands. Incredibly, the BLM claims that the removal of horses is necessary to restore the 'thriving natural ecological balance,' yet the agency proposes no reduction in cattle grazing to help achieve this goal." (http://org2.democracyinaction.org/0/6931) For other such timely alerts go to www.stophorseroundups.org.

A WARNING

Combining federal and state lands where livestock are permitted to graze yields a whopping 290,635,550 acres—nearly 300 million (Wuerthner and Matteson 2002). And, of course, adjacent private lands certainly complete the 300-million figure and greatly expand it. The livestock industry's stranglehold here in the West, as elsewhere, is monstrous in proportion, and so is the industry's contribution to the decline and fall of life on Earth. We would do well to contemplate the vast amounts of soil erosion; spring, stream, and associated riparian overgrazing, trampling and pollution; and the prodigious quantities of heat-trapping methane, nitrous oxide, and other gases that are emitted by livestock in their ruminant, multi-stomach digestive processes. It should be clear which traditions—however long or blindly accepted—should be targeted for major reduction or elimination in many regions where they simply do not belong (de Haan et al. 2006; Rifkin 1992; Ferguson and Ferguson 1983; Jacobs 1991).

SIDEBAR: TEN TIMELY AND CRUCIAL POINTS FOR THE WILD HORSE & BURRO MOVEMENT

In January 2002, in a speech in Carson City, Ms. Karen Sussman, the president of the International Society for the Protection of Mustangs and Burros (ISPMB), presented a number of revealing points that I have taken the liberty to update and expand upon for the sake of the Wild Horse and Burro movement:

(1) Scientists substantiate that America's wild horses are the strongest, healthiest, most diverse horses in the world—let's restore their numbers in the wild so they can remain this way;

(2) In 1859 there were between two and three million wild horses on the plains, prairies, deserts, and mountain ranges of the U.S., but by 1976, only about sixty thousand remained (Pittman 2008). Though seventeen thousand is the official figure given by BLM for wild horses on the public lands at the passage of the Wild Free-Roaming Horse and Burro Act in 1971, this is widely considered to be low by at least a factor of two. Even a population of sixty thousand individuals is very few compared with the other wildlife species, including those judged to be endangered with extinction, such as the African elephant, whose members number in the hundred thousands.

(3) In 2008, there were an estimated twenty three thousand wild horses and four thousand wild burros left on public lands (Pittman 2008). This is less than what remained at the passage of the Wild Free-Roaming Horses and Burros Act of 1971 when, according to the act's preamble, the U.S. public was alarmed at how these animals were "fast disappearing from the American scene."

(4) The American Veterinarian Medical Association (AVMA) estimates that ninety thousand horses were killed at three U.S. slaughter houses in 2005. Many of these were wild horses. Also according to AVMA, fifteen months after the Congress banned support for horse slaughter inspectors in the U.S., the number of horses transported to Mexico for slaughter increased by 312% and Canada was also responsible for the increased slaughter of U.S. horses, having one of the world's largest horse slaughter industries. Truck drivers have testified that formerly free wild horses from the U.S. public lands are frequently hauled to Canada for slaughter and processing for the international market. (This fact is also verified by long-time Fallon(Nevada) livestock holding facility manager Nick Illia.)

(5) Citizens of Japan are the number one consumers of horse meat, followed by France, Italy, and Belgium. With the recent major 2011 earthquake and tsunami in Japan, Japanese buyers are now stepping up purchases of horse meat; the forty-three thousand wild horses now in holding may already find themselves targets of such (*The Milkweed* 2011; Nick Illia, April 2011, pers. comm.).

(6) Though popular, the Equine Anti-Cruelty bill was defeated in the 111th Congress. It would have outlawed slaughter for commerce and other cruel practices. As of August 2011, Senate Bill 1176, the American Horse Slaughter Prevention Act of 2011 (Senator Mary Landrieu, chief sponsor, D-LA) seeks to resurrect the Equine Anti-Cruelty Bill, but no counterpart to the ROAM (Restore Our American Mustangs) bill has yet been drawn up – a shame considering this is the 40th anniversary of the act!

(7) The Restore Our American Mustang (ROAM) bill passed the U.S. House of Representatives by a substantial majority (239 Yea and 185 No) in the spring of 2009, but was let to die by the U.S Senate. It specifically sought to restore the overly reduced wild horse and burro herd in the West and to overturn the nefarious rider (introduced by Montana Republican Senator Conrad Burns) to the federal omnibus Appropriations Bill in late 2004. Without

open debate, this sneak attack permitted sale to slaughter of wild horses and burros removed from their legal herd areas. Though efforts were made in the Fall of 2010 to eliminate the loopholes and pass it out of the Senate Subcommittee on Public Lands within the Committee on Energy and Natural Resources, these efforts were repeatedly blocked. A similar but improved bill must now be formulated and reintroduced. This should include the basic tenets of reserve design (see Chapter IV, 124-132). Senators likely to support this bill include Landrieu of Louisiana, Launtenberger of New Jersey, Boxer of California, and Lantry of Vermont. The BLM's wild horse and burro program must be checked in its policy of overkill and a new directive given to restore wild horses and burros as "national heritage" species throughout the western United States, bringing also into effect provisions of the National Heritage Protection Act.

(8) Speaking positively, the current prescription for wild horse/ burro demise will be replaced by a benign and well-integrated plan for restoring our wild equids upon their legal and other suitable lands in order to assure complete habitats for long-term viable populations following the principles of reserve design. ROAM was introduced by the late Senator Robert C. Byrd (D-WV), who passed away on June 28, 2010. Its revival, perfecting and the passage of a similar bill would be a fitting tribute to this great animal and horse defender and longest-serving U.S. senator. It would also be a most fitting celebration of the fortieth anniversary of the act.

(9) Due to recent federal cuts to American Indian tribes, there has been a loss of lands available to wild horses on reservations. On the Cheyenne River Reservation, the last survivors of two genetically distinct races of mustangs from the Southwest U.S. still were clinging to life as of 2005 thanks to the tribe's and ISPMB's valiant efforts. But federal government cutbacks have now broken up these populations, threatening their demise.

(10) From fiscal years 2000 to 2009, a total of 94,280 wild horses and burros were reported to have been removed from the public lands, while 57,225 were reported to have been adopted out (Vincent

2009, 8). According to Vincent's figures, ca. 37,055 remained in the wild after the 2009 roundups. But many question these figures due to the blanket application of the 20% rate of population increase by BLM officials and failing to consider inflated censuses and major mortality factors, such as illegal killings. In more stable wild-horse/burro-containing ecosystems, the rate of increase is much less than 20%, even 5% or less, according to studies performed in Wyoming during the early years of the act (National Research Council 1980 and 1982). The newly revised plan of Interior Secretary Salazar is to place the captured equids as non-reproducing herds principally in ecosanctuaries and to continue to nearly eliminate wild horses and burros from their rightful herd areas and territories throughout the West. It seems that where the ecosanctuaries occur on legal HMA land, the number of non-reproducing horses/burros will be subtracted from existing AMLs (Laura Leigh, pers. comm.). This would further undermine the wild populations.

SOME REAL POLITIK

The wild horse conspiracy is as perverse as it is intentional. The attitude of many profiting on wild horse suffering and death, including public officials with their large salaries and benefits, is indicated by bottom-line statements I have heard such as: "18,000 tons of horsemeat valued at $61 million" (Pittman 2008) or "the only good wild horse or burro is one made slave or dead." Sound familiar? Well, it should, for similar coarse statements regarding naturally living Amerindians or Afro-Americans were made not that long ago. And similar derisory statements targeted/still target the wolf, bear, bison, puma, prairie dog, condor, coyote, even eagles—and the list goes on.

Since the passage of the Burns Amendment in December 2004, many thousands of wild horses have been shipped over the border from the U.S. to Canada and Mexico. Though only God knows exactly how many, registers of international commerce list them simply as "horses." Many in the know, such as members of the Animal Angels NGO, are certain they are the very wild horses that our livestock-government conspiracy has unjustly over-gathered from their legal areas. For those who survive the tortuous transport, their fate in Mexico is apt to be so filled with suffering, misery, and horror that those who die along the way perhaps are the more fortunate. In February 2011, I personally encountered evidence of illegal trafficking of equids over the Rio Grande River in Texas' Big Bend region and was informed by locals that the drives over the river to Mexico included both domestic and significant numbers of wild horses and burros. Near Presidio, Chihuahua, Mexico, one hell-hole that has been the subject of recent outraged protest both in Mexico and the United States is the San Barnabe auction yard.

Recap Concerning the Injustice to the Wild Ones

BLM and USFS officials seem always to be looking for one excuse or another to eliminate wild horses and burros from their legal herd areas and territories. Clearly forgotten is their legal mandate to uphold the law by treating these remnant wild horses and burros as the "principal" presences in these areas. Though the latter constitute only about one-sixth of the vast BLM and USFS public lands, even these lands are in their great majority given over to various exploiters and disrupters of ecological harmony. On BLM and USFS lands, a full 260-million acres are leased for livestock grazing, while the original wild horse and burro herd areas sum only 53.5 million acres according to BLM, or ca. 20% of the former, though the U.S. Geological Survey reported 88-million acres of original 1971 legal wild equid lands (Animal Welfare Institute 2007, 8). This 88-million-acre figure is much closer to the truth, given the sabotage of the law that I have substantiated in this chapter and in this book. In spite of this great inequity, those areas actually still planned for wild horses and burros, i.e. herd management areas, have been reduced to only 26.6-million acres, or about 10% of the land grazed by domesticated livestock on BLM and USFS lands combined, and much less in relation to public lands as a whole. *And a further outrage is that even within this remaining small percentage, wild horses and burros continue to be marginalized, reduced to a small minority in relation to livestock and big game—and entirely contrary to the law.* This is a vicious downward spiral for horses and burros in the wild, and we must bring it to an end on this the fortieth anniversary of the still intact Wild Free-Roaming Horses and Burros Act of 1971. **We can do it if their freedom and their life here on this planet Earth we share with them as home means enough for us to act!**

CHAPTER IV:

BETTER FUTURE WAYS: LEARNING TO VALUE & RESTORE LIFE'S FREEDOM

RESUSCITATION

America's wild horse and burro herds have either been reduced to non-viable population levels or totally eliminated in most of their ca. 350 original, legal herd areas. Though these natural habitats were established by the Wild Free-Roaming Horses and Burros Act in 1971 on both Bureau of Land Management (USDI-BLM) and the U.S. Forest Service (USDA-USFS) lands and by the unanimous vote of Congress, it is due to a very persistent attack upon these animals in their free-roaming, natural state—as well as upon their supporters—that the true intent of Public Law 92-195 has been so grievously subverted today. The enemies of wild horses/burros consist chiefly of livestock ranchers but include much of the big game hunting establishment, as well as some mineral and energy extractors, and even otherwise well-meaning conservationists, misled on this issue. The smear campaign against these animals in the wild and the ruthless infiltration and evisceration of government programs by their enemies count among the most dishonorable and unsupportable happenings today.

Nevertheless, the movement to save America's last wild equids in the wild has been and remains powerful. Wild Horse Annie intelligently crafted this progressive reform in response to unspeakably cruel abuses and in recognition of the noble principle concerning life's basic freedom. Her great achievement, however, has been countered by deliberate lies and selective interpretations and distortions of facts that have insinuated themselves into the governing platform today. Through twisted interpretations of the act and of subsequent laws such as the Federal Land Policy and Management Act (FLPMA) of 1976 and the Public Rangelands Improvement Act (PRIA) of 1978, the noble intent of the law has been subverted. Such "extreme prejudice" ignores the horse/burro family's, genus' and very species' origins and long-standing evolution in North America and the many consequent benefits that both wild horses and burros confer upon their fellow co-evolvers. These include myriad plants and animals, microorganisms, and even people—if we would only learn to respect their freedom and allow them to fulfill their role.

However seemingly set in concrete America's relation with wild equids seems to have become, the way forward must correct the imbalances and injustices. Our steps must be governed by a clear vision of and for horses and burros, one that appreciates their true value in nature and the meaning of their presence here. We must respect and restore their natural freedom, as well as the freedom of our own kind to explore better possibilities for a mutual sharing of planet Earth. By awakening a higher conception of and identification *with* the Rest of Life, *not man apart*, a solution to our present predicament will surely emerge, one fair to horses, people, and all interrelated kinds.

The law of the land must be truly respected and applied, as horses and burros are reinstated where at all possible in their legal herd areas established in 1971 and/or other appropriate areas. And the latter must not be defined by their enemies, as has been the case. The web of deception that has so ensnared the program must be dismantled, as new officials who are truly appreciative of wild horses and burros and their natural freedom methodically take charge to rectify all that has gone so awry. These will be individuals with sufficient courage to exert their authority on behalf of wild equids in their legal areas, where by law they are the "principal," not marginalized, presences.

In spite of the act's mandate, over 27 million of the admitted 53.5 million herd area (HA) acres have been or are about to be zeroed out by the BLM and USFS in order to establish 26.5 million acres of herd management areas (HMAs) (Animal Welfare Institute 2007). Then, to add insult to injury, after reducing the original ca. 350 HAs to 180 HMAs on BLM land, our "public servants" have proceeded to approve of appropriate management levels (AMLs) that are in most cases non-viable in each given HMA. As mentioned in Chapter III, most of these levels do not even meet the questionable requirements for minimum viable population of 150 horses/burros per herd commonly recognized by the BLM and, of course, fall far short of the 2,500 individuals recommended for a viable population by the Equid Specialist Group of the IUCN Species Survival Commission (Duncan 1992).

Of the 180 greatly reduced HMAs throughout the BLM West, a glaring 130, or 72%, have AMLs of less than 150, and many of these are much less than 100, even numbering in the teens. According to BLM's own standard of 150, in California 19 out of 22 HMAs have non-viable AMLs; in Utah, 17 out of 21; in Idaho, 5 out of 6; in Montana, 1 out of 1 (6 of the original 7 HAs having been zeroed out); and in Nevada, 67 out of 90 of the scant remaining herds are similarly non-viable (Animal Welfare Institute 2008, 22; also see Chapter VI).

The Congressional Research Service reports that, in FY2005, forage eaten on BLM lands by livestock summed up to ca. 6,835,458 animal unit months (AUMs), contrasting with wild equid consumption of only 381,120 AUMs, or 5.6% that of livestock. On USFS lands, livestock devoured 6.6 million AUMs worth of forage, much of this in vital headwaters, while wild horses and burros got by on a meager 32,592 AUMs, or .5% (Animal Welfare Institute 2007, 13). For years, it has been the all-too-easy custom for established interests to "scapegoat," or lay the blame, for overgrazing, erosion, threats to native species, and other ecological abuses upon wild horses and burros wherever they occur by magnifying their effects out of proportion, all the while conveniently ignoring their own—and I admit some of my own—enormously destructive traditions.

A New Approach to Living

Mankind's treatment of wild horses and burros today counts among the most reprehensible of any group of animals. The prejudiced system that perpetrates this has targeted horses and burros when living as free, naturally restored inhabitants of our planet—their normal way of life by any objective, long-term view. This intolerable situation should be changed swiftly, and justice restored for these noble animals as realized upon some fair portion of their ancestral home.

Certainly more harmonious ways exist for people to live and relate to the other life forms than are currently being realized. And we had better put these into practice soon, since our human numbers have leapt from six billion to seven billion in just the past twelve years according to the United Nations population division! As an example, in the Great Basin by moderately harvesting nutritious nuts from the pinyon pine, much more healthy food would result with much less ecological impact (Wheat 1967). By harvesting equally nutritious nuts from *Jojoba* bushes in the more arid deserts of the Southwest, more harmonious food could be obtained. The bulbs of sego lilies are another staple that was used by western Amerindians as well as by Mormons and could be again with moderation. Whatever we choose as our path to reform, what is certain is that we must not continue to blindly impose masses of ill-adjusted livestock and other monocrops, both plant and animal, upon the land as we have in the past.

In diverse ways, including additional harmonious Amerindian traditions as well as new lifestyles guided by the modern science of ecology, we can find a way out of our seemingly impossible predicament. Our dilemma has been brought on by a far too human-centered attitude that excludes the Rest of Life from a benign view. The solution lies with our first recognizing and then changing this narcissistic value system. Along with other species, wild horses and burros have much to teach us in this regard, *if* we will only show them respect and listen to and observe what they are communicating, most of all through their splendid example when *living free*.

Our approach to living in North America provides the key to restoring wild horses and burros to their natural freedom here. There are many possibilities open to us that will permit harmonious interspecies living. As just mentioned, we can collect and relish those nutritious pine nuts that grow in the extensive pinyon pine forests of the Great Basin in lieu of foisting numerous cattle and sheep on these same ecosystems, often after first removing these forests. We would procure more food and greater health for ourselves and restore the native biome in the process. And we could moderately and selectively remove some of the trees for our wood needs without overly affecting the forest. We would allow a greater variety of native plants and animals, including pinyon, juniper, and other diversely coevolved trees and bushes. These would shelter the wild equids, deer, pronghorn, elk, sage hen, etc., from intense summer sun and harsh winter storms. And they would provide food and nesting areas for a great variety of smaller creatures, including birds, lizards, amphibians, rabbits, and rodents.

Judicious use of the tart juniper berries would be another mutualism we could develop. Junipers are becoming increasingly abundant relative to pinyon pines due to global climate change (Kunzig 2008), but are being unwisely targeted for removal by BLM and USFS to provide more forage for livestock. Thousands of these magnificent trees are being sawed down and left to rot or for wood gatherers throughout the West due to our federal government's misguided policies that promote their destruction (as well as of pinyon) in the name of increasing patchiness of habitat but overlook the many values and ecological services of the pinyon-juniper woodland in its own right: stabilization of soils and slopes, buffer against winds, water retention, providing food, shelter and other habitat needs for many wildlife species, beauty, etc.

Modern man has so much to learn from the ancients—and to revive! The so-called "digger" Indians of the Great Basin, including Paiute, Ute, Shoshone, and the smaller tribe of Washoe Indians inhabiting around Lake Tahoe and western Nevada, had "1,001 uses" for native plants and animals. The sagebrush seed (*Artemisia tridentata*) could be ground into a nutritious meal, or mush; and, as just mentioned, the sego lily's tuber (*Calochortus nuttallii*) provided another staple in times of scarcity. Deer, pronghorn, and rabbits could be hunted in a judicious and humane manner so as not to overwhelm any one species. Fish could be moderately and humanely caught and smoked for winter sustenance. In regard to the Paiute, Wheat (1967, 74) notes: "Before the early settlers reduced the number of predatory animals, deer populations in the Great Basin were small, and kills by the Indians were infrequent. Antelope and mountain sheep, although more numerous, were the prize of only the most diligent hunter." Desert roots supplied a major portion of the diet–hence the derisive name "digger" was applied to them by some whites. Even tiny insects, like grasshoppers or termite larvae, provided protein-, carbohydrate-, and fat-rich food. As they say: variety is the spice of life. And, I might add, not only is it the spice of life, but by diversifying our foods and diminishing our consumption of any single food source, such as wheat, corn, rice, sugar, beef, chicken, milk, cheese, butter, eggs, etc., we could restore balance and assure the healthy continuation of life on Earth. What greater satisfaction for relatively minor sacrifices?! One point is clear: we must take action now to change how we live. We must become bio-regionally identified and integrated, learning to relate to the unique life community where we live and to harmoniously derive our living and in turn contribute to the well-being and perpetuation of this special home. Too much is at stake for us to fail to act.

EARTH'S VANISHING MAMMALS, ETC.

In recent times, the high rate of disappearance of large mammals from the earth's various biomes has become alarming (Morrison et al. 2007). A comparison of historical (AD 1500) range maps of large mammals with their current distribution reveals that less than 21% of the terrestrial globe still contains all of the large mammals (greater than 20 kg in weight) it supported several centuries ago. This study measures the tremendous ecological impact people are having on the planet. The concurrent die out of most of the species of an entire class of vertebrates: the Amphibians[9] (frogs, salamanders, newts, etc.) from all

---

9 Evolving from fish, they were the first vertebrates to occupy land a few hundreds of millions of years ago; and they gave rise to reptiles.

continents where they occur represents a very serious unraveling of the global web of life. And amphibians are a major prey species for many mammals.

Among groups of large mammals most affected figure the horse family, genus and species: namely, Equidae, *Equus* and all species in this genus, including the modern horse, *Equus caballus*, in the wild. Other species severely affected are the Przewalski's, or Mongolian, horse and several species and subspecies of zebras, onagers, and asses. The contraction of former occupied geographical ranges of such large equid species is 72% on average. According to the study, the range of wild *Equus caballus* ca. AD 1500 was 13.5 million square km compared with its current range of only 3,070 square km, representing a loss of almost the entire distribution (Morrison et al. 2007, Table 3). However, it appears that this study did not recognize the wild horses of the West, whose inclusion would make this proportion considerably larger (add ca. 40,000 square miles), but still alarmingly small as concerns species survival.

Since the horse has a long coevolutionary history with many diverse plant and animal companions in a variety of ecosystems and over an extensive range, its disappearance constitutes a major ecological setback (Downer 2005). As a major *climax* species, or member of the more stable, long term, and biodiverse life community that establishes itself over time, the horse has helped to characterize and to assist so many of the earth's ecosystems including by its:

> 1. grazing of grass, extensive pruning of vegetation (including forbs, shrubs, and even trees), and consequent bolstering of annual plant productivity;
>
> 2. successful intact seed dispersal of hundreds, even thousands of plant species through its feces, that also greatly build the moisture-retaining and nutrient-releasing humus content of the soils;
>
> 3. major role as a prey or scavenged species for lions, puma, wolves, bears, foxes, raptors, vultures, and smaller animals;

4. role as a trail breaker through dense vegetation and as a breaker of frozen snow and ice, and also as an opener of tiny seeps to create ponds thus made accessible for other smaller species during dry seasons (all by virtue of its powerful physique, strong legs, and soliped hooves); and by its

5. creation of natural water catchments through its wallowing habit, particularly important in desert areas and especially during the dry seasons when cloudbursts occur.

All this has and should continue to aid literally thousands of plant and animal species through mutual symbioses that have been millions of years in the making. When the horse is suddenly removed, as through massive helicopter roundups, or killed off by man, it leaves a big gap that upsets the equilibrated life-support system. And many remaining commensal species find it hard to readapt in the modern era of species displacement; chemical pollution of air, water and soil; and global climate change. As concerns the latter, carbon dioxide from vehicles, factories and coal-burning power plants, methane from hordes of livestock, chlorofluorocarbons, nitrogen oxides, sulfur oxides, among other ecologically excessive and unbalanced gases, as well as the attendant melting of the polar ice caps and permafrost, all contribute to an ever exacerbating and ecologically destructive vortex.

WILD EQUIDS AND GLOBAL CLIMATE CHANGE

The reestablishment of the horse and burro in the North American Great Basin, Great Plains and prairies, as well as in many suitable western mountains and valleys can help to combat the noxious effects of global climate change by greatly balancing and enhancing the native ecosystem. By no means should horses and burros be merely labeled feral exotics, since their return is certainly the restoration of a native species in the case of the horse, and very likely the burro as well (Klingel 1979; also see Chapter I). In fact, all three extant branches of the horse family (and genus) originated and had their long-standing evolution in North America (MacFadden 1992). As with the horse, the desert-dwelling burro should be recognized for its many positive, ecological restorations, ones that are similar to those contributed by horses, but generally in drier areas.

THE PLIGHT OF THE HORSE FAMILY

Another member of the ass branch of the Equidae is the Onager (*Equus hemionus*). These hardy, large-headed equids inhabit vast, dry stretches of the Near and Middle East. In spite of their great antiquity, they have been exterminated from all but a tiny fraction of their former range. In AD 1500, their population was estimated at 13.5 million individuals. With a current range of 411,000 square km, onagers have disappeared from almost all of their former occupied range. They are classified as endangered with extinction by the IUCN Species Survival Commission (Duncan 1992), as are most of the species and subspecies still surviving in the horse family, including zebras of diverse stripes (both the Grevy's Zebra and the Mountain Zebra are Endangered), and the asses, including the burro when considered *in the wild*. Why then should not wild horses also be considered endangered, since this is the branch of the modern horse species that is, in fact, preserving the long-term survivability—the true vigor—of its species precisely because it lives in the wild? I can think of no species more worthy of being part of future life on Earth. And not just because of all it has done for man (Downer 1977).

Authorities should consider the plight of the ancient horse family taken as a whole in the world today. Its origin dates back ca. 58 million years, to the base of the Cenozoic era (right after the age of dinosaurs) in the late Paleocene epoch, but as members of the family Homidae, we humans are relative newcomers on Earth dating back only a few million years. We should do all that we can to protect and restore all species of Equidae in suitable habitats of the Americas, Eurasia, Asia, and Africa where they have played an important role for thousands of generations involving millions of year—especially in North America.

RESTORATION URGENTLY REQUIRED

Wild horses and burros should be restored to their original herd areas (HAs) throughout the West. The legality of their refuges is based upon where they were found in 1971, and this should be interpreted as meaning year-round habitat. But these areas are today largely empty of wild equids: a fact that, on the face of it, evinces the gross injustice with which these marvelous animals have been treated (see Figure 5 on page 53).

For example, one of the most compelling cases of injustice I have heard reported concerns the Carter Reservoir HMA mustang herd in northeastern California. Here, for 23,000 acres of legal habitat, the Surprise BLM office (located in Cedarville) decided to declare an appropriate management level of only 35 horses and then proceeded to nearly eliminate the herd by helicopter. A local couple who used to conduct guided mustang tours to Carter Reservoir HMA and knew it like the back of their hands had only been able to find ten remaining horses as of October 2009, when I spoke to them. They greatly lamented the evisceration of this once spirited and awe-inspiring population, not only because of their loss of livelihood and affection for the individual horses, but also because, of all the herds in the United States, it had the most authentic Spanish mustang genetic markers, as tests had revealed. Local newspaper reporter and writer, Jean Bilodeaux denounced the callous disregard that BLM officials had demonstrated by their plans and actions in this and other HMAs, e.g., the Bitner HMA herd where for ca 50,000 legal acres an AML of 25 wild horses was assigned and the estimated population in FY2009 was only 32. She felt that BLM was literally destroying the special Spanish mustang population in this beautiful part of our nation. To these sensitive humans, it seemed the majority of these once free wonders lived on only in memory. BLM had censused 104 Carter Reservoir mustangs in 2008. If the tour guides are correct then where have 94 mustangs gone, indeed? This area is know for much defiance of the law and crimes against the wild horses, including illegal capturing and killings.

In westernmost Nevada, in the extensive, biodiverse Pine Nut Wild Horse HA, previously considered, the present HMA represents only ca. 40% of the original 250,000 acres. Additionally in Nevada, the Little Humboldt HA has been reduced from 52,538 acres to a mere 15,734. Certainly a state's having a substantial number of legal wild equid acres on the books does not signify it has a fair number of wild equids. Again, for example, Colorado lists ca. 281,000 legal HA acres, but only 176 remaining wild horses and no wild burros in its 2008 statistics. Of course, many of the HAs have simply been zeroed out, their wild horses and burros declared inconvenient to vested interests or planned projects and removed. Two of the four herd areas in Colorado—Douglas Mountain and Naturity Ridge—have been zeroed out, while the North Piceance HA has only ca. fifteen wild horses left. BLM is now proposing zeroing out the only herd still with any fair number in Colorado: West Douglas Creek. As a consequence, it was successfully sued by The Cloud Foundation and the Colorado Wild Horse Coalition, for abrogation of responsibility. In spite of this drab scenario, we must not forget that in all legal herd areas in Colorado and other states throughout the West, the wild horses and burros can be legally restored (Figure 7).

State	Horses	Burros	Both	#HAs	Additional	Total Horses & Burros
Arizona	35	540	575	8	1000	1575
California	2005	303	2308	15	5000	7308
Colorado	659		659	7	1000	1659
Idaho	81		81	4	1000	1081
Montana	294		294	6	1000	1294
Nevada	5200		5200	31	4310	9510
New Mexico	166		166	3	334	500
Oregon	2240	10	2250	28	1750	4000
Utah	1085	17	1102	18	1085	2187
Wyoming	7425		7425	29	2575	10000
Totals:	**19190**	**870**	**20060**	**149**	**19054**	**39114**

Figure 7. Numbers of Wild Horses/Burros that can be Restored by State and as Totals.

Replacing wild equids are cattle, sheep and, in some cases, big game such as elk, though most of the latter are primarily bush and tree browsers, such as deer, while horses are primarily grass grazers. Also entering into the equation are, in major fashion, oil and gas drilling, pipelines, hard rock and open-pit mining, subdivision development, dams, off-road vehicles, golf courses, alfalfa fields, among other nature-manipulative, ecologically disruptive and extractive activities, i.e., those that take but do not put back. (For your information, the Ruby Pipeline path recently constructed across northern Nevada is now overrun with exotic cheat grass, and the wild horses have been nearly all rounded up. – Expect a fire!)

SIDEBAR: PICKENS'S OFFER AND BACKGROUND OF A TRAGIC SITUATION

Since 2001 under the administration of Presidents George W. Bush and Barack Obama, BLM and USFS have been removing so-called "excess" wild horses and burros at an appalling rate. In spite of President Obama's pledge to reform government policy to be fairer to the interests of the general public, the wild horses and burros continue to be eliminated under his administration, as he turns a deaf ear to the outcry of many thousands of Americans. The total that was removed during the eight years of the Bush administration is ca. seventy-five thousand. The consequence is that, as of late December 2008, there were more wild equids (ca. thirty-five thousand) languishing in holding facilities than there were remaining in their legal areas, a little over thirty thousand according to government sources. The April 2011 numbers in holding (short- or long-term corrals or fenced pastures chiefly on private, inscrutable land) are ca. forty-three thousand wild equids, while those still on the public lands have been greatly diminished. Though BLM claims this is in the mid-thirty thousands, independent assessments put these at less than twenty thousand (www.americanherds.blogspot.com).

If a recent anonymous tip proves true, even those being held may not be safe. This concerns our government officials' intention to massively kill and secretively dispose of the wild equids, a plan originally announced at a Reno meeting of the Wild Horse and Burro Advisory Board in July of 2008. Horrified by such rumors, Madeleine Pickens, the wife of Texan billionaire T. Boone Pickens, offered to take all of the held horses and provide a wildland sanctuary for them somewhere in the West through the purchase of ranches and their grazing permits. This offer was made at the Wild Horse Summit in Las Vegas on October 12, 2008, and was widely reported by the national and international media. It was overtly accepted by BLM officials but only as a possibility. In early March, 2009, BLM officials reported that northern Nevada ranchers and the county governments that represent them were resisting the

Pickens's proposal, particularly the Elko County commission, which voted to oppose the conversion of cattle grazing leases to horse grazing leases on the public lands within their county.

Meanwhile BLM proceeded to sterilize the horses it had captured, so even if Pickens would be able to preserve their lives, the wild horse enemies would have already accomplished their goal of managing for extinction and horses would not carry on beyond the present generation. Consequently the natural adaptivity to specific regions of the West by these horses would be lost. This is adaptivity made possible by generations of natural selection, now set back by the thoughtless, massive clearances. And all this is well known though little appreciated by many educated wild horse enemies who have insinuated themselves into positions of power. Their smug cynicism and lack of regard toward the wild horse is detestable.

More recently (October 2010), Madeleine Pickens has obtained the Spruce and Warm Springs ranches in Elko County and wants to start running one thousand formerly wild horses as a non-reproducing herd here. She sees this as a first step toward rescuing many more of the ca. forty-three thousand wild equids now held in captivity, mostly from BLM's contracted short-term holding facilities. So much of this, however, can be viewed as a convenient whitewashing for the gross displacement of wild horses from their rightful herd areas on BLM and USFS land. In early June 2011, after being thwarted repeatedly by BLM, Pickens was finally able to release ca. 500 wild horses who had been gathered off of the Pyramid Lake Paiute Reservation (where I used to be Environmental Director), though as sterile, non-reproducing herds and only on the private land, not the grazing permitted BLM land, of her two northern Nevadan ranches.

MORE WHITTLING AWAY, SOME NEEDED PERSPECTIVE

BLM reduced forage allocations, or AUMs (animal unit months), for wild equids by 17% between 2002 and 2005, citing drought conditions and ignoring: (a) wild equids' pre-adaptation to consume the large quantities of dry flammable vegetation that have resulted from global climate change and so to reduce catastrophic fires, (b) their role in combating global climate change over the earth's vast steppe or steppe-like biomes by promoting these biomes (Zimov 2005), and (c) the fact that wild equids are capable of grazing much steeper and more rugged areas farther away from water than cattle, which tend to concentrate their activities around water sources.

Cattle and sheep grazing on U.S. public lands contributes substantially to global climate change through the release of enormous quantities of methane gas and nitrogen oxides involved in ruminant digestion and through the widespread degradation of ecosystems, especially riparian (Hudak 2008; de Haan et al. 2006). Yet, the reduction for livestock in drought-stricken areas has been only 4% even though they greatly outnumber the wild equids that have been reduced by 17% and as of fall 2011 perhaps the double of this.

Permittees only pay a small percentage of fair market value, at present amounting to about 9% to 12%, in order to graze their livestock on the public lands. This has just been reauthorized (March 2011) at the minimum required by law: $1.35 per AUM, a measurement that includes a cow and her calf (and genetic breeders are making ever larger cows that consume ever more forage on the public lands). Only recently has a foal less than one year of age been included with its mare to equal one AUM (Sussman pers. comm.). The Government Accountability Office (2005) reported that the government lost at least $123 million in order to prop up public lands livestock grazing, while real costs have been estimated as at least one-half billion dollars per year, adding in ecological damages (Center for Biological Diversity 2002). To put the situation in perspective, there are nearly twenty-two thousand public lands ranchers in thirteen western states, about one for each wild horse or burro that the federal government is now planning to leave as its unfairly conceived, nationwide appropriate management level. And the top 10% of the ranchers—often large corporations, wealthy bankers, lawyers, and doctors—own over 65% of the livestock grazing the public lands. (Rogers & La Fleur 1999; Wuerthner and Matteson 2002; Jacobs 1991; D. Ferguson and N. Ferguson 1983; Rifkin 1992).

RECKLESS DISINFORMATION, DENIAL, DISHONESTY, AND DESTRUCTION

The unjust treatment of wild horses and burros in their legal areas has everything to do with imperceptive, greed-driven tradition and the monopolization of public lands by exploitive interests, including livestock, mining, hunting, etc. It is based on a mentality that ignores the greater truth concerning horses, burros, and their place in the natural world. This more complete picture can be obtained from the wider array of scientific facts available today, but so many of these are being overlooked, or conveniently distorted by partial interpretations. Many are obnoxiously denied by established interests whose aim is to discredit horses and burros in the wild—this naturally free life they have led for over 99.999% of their duration on planet Earth, and, by far, mostly right here in North America (MacFadden 1992). It is absurd to say the horse or burro is merely man's creation and cannot quickly revert to harmonious living in the wilds of America, its ancient cradle of evolution.

Yet, this is precisely the philosophy BLM wild horse/burro officials such as 38-year veteran of the program Lily Thomas present. During a tour of Broken Arrow (a newly constructed primary wild horse holding facility for BLM gathered horses located on private land north of Fallon, Nevada), she arrogantly told me: "This is where they belong!" in reference to the dispirited, freedom-deprived horses we were viewing. She also told me that the pinto and paint colorations in horses were a creation by man, though as a wildlife biologist, I well know the meaning of "disruptive coloration" that occurs in many wild animals (e.g., the Malaysian Tapir) to break their outline and be less easily recognized by a predator, and it has been around for a lot longer than mankind itself on our planet.

Another major official who has displayed this demeaning attitude toward wild horses in the wild is Nevada BLM's lead for the wild horse and burro program Alan Shepherd. Though Shakespeare proclaims "[h]is neigh is like the bidding of a monarch, and his countenance enforces homage," Mr. Shepherd told me that he was perfectly fine with the zeroing out of the earlier discussed 1.4 million acres on twelve legal wild horse herd areas in the Caliente area in southeast Nevada. He tried to reassure me that there would always be a few wild ones left here and there and further communicated that the ones removed would be as content as clams in Midwestern and Eastern pastures as non-reproductive herds with plenty of knee-deep grass to eat and water to drink—as though this were all the horses cared for! As concerns the claim by some Nevadan state senators and representatives, ranchers and hunters, that the wild horses and burros have no legal right to water in the state, Shepherd merely indicated that the law was on their side, totally ignoring the Implied Federal Water Rights that came with the passage of the act. Out at the Black Rock East roundup on December 31, 2009, when I brought up section 6 of the act allowing cooperative agreements with other private and public agencies to further the mandate of the act—meaning securing the horses' freedom to a fair and viable degree—Shepherd tried to brow beat me in front of ca. 20 others present with the statement that I "should know this wasn't true." I was truly flabbergasted that he could be so in denial of the positive possibilities of the act for the wild horses and their freedom. On another occasion at the Calico Mountain trap site, when I brought up that very spirited wild horses like the black stallion "Freedom" who had leapt the corral should be left in the wild and as BLM regulations themselves allow, Shepherd totally ignored my point and merely stated that they had their capture quotas to fill. When slender but stalwart humane observer Elyse Gardner had a handful of hay violently ripped from her hand by Dave Cattoor (the principal contractor in the Calico roundups) who then muttered some profanities and stormed off, Shepherd merely stood on the side and said nothing. You can bet that if it had been a wild horse advocate who did this to any of the officials or roundup contractors, there would have been hell to pay, as the armed and glaring BLM law enforcement agents and local county sheriffs often reminded us roundup observers. We were usually kept much too far from the captive horses to obtain a precise idea of what was happening to them, e.g., measure respiration rates and durations, examine wounds sustained during roundups.

Nowhere has the government's intentional sabotage of the wild horse program been more proven than during the Reagan administration when it intentionally "fouled up" several years of research by the University of Wyoming during the first few years of the act. As chairman of the National Academy of Sciences' Wild Horse Research Committee, Dr. Fred Wagner strongly denounced BLM for doing this. Though the BLM Wyoming State Director Max Lieurance tried to cover this up, those in the know realized that the roundups were a deliberate sabotage designed to squash many positive findings. These concerned the ecological contributions of wild horses and their ability to self-stabilize and to come to harmonious terms with their environment. In the words of Wagner, "The horse drive destroyed the known distribution and completely disturbed the natural distribution and movement patterns" of the wild horses being studied (United Press International 1981; National Research Council 1980; University of Wyoming 1979). (See Sidebar below.)

SIDEBAR: INTERVIEW WITH RETIRED BLM WILD HORSE/ BURRO OFFICIAL JOHN PHILLIPS:

In an interview with 30+-year retired BLM wild horse/burro official John Phillips on August 8, 2011, I gained considerable insight into what has gone so dreadfully wrong with America's wild horse and burro program. He reiterated that on BLM lands alone there were 90,000 square miles of legal wild horse and burro herd areas at the passage of the 1971 act (see his interview in film "Stampede to Oblivion" [2009]). Given 640 acres per square mile, this is equivalent to 57,600,000 acres. This makes it easy to believe that the until-recently-published USGS figure of 88 million acres is valid when U.S. Forest Service wild horse/burro territories are added on to those of BLM. From this we can deduce that there were 30,400,000 acres of 1971 U.S. Forest Service wild horse/burro territories at the passage of the act.

Mr. Phillips expressed a profound disgust at what has happened to the program and revealed some intricacies of what went on that, while not surprising, were none-the-less disturbing. He swore that much of the initial impetus to destroy the program began in California and with the hunting establishment associated with this state's fish and game department. In particular, a biologist named Richard Weaver misused his position of authority to disseminate pseudo-scientific articles and addresses that were shamelessly biased and motivated solely by an animus against the horses and burro in their wild and free state. Weaver was particularly upset by wild horses' and burros' having gained any legal status and by the state's having to share natural resources other than for hunted game animals such as deer or bighorn. Phillips emphasized that among professional wildlife departments and academic institutions the lion's (and the liar's) share of the campaign of negativity against wild horses and burros stemmed from the nefarious slings and arrows of this very vindictive man.

Among BLM state offices during the 1970s, Phillips signaled New Mexico, Nevada, and Colorado as being the least honest, while Wyoming, California and Arizona were more honest. He said that it was during the 1980s that the most damaging and dishonorable decisions and acts befell our nation's wild horses and burros and the federal program to uphold the act. Too often BLM state directors adopted the policy that state estray laws superceded the Wild Free-Roaming Horses and Burros Act, such that if a private rancher claimed the animals, BLM did not challenge state livestock inspectors when they allowed tens of thousands of wild horses/burros to be claimed as saddle horses and sold to the killer market. Phillips adamantly insisted that the act carries with it *Implied Federal Water Rights*, as is the case with other acts establishing wildlife refuges, Indian reservations, etc., and that the BLM and USFS are not upholding viable wild horse and burro populations with adequate entitled water in the legal wild horse/burro herd areas. He said the officials have been shirking their public trust duty as they deliberately betray the animals, their public supporters, and the very act and unanimous will of the senators and representatives of the American people. As it turns out, lack of water is a primary excuse given for zeroing out herds, yet the water is often present, it's just that our federal officials refuse to assert the wild equids' right to it. He also revealed how since the 1980s, BLM has refused to form positive cooperative agreements with other government agencies, such as the National Park Service, US Fish and Wildlife Service, military bases, state and local governments, etc., in order to provide complete and natural habitats for healthily sized populations of wild horses and burros at genetically viable levels. Drawing near to the end of the interview, he signaled Peter Sanchez, one time director of the Death Valley National Park, as being another virulent enemy of wild burros and horses and his use of Weaver's biased publications to pseudo-justify discrediting and eliminating these animals from the park. Phillips also pointed out the Coastal Game Range of Arizona as an extreme example where over zealous USFWS officials had fenced off major water sources so burros could not drink, inadvertently resulting in the deaths of many other big game species such as deer, as well as the burros themselves. He finally expressed his utter disgust for people who blame wild burros and horses for despoiling water holes and western habitats that livestock such as domesticated cattle and sheep have utterly trashed, not the wild equids. I told him to be on hand to testify.

But there is no sense "beating a dead horse" by merely bemoaning this injustice. This is an all-too-familiar story as concerns too many of Earth's species. I am cognizant of the role that the cattle/sheep culture has played in destroying indigenous Andean wildlife, especially the endangered mountain tapir, now reduced to only ca. two thousand individuals in Colombia, Ecuador, and Peru (see www.andeantapirfund. com). Enormous ecological damage has been done throughout the Americas, especially since the arrival of Europeans, but also before by some groups of Amerindians, though not to nearly the degree. In the U.S. west of the Mississippi River, ca. 700 million acres of grassland have been degraded due to overgrazing by uncontrolled millions of cattle and sheep; yet left to their own devices, these animals would either harmoniously adapt or perish. In 1884, the region of today's western states held ca. 40 million cattle in addition to sheep. It was not until 1934 that this cancerous destruction was in any way checked through the Taylor Grazing Act—yet, unfortunately this act perpetuated the control of our public lands by private livestock interests.

THE PEER REPORT

In 1997, Public Employees for Environmental Responsibility did an investigation of BLM's wild horse program. It is entitled *Horses to Slaughter—Anatomy of a Coverup within the BLM* and uncovers this agency's "... toleration and facilitation of illegal trafficking of the wild horses supposedly under its care to slaughter." This unsettling document reveals how BLM higher-ups obstructed their own agency's law enforcement branch in its legal duty to expose ongoing and large-scale commercial wild horse/burro theft, fraudulent adoption schemes, and bogus "sanctuary" herds. All of this, or course, facilitated the draconian reduction of America's already sub-viable wild horse/burro populations. The report reveals that, contrary to BLM's legal obligations to uphold wild horse/burro freedom on a relatively minor portion of the public lands, "political pressure from the livestock industry creates a powerful institutional incentive within BLM to remove wild horses from the range whenever and wherever possible." PEER further reveals that "... the lucrative market for horsemeat creates an irresistible economic opportunity for theft and fraud" and "the agency has embraced the fiction that very few horses under its legal jurisdiction are commercially exploited, publicly maintaining in February, 1997, that less than one percent of wild horses go to slaughter despite current well-documented evidence to the contrary."

Though in 1993, BLM National Director Jim Baca initiated an investigation and crackdown on these illegal operations, he was abruptly dismissed in 1994, largely because of this. BLM investigators had amassed substantial evidence of:

> (1) theft of wild horses during BLM contracted roundups;
>
> (2) phony double branding so duplicate branded horses could "disappear" without a paper trail;
>
> (3) single individual's in effect adopting many more horses than legally entitled through the use of proxies and in order to profit from maximized wild horse sale to slaughter;
>
> (4) evasive use of satellite ranches as stopping points on the wild horses way to slaughter; and

(5) fraudulent use of wild horse sanctuaries subsidized by the federal government for unadoptable wild horses as fronts for commercial exploitation.

Though Baca's investigation had found conclusive evidence concerning these illegal activities and was accepted for analysis by the U.S. attorney general's office in the Western District of Texas, the legal process was obstructed by certain implicated BLM managers. The latter also tampered with witnesses by use of threat. These same managers also exposed the identities of undercover investigators—a serious violation of federal law governing betrayal of confidence and mission and one posing considerable danger to the investigators.

Once Baca was removed, the corrupt officials in the U.S. Department of Interior (USDI) took immediate steps to prevent the already convened grand jury from hearing the case. Pressure was exerted to limit the investigation to local level BLM employees. With the aid of certain lawyers from the USDI solicitor's office as well as civil legal representatives in the Department of Justice, anti-wild-horse BLM officials used bureaucratic *sleigh-de-main* to assign new, more lax investigators while dismissing the original law-defending ones. Miscreant agency lawyers then blocked the execution of subpoenas, thus effectively killing the grand jury probe. A Department of Justice lawyer revealed that the involvement of BLM personnel in the wild-horse-to-slaughter trade was so pervasive that the investigation would have led to a major ouster among BLM personnel (to which I say "So be it!"). In spite of objections by the assistant U.S. attorney general, the recommendation to drop the case was conveniently—though dishonorably—accepted. As PEER goes on to state: [though] "... the Office of the Inspector General (OIG) of the Department of Interior is supposed to be an independent monitor of agency actions...when it came to wild horses this watchdog ran for cover. The OIG then declined a request for assistance from the Chief of BLM Law Enforcement, who acknowledged that his program lacked the independence to investigate its own agency." As would be expected, subsequently OIG ignored complaints from individuals employed by the BLM concerned continuing illegal activities within the wild horse and burro program. To again quote from the PEER report: "The problem stems from failure to faithfully execute the law regardless of political consequences." True to form, in 2010 OIG again covered for BLM's corrupt wild horse/burro roundup program and the largely unnecessary suffering and death of these animals.

Every year BLM officials present before Congress the same lies and distortions—or should we call them "fractional truths"—concerning the wild horses and burros. This is in order to get ever more millions of dollars for wild horse and burro roundups and to "achieve" other serious compromises of the Wild Free-Roaming Horse and Burro Act including zeroing out and fencing within their legal areas. All this is in place of positive actions that should be designed to secure the place of wild horses and burros in the wild, such as: (a) establishing permanent sources of water for them (through exerting the Implied Federal Water Rights that go with any act of Congress setting up a special area for special species), (b) removing fences impeding natural movements, and (c) buying out conflicting rancher grazing permits. In so perversely acting or failing to act, and usually under the direction of the Secretary of Interior himself, BLM officials abrogate their responsibility before the U.S. public as they continue to pander to wild horse enemies, chiefly public land grazers and hunters, as well as to other enemies who see horses as being in the way, including mining and energy interests. Many are, of course, also motivated by their desire for job security in a corrupt bureaucracy with enormous budgets to very poorly "play God" on the public lands. By pushing the false wild horse "over-population" and "destructive exotic" myths, BLM assures itself of ever bigger budgets to prop up the very ecologically damaging and economically losing livestock industry that monopolizes the glutton's share of our public lands today, as it has for at least the past one-and-a-half centuries, along with other destructive industries such as massive open-pit mining. But with the fortieth anniversary of the act, it is now high time for reform.

PROPOSED SOLUTION—A WAY OUT

Let us not dwell upon the negative. What matters is that we learn lessons from past experiences at each stage along life's way, for our doing so veritably redeems the past. In this vein and remembering Jacob's ladder (Genesis 28), I present a workable solution. This will be to restore wild equids in their legal herd areas and territories, and in all ecosystems where they play a crucial role. Let us plan a *modus operandi* by which to reestablish wild equid herds at long-term-viable population sizes within long-term-viable habitats, adequate in all respects as to size, water provision, food availability, shelter, mineral requirements, and elevational gradients. The latter will allow for seasonal migrations to higher areas during the summer and to lower areas during the winter. In these areas, wild equids will be treated as the "principal" presences as the Wild Free-Roaming Horses and Burros Act of 1971 intended; they will no longer be given secondary or even last priority by the very authorities whose duty is to uphold—not subvert—the federal laws protecting them.

Employing principles of reserve design (Downer 2010, Peck 1998), the following directives will serve to guide us:

(a) Let wild horses/burros reoccupy their full legal herd areas wherever possible and in no case less than 75% of the original legal area. And where a reduction in equid occupation of the original herd areas is deemed necessary, there must be a compensatory acquisition of wild equid habitat of equal or greater value as judged by competent, independent wildlife ecologists with particular knowledge of wild horse and burro requirements and unbeholden to wild equid adversaries. To accomplish this reoccupation, federal officials should employ Codes of Federal Regulation 4710.5 and 4710.6 to reduce or curtail livestock grazing within legal herd areas and territories. Also, they should authorize the purchase of grazing permits/base properties/water rights that are conflicting with the sound establishment of legal wild horse and burro herds. And they should not forget to insist upon the Implied Federal Water Rights that come with the legal herd areas or territories.

(b) Where possible and/or necessary, employ natural barriers or, where such do not exist, semi-permeable, artificial barriers, in designing each wild horse/burro herd area/territory as the true sanctuary the law intends. These barriers will act as limits, or impassable boundaries, to wild equid expansion. These will help contain each wild equid population within its legal domain, as legally expanded where necessary to provide long-term-viable habitat and to keep wild horses/burros out of harm's way, i.e., out of areas where they would be in clear and unavoidable conflict with human activities. Here I particularly recommend the employment of special Strieter-Lite light reflectors that prevent nighttime collisions of animals with automobiles wherever major roads or highways transect the wild equid herd areas/territories. Also, intelligent use of drift fences can serve to effectively contain horses at strategic passes, etc. But none of the foregoing shall be used to restrict the wild horses/burros within their large, viably sized, and complete habitats.

(c) Design and employ buffer zones around the wild horse herd areas/territories. Here a gradual tapering off of wild horse or burro presence would occur through the implementation of discouragements to their transiting into areas where danger exists for them, such as in farms or cities. This may involve the use of what wildlife managers term "adverse conditioning" that need not be overly harsh to be effective. The effectiveness of buffer zones depends to a high degree on public education, on working agreements with the people who live in or around each herd area/territory. These agreements will foment win-win relationships for both wild equids and people. Locals would monitor and protect the herds and derive benefit for doing this as well as from ecotours, and would be encouraged not to feed the equids. These buffer zones would be established according to principles of reserve design and in a positive manner respecting the wild equids.

(d) Allow each wild horse/burro herd to fully fill its ecological niche within each given legal herd area/territory bounded by natural or where necessary artificial barriers, and by buffer zones. Then allow each specific herd to self-stabilize, or auto-regulate, its population within this area.[10]

---

10 Such auto-regulation can occur if we humans allow. Both horses and burros are *climax* species, which is to say, members of the climax successional sere, or stage, and do not expand out of control to destroy their habitat and ultimately themselves, as humanity is presently doing. In other words, each band within a herd population is usually governed by a lead stallion (*patron*) who watches out for and defends the band and does most of the breeding, as well as by a usually older, lead mare. The latter is very wise as to where the best foraging, watering, mineral procurement, sheltering areas, etc., are located. She leads the band along paths uniting these habitat components. These include longer seasonal migratory routes between higher summering and lower wintering habitats. Both patron and lead mare socially inhibit reproduction among younger members of their band.

Each band establishes a home range within and/or outside the legal herd area/territory, according to its survival necessities. And all of the bands taken together form a mosaic of somewhat overlapping but generally distinct home ranges. Given enough time to work out their individual and collective differences, wild horses reach a more stable state in relation to their bounded habitat. They do not overpopulate and destroy this habitat but rather auto-limit, achieving a balance with the natural resources of their herd area/territory. Of crucial importance here is the optimal size of habitat that should be made available to each wild equid herd in order to provide for an optimally viable population. To be minimally viable and considering today's political constraints, I recommend that each herd contain at least five hundred and to be optimally viable for long-term survival over the generations, each herd should be well over one thousand interbreeding individual animals. Remember that the IUCN SSC Equid Specialist Group recommended a minimum size of 2,500 individuals in order to achieve long-term viability for a wild equid population, and a minimum size of five hundred for a carefully managed domesticated population (Duncan 1992, 5). Again, equids possess means of limiting their own reproductive capacities, either socially or biologically, when resources, including space, become limiting. This involves stress and hormonal factors (Rogovin and Moshkin 2007).

(e) In order to realize healthy, balanced wild horse/burro-containing ecosystems in each of the herd areas, as full a complement of plant and animal species, each filling its specific place and role, should be allowed. Wherever possible, this should include large carnivores/omnivores native to the region in question, such as puma, wolf, and black or brown bears. These will provide a natural control on the equid population (Mitchell 1986), one that will act through natural selection to make any given population more fit for survival in the wild and more adapted to its particular ecosystem. And the refuge should also include as large a variety of other large, medium, and small herbivorous, carnivorous, and omnivorous species as possible: rabbits, mice, prairie dogs, foxes, coyotes, deer, pronghorn, beaver, skunks, weasels, raptor birds such as hawks and eagles, scavenger birds such as vultures, song birds, and myriad lizards, snakes, rodents, amphibians, and insect species. This animal complex will, of necessity, be based upon a similarly diverse collection of plant species, including a complex mixture of grasses, herbs, shrubs, and trees, tending as much as possible to the autochthonous, or native, and supportive of a complete series of inter-complementary animal pollinators, seed dispersers, decomposers, species related as predator-prey, etc. Thus, the safeguard of greater biodiversity in the web of life will be allowed to make a comeback and be further enhanced.

REPRODUCTIVE INHIBITORS AND RESERVE DESIGN

In March 2008, BLM officials were considering castrating wild stallions in their legal herd areas to prevent their reproduction. I complained that this could precipitate inbreeding, because fewer stallions would actually fertilize the mares. Since horses naturally form harems, the dominant stallion of each does the majority of the breeding; however, a certain percentage of the breeding may be done by subdominant stallions (Berger 1986). Given castration, the male contributors to the gene pool would be greatly reduced and the specter of inbreeding would loom, as survival prospects for any given population would grow dimmer. Also, castration has caused stallions to be socially ostracized, attacked by kicking, and generally marginalized from the wild horse social groups in which they would otherwise be accepted (pers. obs.).

At BLM's Wild Horse and Burro Advisory Board meeting on February 25, 2008, in Tucson, Arizona, board member Larry Johnson proposed castration as a way of reducing wild horse reproduction. Johnson had been a very effective enemy of wild horses/burros in the wild and chiefly advocated for big game, especially bighorn, and their maximization on the public lands (bighorns greatly outnumber wild equids, yet are treated by government agencies as endangered). Castration would prove the ultimate cruel set up, or "managing for extinction," if adopted as policy and entirely contrary to the true spirit and intent of the act. Johnson is now off the board, as are a few other old-timers, but it remains to be seen whether the new board will become true advocates of wild horses/burros in the wild and work for their restoration.

As of July 29, 2011, Wyoming's BLM had decided to victimize the wild horses in the one-million acre White Mountain and Little Colorado

HMAs by removing 90% of them and returning only castrated stallions. Fortunately the Western Watersheds Project and American Wild Horse Preservation Campaign threatened suit to stop this cruel and outrageous "managing for extinction" BLM had scheduled to start in mid August 2011. Though BLM backed off on castration, it is still planning to drastically reduce the herds. A scientific analysis was just prepared by a retired BLM range manager examining the justification for Wyoming BLM's continued obstinacy, and it is hoped its findings that support greater numbers of wild horses will result in a fairer plan for the spirited Rock Springs mustangs (Edwards 2011; www.wildhorsepreservation.org/news/2011/07/29/).

BLM plans to use "aggressive birth control" to prevent the expansion of the wild horse/burro populations that remain. Chief among the drugs to be used is PZP (*porcine zona pellucida*). This injected drug covers the eggs, or ova, of mares, preventing sperm from fertilizing them. It is experimental, however, and has some questionable effects upon the horses themselves, both individually and collectively. For example, its effect leads to mares' repeatedly recycling into estrous, thus stimulating stallions to repeatedly mount the treated mares—all to no avail. This frustrating situation causes much stress among individuals of both sexes and a general disruption of the social order, both within bands and, as a consequence, within the herds[11] themselves.

Other unintended consequences of PZP are out-of-season births occurring after PZP's effect has worn off after a year or two. These births have been observed during the colder late autumn and winter seasons (e.g., Pryor Mountains herd by G. Kathrens) and their un-timeliness causes suffering and death among both foals and their mothers. Also the main humane organization that BLM officials have consulted for the Pryor Mountain herd is the Humane Society of the United States—the very patent holder on PZP that may stand to gain on the product's purchase by the government, according to Cindy MacDonald of www.americanherds.blogspot.com. This would clearly be a conflict of interest.

---

11 A herd is a more-or-less isolated group of interbreeding bands separated from other such herds by barriers such as tall mountain ranges; broad, deep rivers and canyons; vast, arid expanses bearing little to eat or drink; or human occupied areas (all components to be considered in reserve design).

The current experimental use of PZP delays the fertility of thousands of mares dispersed throughout many wild horse herds. It is another way BLM is taking the wild out of wild horses. Along with the very low appropriate management levels BLM has established, this is proving yet another tool for "management for extinction." Both out-of-season births and accelerated, unfruitful estrus cycling undermine wild horses' ability to survive in the harsh climate of the Pryor Mountains and similar places throughout the West, causing social instability both within and among the bands. Remarkably, long-time roundup contractor Dave Cattoor—whose company has received many millions of dollars from the federal government—confirms some of Kathrens's alarming observations, particularly out-of-season births and the excess stress on mares and the stallions who repeatedly try to impregnate the mares in vain. —There is something hellish about this!

The injection of GnRH is a hormonal way of preventing reproduction in mares, but is observed to produce serious suffering and aberrations, just as it does with women, in whom it has been linked to cancer. It is also being considered for use with the wild equids. Another inhumane way involves extraction of ovaries, which has been experimentally employed on the Sheldon NWR's wild horses (see www.humaneobserver. blogspot.com).

The answer to the wild horse crisis is not to be found in these cruel and invasive manipulations that are contrary to the act and its "minimal feasible level" of management tenet (Section 3a). Rather the solution is to be found in proper *wild land reserve design*. As detailed above such involves natural and/or artificial, semi-permeable barriers, natural predators, as well as community-involving buffer zones, among other tools. Future wild horse/burro reserves will contain complete habitats, large enough to support long-term-viable wild horse/burro populations. Accomplishing this will entail making some sacrifices in terms of certain outmoded ways—but is not true progress always thus?

CURRENT ROUNDUPS, BROKEN PROMISES, AND OBSERVATIONS CONCERNING WILD HORSE/BURRO HOME RANGES AND SANCTUARIES

Wild horses form tight-knit stallion- and elder-mare-governed bands. Over time, each band searches out and establishes its own home range, which may cover hundreds of square miles on an annual basis in drier regions. The ecological mosaic that results among all such particular band home ranges in a given herd area prevents overcrowding and overgrazing. Once available habitat is filled, the horse, as a climax species, limits its own population as density-dependent controls are triggered.

In the immediate future, true wild horse- and burro-containing nature sanctuaries need to be established. Here livestock should be excluded or at least greatly minimized and wild horses or burros allowed to establish viable populations in the thousands, not the mere hundreds or less than one hundred. These fairly populated sanctuaries will be viable in the long-term. They will preserve the vigor of the horses and burros they were designed to conserve by letting "God through Nature" work.

The draconian helicopter roundups conducted by BLM contractors (such as the veteran Dave Cattoor of Nephi, Utah) cut wild equid populations to non-viable levels and cause terrible trauma, injury, and death to individual horses, as well as social and ecological disruption for those remaining in the wild. This makes it very difficult for these individuals, their populations, and their ecosystem to recover and stabilize. As of 2010, a high of 10,255 wild equids were removed from the range. And according to Watson (2011), in spite of BLM director Bob Abbey's promise to reduce the level of roundups to 7,600, nearly the same number of wild horses are being removed in Fiscal Year 2011 (October 1, 2010 to September 30, 2011) as in Fiscal Year 2010, i.e., 11,910 being rounded up and 9,620 removed from the range. (In FY2010, BLM removed 9,715 horses and 540 burros from the public land, but was only able to adopt 3,074 of these.) So, in actuality, BLM will only have reduced the "gathers" by 635 animals, or 6%, not the ca. 2,600 reduction promised by Abbey (Watson 2011). As has become all too familiar, wild horses enemies get their way while wild horse supporters are lied to and disregarded! These excessive roundups actually cause an increase in these equids' rate of reproduction—a phenomenon called "compensatory reproduction" that has to do with the disruption of their social structure and increased breeding by younger, immature horses, unguided by the more mature ones as well as desperate to survive both as individuals and as species.

FURTHER THOUGHTS ON LIFE'S FUTURE, THREATS THERETO, & THE ROLE OF EQUIDS THEREIN

Worldwide, the horse family is declining rapidly (Duncan 1992). Restored to their ancestral freedom on the North American continent, any population of wild equids, in fact, returns to its more ultimate place of origin and long-standing evolution. Here these animals should be allowed to regain long-term-viable population levels in regions of adequate size and containing complete habitats. Thus, their true vigor as species will be restored, be this for horse or burro. And in the larger sense, this restoration will be of the very ancient and magnificent horse family itself.

In his acceptance speech for the Nobel Prize in Oslo, Norway, on December 10, 2007, former U.S. Vice President Al Gore warned that if humanity does not heed the current threat of global warming, life on Earth as we know it could soon become a thing of the past. To quote Gore: "We are recklessly burning and clearing our forests and driving more and more species into extinction. The very web of life on which we depend is being ripped and frayed." While Gore mentions carbon dioxide (CO_2) emissions by automobiles and factories, equally alarming are the enormous quantities of methane (CH_4) and nitrous oxides (N_2O, etc.) that have and continue to be generated by enormous hordes of domesticated livestock worldwide. (Perhaps he did not raise this point because he is from a Black Angus bull raising family.) Both of these groups of gases trap heat from the sun; methane does so much more intensely than carbon dioxide. In fact, methane's heat-trapping ability is twenty-three times that of carbon dioxide, while nitrous oxide's is hundreds. In this connection, as arctic and sub-arctic latitudes warm today, vast regions of permafrost are being melted, and in the process, these are releasing enormous quantities of methane. According to Henning Steinfeld and Tom Wassenaar (2007), "...livestock currently contributes about 18% to the global warming effect. Livestock contributes about 9% of total carbon dioxide (CO_2) emissions, but 37% of methane (CH_4) and 65% of nitrous oxide (N_2O)." The authors indicate that increased crop-fed livestock production is greatly accelerating this dangerous trend. Cattle raised on the open range are fattened up using farm-produced feed in concentration-camp-like feedlots before being slaughtered.

Those who advocate and practice a vegetarian diet (now including former U.S. President Bill Clinton) should be hailed as true saviors of life on Earth, along with those who do not use carbon-emitting vehicles or products from factories generating heat-trapping gases. For all those who know and care about the life of our home planet, wild equids, including horses and burros, should also be recognized as saviors of the biosphere, for they have a crucial healing role to play. If the "equid element," or component, could be restored in North America and domesticated ruminant cattle and sheep and wild ruminant game deer, etc., diminished, much less methane and nitrous dioxide would be generated. As explained earlier, this is because equids' post-gastric digestive system does not as thoroughly decompose consumed vegetation when compared with the ruminant digestive system, that releases voluminous quantities of gas. And, to reiterate, much more of the coarser, dry, and flammable grasses and other vegetation would be eaten by horses and burros and over broader areas, thus reducing fire hazard. This great service could save billions of dollars worth of property, vegetation, and fire fighting—all free of charge. All we have to do is learn to live in harmony with such wonderful animals! Evolutionary history demonstrates how well equids adapt to life in arid and semi-arid regions. Think of the Arabian Peninsula, North Africa, Central Asia where horses dwelt for millennia. Their unique experience of life over millions of years pre-adapts them to such austere wide-open places.

Wild horses and burros should be declared UNESCO World Heritage, as well as the national heritage species they have already been, in fact, proclaimed by the act. Wild horses' genetics combine early Spanish horses of Andalusian stock (a combination of Berber, Arab, and northern races) with horses from all over the world. These include the

Bashir curlies brought over by Russians to the northwest Pacific. In fact, the hardy wild horses and burros have much the same diversity and hybrid vigor as American people. Thus we Americans can say they are a reflection of ourselves. Living in the natural world, they are submitted to the rigors of natural selection that adapt them to more constant as well as changing environmental conditions. Thus, many adaptive traits may emerge that do not manifest in captivity, where genetic diversity, particularly among males, is greatly reduced (since fewer males are chosen to breed). One great example concerns their remarkable hoofs. These are kept in perfect, unshod condition on wild, rocky terrain and greatly assist in the circulation of blood through a sort of pumping action involving the suction cup effect of the hoof's bottom as the horse walks or runs. Equids living in the wild become their own person, so to speak—a truly quickened and striving presence! When people dismiss them as misfits here in North America, their cradle of evolution, they prove the old saw, "There are none so blind as they who will not see."

Though horses and burros have made civilization possible for mankind, their origin, long-standing development and greater role in relation to all of life is realized in the natural world. To deny such magnificent species their place in nature, their right to carry on their own special evolutionary paths, to treat them as mere slaves, worse yet as mere objects to possess and manipulate, epitomizes injustice.

How many people will only value a horse when he is enslaved, confined behind a fence or in a tiny corral, but when he is free to roam the wide, unfenced expanses, then suddenly there is something dreadfully wrong with him to their way of thinking? He becomes in their eyes a mere misfit, vermin, something beneath man's consideration and to be eliminated, or enslaved. This mindset has prevailed among certain political establishments for many years, particularly in the West, where draconian rancher hegemony has held sway in states such as Nevada and Wyoming, Idaho and Utah, Montana and Colorado, Arizona and New Mexico. Most ranchers, it seems, are obsessed with possessing the land and resources to maximize livestock production. All else on the land is viewed as secondary, with the most concessions being given to game production and harvest by hunters, especially deer and including truly exotic chukar partridges from Central Asia, or logging enterprises that clear the land of forest and, thus, expand open grassy areas for livestock.

Mining operations often despoil and contaminate the land, water, and air for generations to come, thus, affecting all wild species including wild equids—and people too, of course, are not immune. The widespread ramping up of oil and gas drilling operations throughout the West is doing much damage and is used as a pretext to zero out many wild horse herds from their legal areas contrary to the law (Fuller 2009, map on 107). This is very evident in eastern Nevada and southern Wyoming where some of our nation's greatest wild horse herd areas occur, as well as in western Colorado. The massive Adobe Town HMA roundups that occurred in October 2010 were related to oil and gas extraction. And the Triple B HMA, whose wild horses have recently (7-8/2011) been drastically reduced by helicopter roundups, is home to the enormous Mount Bald open pit mine that drains and contaminates enormous quantities of ground water in the region (contact author for photos; see Coffey 2010 b).

Other major displacers of wild horses and burros are farmers and land developers. Both effect the near total removal of the original, native ecosystem to supplant this with irrigated fields or housing tracts, business centers, shopping malls, industrial parks, etc. Often these require the monopolization of natural water sources. Similar to pioneer ranchers, these tend to secure local water rights, which, in fact, they often purchase from these ranchers. Like the ranchers, they often cap natural spring sources in the mountains and pipe this water down to their fields, golf courses, or buildings. This happened on a gargantuan scale in the central Sierra Nevada mountains when the Los Angeles Aqueduct project was forced through in the early twentieth century and the eastern Sierran mountains, foothills, and valleys were greatly diminished, including wildlife and rural communities, by draining their water. A grassroots campaign and legal suit brought by the Save Mono Lake Committee, spearheaded by the late biologist David Gains, whom I met, was finally successful in saving the giant, salty lake, home to many unique and endemic life forms such as brine shrimp and an important migratory bird stopover—but so much in the way of the native ecosystem was lost. (Incidentally, my grandfather Thomas Benson Downer was one of the engineer-surveyors who laid out the L.A. Aqueduct.) A similar outrageous "water grab" is now afoot in Nevada to continue the insane expansion of megalopolis Las Vegas. The Southern Nevada Water Authority proposes to drain, or pump, the aquifers from a vast area of eastern central Nevada and parts of western Utah in order to import 176,655 acre feet of groundwater annually. This would devastate the natural ecosystems of this region, including those harboring wild horses and burros (see www.blm.gov/5w5c; http://greatbasinwater.net) and be a further nail in the coffin of Mother Earth as a whole. (I protested this proposal at a BLM hearing on August 18, 2011, in Sparks, Nevada.)

The bigger picture concerning threats to the West was reported in *National Geographic's* article "Drying of the West." Here Kunzig (2008, 90–103) reveals that the Southern Nevada Water Authority has been purchasing ranches in central and eastern Nevada to secure water rights. The idea is to pipe the water to Las Vegas, whose population is projected to expand to over three million inhabitants in coming years, though with the current economic recession putting Nevada, including Las Vegas, at the number one position in the nation for home foreclosures and unemployment, it seems the projection of unbridled expansion was premature. Nonetheless, it seems the temptation of big money is too much to resist for many Nevada ranchers, same as it is with chauvinistic pie-in-the-sky developers. Also painfully lacking is the willingness on the part of public officials to secure water and habitat for wild horses and burros in perpetuity in their extensive legal herd areas/ territories throughout eastern and central Nevada. This would benefit all species of wildlife within nature-enhancing, wild-equid-containing ecosystems.

Though the Nevada Department of Wildlife (NDOW) has complained about Las Vegas's move to take over a major portion of Nevada's watershed, it remains to be seen whether it can stop this juggernaut. The natural ecosystem is being forgotten, devalued, and will become even more devastated if natural aquifers are drained by anywhere from five to a few hundred feet. Clearly needed is a sober willingness to change our priorities and lifestyles to become more conservation conscious. We need to make sacrifice of the less perfect for a more just and equitable way of life. In order to do this, we need to abandon humanity's narcissistic self-absorption for the sake of a more refined path in life, one that identifies with life's greater community.

A REMINDER ABOUT THE FOREST SERVICE

The U.S. Forest Service has been even more renege in implementing the act and has finagled since the act's inception to eliminate its wild horse and burro herds from at least 53% of their legally mandated "territories." Those relatively few territories that still possess wild equids have in most cases been given over to the BLM for management and have cripplingly low AMLs. One example is the Cherry Spring Territory in eastern Nevada just to the south of the Ruby Lake National Wildlife Refuge. Its already tiny numbers of wild horses on a tiny acreage were being drastically reduced by recent helicopter roundups as of August 2011. A particularly outrageous example of how the U.S. Forest Service has abandoned its obligation under the law occurred in the Lassen National Forest in northern California, in the only federal wild horse area west of the Sierra Nevada. The Brushy Mountain Wild Horse Territory had been legal home to at least 100 wild horses since before 1900 and until the 1980s. But according to local sources, officials, including Lassen N.F. Superintendent Dick Henry, not only condoned but aided (through helicopter spotting) both ranchers and hunters in shooting nearly or perhaps all of this agile and graceful herd. These nefarious shootings occurred mainly in 1982 in order to give more grazing resources to just one rancher. In 1987, inspectors from the national forest and the nearby Wild Horse Sanctuary found seventeen horse skeletons, one whose skull was pierced by a bullet. The rest were probably "gut shot". Along with his hunter accomplices, the rancher shot the great majority of the Brushy Mountain herd in 1982, then in 1987, just before losing his ranch, he shot the remaining ten horses on the far side of his land. –This keenly missed herd should be restored and protected now!

POOR TREATMENT OF MONTANA'S PRYOR MUSTANGS, U.S. FOREST SERVICE'S INTRANSIGENCE, WEIGHTY PROTESTS & OPPORTUNITY FOR RESTORATION

Though the Pryor Mountain Wild Horse Refuge was the second so declared by the U.S. Congress in 1969 (the first national sanctuary is the Little Book Cliffs of Colorado declared in 1967), its AML is outrageously low. BLM's Billings office in Montana has set this at 92 to 117 horses on 37,147 legal acres. In part stemming from escapees from the Lewis and Clark Expedition of 1804-1806, these mustangs[12] have been reduced to a genetically non-viable population level through over-management, yet they had stabilized as a modest population of ca. two hundred due to natural mortality factors. The latter include harsh winters, significant predation by pumas, and natural boundaries such as the steep canyon walls of the Little Bighorn River present on the northern side of the refuge, which I photographed in June 2003.

Contrary to their duty under the act, officials of the Custer National Forest have declared a policy of wild horse elimination from a vital portion of their original, legal 1971 wild-horse-occupied area in their public forest. This is putting an unnatural squeeze on the horses' annual movement patterns and reveals a pointed hostility. In the fall of 2010, forest officials constructed a fence to keep the wild horses from occupying the highland meadow that they clearly occupied at the passage of the 1971 act. And though The Cloud Foundation was granted the right to sue USFS concerning this illegal fence, the suit did not halt the fence's construction. Though USFS officials regard wild horses as a detriment to wilderness values, the horses act as a significant prey or scavenged species for puma, bear, eagles, and a variety of animals. Officials also overlook the mutualism of these "returned natives" that includes soil building and seed dispersal, breaking ice and snowy crusts to provide access to food and water during freezing weather, as well as their role in reducing dry flammable vegetation while stimulating increased growth of more tender sprouts that are more suitable for ruminant grazers. Award-winning filmmaker Ginger Kathrens has abundantly and sympathetically documented the life of the Pryor

12 Oelke (1997) considers the Pryor Mountain mustangs along with the Kiger mustangs of Oregon and a few other herds to be the last hope for survival of the ancient Sorraia lineage of Spain.

Mountain mustangs since 1994, especially in relation to one charismatic white stallion she dubbed Cloud (see www.thecloudfoundation.org); and this herd is world famous, though still treated by officials as a kind of joke.

By branding them as exotic misfits in designated wilderness areas, USFS officials ignore conclusive evidence proving the horse's native status in North America (Kirkpatrick and Fazio 2008), much of which comes from Pryor Mountain fossils or nearby. Custer National Forest officials would do well to visit Hagerman Horse Fossil Beds National Monument in southern Idaho where substantive evidence for the modern horse's North American native status is presented. Here is graphically illustrated how *Equus caballus* originated in North America at least 1.8 million years ago and how the entire horse family has its roots in North America, including both ass and zebra branches, as well as the caballine horse branch (Chapter 1).

A letter of July 2, 1992, by E. Gus Cothran, Ph.D., director of the Equine Blood Typing Research Lab and directed to Mr. David Jaynes at the BLM Office in Billings, Montana, proves revealing. While conciliatory in tone, Cothran obviously felt compelled to emphasize: "...the revision documents do not address the potential concerns that exist for the herd based upon the recommendations in my report on the genetic status of the herd. The main point is that a breeding population of 50 [from a total population of 150] is a minimum number, therefore there is little room for error when managing the herd at this size. Second, the population subdivision was a strong point for maintaining genetic variation in the herd. If this is no longer possible, then there is potential [negative] effect." This veterinarian then goes on to blunt his point. Without being so bold as to openly contradict his BLM contractors, Cothran seems to be issuing a warning to BLM officials about the serious consequences of reducing the wild horses of the Pryor Mountains to such a sub-minimally viable population level as the agency plans. That the BLM has not heeded his warning is evinced by their proposal of February 2008 to reduce the total herd to the lower AML limit of ninety-two horses. This would equate to an effective breeding population of just thirty-one horses, well below that for a minimum viable population, even by BLM's overly low standards. Since this time, a 2009 roundup has taken place, and the herd was brought down to a lower level though not quite as low as BLM planned. As of August 2010, another roundup was being proposed by BLM to further reduce the herd of 158 mustangs again to the sub-viable level of 92, and The Cloud Foundation has been urging that protests be sent to Billings BLM office.

As a member of Wyoming's pioneer Tillett family, Jerri Tillett maintains the tradition of fending for the Pryor Mountain mustangs (Ryden 1999). Without her family's efforts, it is probable that all these unique and valiant survivors of the centuries would have been eliminated to make way for more livestock and game animals, mines and mayhem. Here I excerpt portions of her December 13, 2007 letter directed to Mr. Gene Terland, Montana BLM state director. This concerns this agency's new (2008) plans to greatly reduce the herd:

> I noted that the BLM's stance is pretty much what it's always been....[because] I've...noticed over the years that the BLM isn't really interested in what I have to say, I shan't waste my time nor the BLM's...in further observations....Concerning BLM's Conclusion 'The AML should be maintained at a level between 92 and 117 adult wild horses.' ...for the past number of years I've been utilizing the IBLA Process [of legal appeal] extensively, and they have, indeed, been supporting your [BLM's] agenda 'across the board' and I expect they will continue to do so. However, that doesn't mean that I failed to show that the BLM committed an error....I did show that the BLM and the IBLA have committed grave errors in judgment in violating the LAWS OF THIS LAND extensively...[and] WITH FULL KNOWLEDGE THEREOF....the fact that the BLM State Director personally 'signs off' on all correspondence to me after consulting with the Solicitor, indicates that the BLM recognizes the validity and seriousness of the BLM's previous arrogant 'lack of judgment' concerning the LAWS OF THIS LAND. The way the BLM has previously conducted its response to observations

that differ from...[its] stated Objective/Agenda has only compounded the...Original issue (AML's and Wild Horses)...[and]...broadened the field extensively into other Issues of Major Concern i.e. Malfeasance and Civil Rights Violations. Therefore, I expect the result of this endeavor to be no different than what I've observed for the past 15 years: A 'DONE DEAL DANCE'. The BLM/IBLA will do whatever is necessary to ensure [their] Agenda is approved and I'll again get my 'Ass royally kicked'. Such is life!

Ms. Tillett speaks for thousands, even millions of people who have fought the corrupt politicos working against the wild horses and burros in the wild and whose aim is to subvert the true intent of the Wild Free-Roaming Horses and Burros Act of 1971. Along with the Endangered Species Act and the Wilderness Act (acts that should be viewed as compatible with wild horses), this progressive law demonstrates caring by humans for a species other than man and an appreciation for its natural freedom and habitat. May time prove Ms. Tillett's words not to have been uttered in vain.

Before leaving this subject, it should be recognized that the Pryor Mountains were terribly overgrazed by sheep between the mid 1800s and the late 1900s. This thoughtless plunder has left soils denuded and slow to recover (Dr. Jay Kirkpatrick, pers. comm.)...a process where horse manure can greatly help (see Chapter 11). Also let's not forget that out of the seven original herd areas established by the act in Montana, the Pryor Mountain HMA is the only one that still has any horses left, probably because it was a national wild horse sanctuary even before the act. Nonetheless, Montana BLM officials persist in their aim to reduce the herd to a sub-viable level. And their decision has come in spite of ample forage and water due to an increase in precipitation in recent years. Also suspect is the decision to renew puma hunting in the area, since pumas act as natural horse predators and a natural curb upon and toner of wild horse populations, and this mustang population had been self-stabilizing before renewing the puma hunting season (Ginger Kathrens, pers. comm.).

Though one of America's most famous and visited herds, the Pryor's wild horses have been suppressed to artificially low population and genetically non-viable numbers, as attests Sandra Brooks, former BLM field manager for this region. Bounded by cliffs on the north and east sides, this sanctuary is a perfect candidate to implement reserve design; hence this is where a naturally self-stabilizing population at a higher, more truly viable level can come to be. So let's just do it, meaning let's just let it be!

CLAN ALPINE AND VICINITY

An area in many ways even more impressive than the Pryor Mountains, the forty-mile-long, southwest-to-northeast running Clan Alpine Range occurs east of Fallon and west of Austin in west-central Nevada, where I have spent many days hiking. The subtle charm of this region has been noted by many, and the nearby New Pass-Ravenswood and Desatoya wild horse herd areas, each ca. thirty-miles long, also present intriguing views to passersby on U.S. Highway 50, officially labeled "America's Loneliest." Just north of the Clan Alpine Range is the Augusta Mountain mustang herd and just north of the New Pass-Ravenswood survive concentrated remnants of the great South Shoshone herd. Several thousand horses could easily be sustained in this extensive complex, but since 1981, helicopter roundups have become ever more frequent as increasingly unfair appropriate management levels have been assigned by our supposed "public servants."

In 1981, BLM officials promised me, as representative of the Animal Protection Institute, that the Clan Alpine would always remain a substantial viable herd of around 1,500 horses (Milton Frei, pers. comm.). But due to constant pressure by certain ranchers and the Nevada Department of Wildlife, this vast herd area now contains only a small remnant of 612 horses—well below its AML of 979 (U.S. Department of the Interior 2008). Yet this remains one of America's largest herds—though its vitality/viability has been further compromised because of PZPed mares.

In all of the above areas, survivors of the once numerous Shoshone herd sport their striking pinto, paint, and medicine hat colorations (see Figures 8 & 9). In relation to this herd, I knew the wily old mustanger Jimmy Williams of Austin, who operated for several decades here. Though he profited from periodic roundups for many years, to his credit he limited his take in order to keep the mustangs in the thousands. In his last years, he protested the conspiracy among wild horse enemies to eliminate so many of the herds, including this historic remnant (Williams 1978). The Shoshones had tended these horses from the mid-1800s, allowing them a large degree of freedom amidst these bewitching mountains and valleys. They would capture and ride the horses for periods of time as needed then set them free again, and their relation to the horses was governed by a mutual respect and keen appreciation of their benefits to the life community. I can just imagine the natural way of life that prevailed then: the agile Shoshones and the wild horses living side-by-side, more as companions and sharers of freedom than as masters and slaves. This was a time before livestock operators had secured their stranglehold on this vast and stark desert "basin and range." More of a pristine quality existed back then—in reality not so long ago. But the good news is that this wonderful quality can be restored.

Figure 8. Reese River Pinto Mustangs, central Nevada. 1981 by author.

To this day, this historic remnant possesses a special aliveness palpable in places such as the northern Clan Alpine Range around Shoshone Meadows. Here a fantastic landscape sports various yellow, orange, and purple earths set amid a labyrinth of rolling hills, and each arroyo is a microcosm with its own gurgling spring and meandering rivulet. Here a series of step-like meadows has been fashioned over time, and the wild horses judiciously rest rotate their grazing pressure among these riparian habitats, not camping on and devastating them, as do cattle and sheep, or rather their insensitive human masters who foist these innocent animals here in unnatural concentrations and prevent them from harmoniously adapting as they would if left alone.

GETTING THE WILD BACK INTO THE ACT & INTO PRACTICE – WHAT *Will* BE DONE

Major reform in America's wild horse and burro program is clearly and urgently called for. Selfish and overbearing interests who have displaced wild equids from their legal herd areas/territories must withdraw, as wild equids are reinstated as viable herds. Simultaneously, a well-based, in-field protection and management program must be instituted. Speaking positively, this program *will* place major emphasis on establishing healthy, viable, and naturally self-stabilizing populations in and around each legal area. Each area *will* have a strategic plan specifically designed to suit its unique ecosystem and herd. This plan *will* incorporate natural barriers and predators to the extent possible, as well as semi-permeable, constructed barriers where necessary. Also emphasis *will* be given to buffer zones as prescribed by reserve design. All of the foregoing *will* keep the wild horses/burros out of harm's way. Wild horse/burro areas *will* be as large as possible, encompassing hundreds, even thousands of square miles; and the wild, naturally living horses and burros *will* be treated as the "principal" presences within their legal areas, as accords with the original language, terms and intent of the act. Livestock grazing in these areas *will* be scaled back and even cancelled where possible, as through ranch buyouts; state game departments *will not* be allowed to monopolize the natural resources in these areas, such as by fencing off springs.

Objective studies *will* compare and contrast horse- or burro-occupied areas with those without equids. Those conducting them *will* consider a more complete set of factors operating upon the wild equids and their habitats and incorporate the past history of ecological disturbance in each given area into their evaluation. This *will* give factually substantiated information concerning the ecological niche and role of wild horses and burros, information that has not been filtered out or given a negative spin.

Further investigated *will be* wild equids' elimination of dry flammable vegetation and their consequent prevention of catastrophic, excessively damaging fires, as well as how their droppings help build a more moist and nutrient-rich, humus-containing soil, a soil with greater texture and absorptivity, as attest many persons familiar with horses/burros (Jeff Roth, pers. comm.). Many of these positive contributions have been shamelessly ignored and, when brought up, denied by established interests, both in private and government circles. Top on their agenda has been to discredit and eliminate free-living horses and burros—species returning to their natural place in the world for which myriad generations of living in the wild has pre-adapted them.

Given proper protection and the provision of complete habitats, wild horse and burro herds *will* become healthy and inspiring examples of continuing life on Earth and, as such, world-class ecotourist attractions, generating a wholesome economic lifestyle in communities around them. And the wild horses and burros will become integrated into a better, ecologically harmonious way of life for us humans—use your knowledge and imagination and dare to try! Ecotours *will* be conducted that do not overly disturb any single band or herd or its occupied habitat. Through a judicious rotation of visits among all of America's herds, there *will* be no over-concentration on any one in particular, disruptive to the wild horses or burros. Such tours *will* also provide much needed public vigilance to defend the wild equids against their unnatural human enemies but not overly from their natural predators. This program *will* be overseen by a wild-horse-caring and -defending cadre of public servants, NGOs, or just plain caring citizens for a change. Where feasible, tours *will* be incorporated into scientific monitoring programs, assisting long-term biological and ecological studies and assuring that the equids' public water sources are not fenced off, poisoned or drained. Public vigilance of the herds resulting from ecotours *will* prevent illegal killings, now on the upsurge, and contribute positively in many other ways (Appendix IV: Excerpts from Investigative Report of St. Valentine's Day 2006 Wild Horse Shootings available by request from author). And *there will be* a near endless list of the benefits of this positive approach to sharing life and freedom with wild horses and burros.

With positive vision of wild equids as expanded through ecotours, observational studies, and a caring approach to the mutual coexistence of man and equid, it *will* be wonderful to witness the new age of enlightenment that *will* ensue. For the West *will* be infused with a much more wholesome attitude, value system, and lifestyle involving wild horses and burros and all the other complementary species of plants and animals. We *will* take greater delight in seeing how all species fit harmoniously together and how all life goes forth in mutually supportive fashion and toward ever greater realizations, according to the time. Our interrelations *will not* be taken for granted. By transforming the relations we have with other species, we *will* also transform the relationships we humans have with each other. For we *will* have learned to value, appreciate and identify with the greater whole of life.

Wild horses and wild burros are of great intrinsic interest to humanity. These two species have been and, in many places, remain humans' working partners and/or life companions (see "The Tartar", poem by author from his book *Streams of the Soul* [2005] through request to author). Over the centuries they have shared in so many of our endeavors, our pains and pleasures, our triumphs and defeats, yet their true origin and longest duration on Earth remains *in the wild* and this: chiefly in a place we call North America. It would be extremely unfair to deny these ancient and closely related equid lineages their legal, moral, and natural right to resume their age-old progression in freedom. And I speak for many when I say that their natural evolutionary process must be preserved—that they be allowed their rightful place under the sun! And we should not be envious when they shine so brightly as they come more fully into their own.

CHAPTER V:

PERSONAL EXPERIENCES WITH THE WILD ONES & FELLOW WESTERNERS

As a fourth generation Nevadan growing up here in the West, I have visited many of the remnant wild horse and burro herds. Several are close to my home in Carson Valley; I have become quite familiar with these. I have also worked with several different animal protection organizations over the years, serving as watchdog for the herds. Since my boyhood, I have observed these remarkable animals during all seasons of the year, braving intensely hot summers and biting, cold winters alike, rejoicing in the spring and mellowing out at autumn. Upon occasion, I have come face-to-face with mustangers in the desert, wondering whether they were going to shoot me outright, or beat and leave me to perish on my own. My friends included the famous Wild Horse Annie (Velma Bronn Johnston) and her coworkers. They would go to battle for the wild horses and burros and their right to live free in adequately sized habitats, and as viably sized populations well provisioned with food, water and shelter, and unfenced and unmolested by man. These coworkers of Annie's, Helen Reilly and Dawn Lappin, used to warn me about ending up at the bottom of some old, abandoned mine shaft at the hands of wild horse enemies.

On wide-ranging visits, I attended meetings alongside fellow wild equid enthusiasts, public lands ranchers, hunters, fishermen, Paiute, Washoe, and Shoshone Indians, recreationalists, ORVers, Sierra Club wilderness advocates, hikers, miners, land developers, and county, state, and national biologists and officials, among other nondescript types. Some of these meetings were known as Coordinated Resource Management Planning (CRMP) workshops, and were organized by the Bureau of Land Management. Sometimes more one-on-one meetings occurred among a BLM official, a rancher, myself and/or another wild horse advocate. I would remind those present that the equids had the legal right to be treated as the "principal" presences in their legal herd areas (HAs) and that here they should be able to avail themselves of adequate: (1) natural water sources; (2) food in the form of palatable grass, shrubs and forbs; (3) shelter in the form of trees and natural formations such as canyons; and (4) an elevational gradient extending from more sheltered valley bottoms and mountain foothills (for occupation during the cold winter) to the upper forested slopes and crowning meadows (for occupation during the hot summers). This partitioning of habitat use involves annual migrations that accord with anciently attuned survival patterns, including innate herding behavior that more evenly distributes grazing pressure, allowing for natural rest rotation.

Though I have given stirring witness to the importance of wild equids and their belonging in the West, sometimes I have encountered animosity for daring to stand up for their freedom. This reflects a harsh, narrow-minded utilitarianism that seems to prevail in many rural areas whose inhabitants can sometimes quickly close ranks when it comes to sharing the land, freedom, or very life itself with the equids. Often I have patiently explained the origin of the horse family in North America, pointed out abundant fossil and genetic evidence, and linked wild equids with substantial ecological benefits to the plants and animals with which they have coevolved. Though receiving positive responses, I have come away from some meetings deeply offended by the closed-minded attitudes of those present. Their philosophy seemed to be "more for me and mine and to hell with the rest!" When confronted with this unwillingness to listen and to compromise concerning their use of public lands, I realized just how rooted the Sagebrush Rebellion was in blind tradition, and how certain attitudes have made some people oblivious to myriad values and presences on the public lands.

I particularly miss the administration of President Jimmy Carter in the late 1970s when government officials displayed more of a willingness to stand up for the legal rights of the horses and burros to occupy their land and live in natural freedom. Subsequent administrations have recklessly allowed the subverting of the Wild Free-Roaming Horses and Burros Act. During the Carter administration, officials had the courage to confront certain overbearing parties. They used their authority to achieve greater respect for the relatively few remaining wild equids and allocated a more just portion of the natural resources to them. In some cases, they even curbed livestock excesses under Code of Federal Regulations 4710.5 and 4710.6 so that the equid herds could become more fairly established, thus achieving a closer approximation to long-term population viability.

But instead of accepting this minimal sharing, a vocal contingent of public lands exploiters childishly lashed out at the government officials who were honorably doing their job. They were bent on continuing their monopoly and determined to get their way through customary bullying. Carter and his administration demonstrated a truer courage when faced with these bullies than any of the subsequent presidencies. This integrity should reincarnate during the present administration of President Barack Obama, though the appointment of public lands rancher and wild horse enemy Kenneth Salazar has certainly not been a step in the right direction. Perhaps Obama will appreciate the parallel between the horse and burro and his own Afro-American people: their struggle to realize their own special place and role—and precious freedom! Sadly, though eight years under President George W. Bush seriously jeopardized the wild equids in their legal herd areas/territories, the Obama administration has actually stepped up the pace of roundups, including many zeroing-outs. This should not be surprising, since many of the same officials remain in charge of the program as under Bush.

EUREKA MEETING

I recall one particular meeting in the quaint town of Eureka in central eastern Nevada. Present were a BLM land manager, a local rancher, and three wild horse advocates including myself. An unfairly low wild horse population level had been proposed for the Callaghan Herd Management Area bordering the northern Toiyabe Range and including an area known as Grass Valley. Dawn and Bert Lappin, of the Reno-based WHOA! (Wild Horse Organized Assistance) and I had requested a fairer population level. Now we had to convince the rancher. Dawn let me take the lead and I believe I fairly well shined in standing up for the horses and their freedom. Mr. Brad Hines, the BLM manager, agreed that the proposed level of around 150 was unfair and that 350 was more reasonable, given the legal priority for wild horses within this vast herd area (ca. 156,000 acres) and the major livestock presence. Pleased that my verbal arguments had at long last produced a tangible result for wild horses in the wild, I thought I could leave Eureka in peace. But not so!

The rancher (John Petrocini, as I recall) was egging for the substandard wild horse population and shared the grazing privileges in this herd area with a man named Paris. When he heard BLM's fairer agreement, he became absolutely irate and directed his animosity mainly at me. Red in the face, he pounded the table, emitted gross obscenities, and even threatened to kill me, yelling "I'll plaster your brains all over the walls!" No armed government agent was present, so all Mr. Hines said was, "You two had better settle your differences outside!" Prepared for a fight, we strode out of the office. Just as we emerged, however, Bert Lappin, Dawn's stalwart husband, sternly told the rancher, "You had better not touch a hair on Craig's head!" all the while showing him a loaded pistol. We proceeded to our pickup, while the rancher stood back a few paces, glaring menacingly. Bert confidently hopped into the driver's seat, ignited the engine, then slowly drove west out of Eureka on U.S. Highway 50. A mile out of town, we noticed the rancher's pickup following us a quarter of a mile off. Fortunately he did not press his luck, and we were able to get back to Reno without further harassment—only the feeling that we should watch our backs for a while. A worthy lesson here: standing up for innocent animals can come with real risks, but these are certainly worth it.

SIDEBAR: RURAL NEVADA & WILD HORSE ATROCITIES: Rural Nevada is a particular hot bed of violence toward wild horses and burros, as thousands of these have been cruelly shot, poisoned, trapped, and surreptitiously trucked to slaughter. They have been fenced off from access to their rightful water sources and prime feeding and shelter areas with relative impunity. Much of the problem lies with lackluster law enforcement by responsible BLM and USFS, as well as local, officials (Jacobs 1991, 297–301). One glaring case in central Nevada came to light in August of 1988 when ca. one thousand wild horses were shot by a conspiracy of anti-wild-horse ranchers (Barber 1989). Many of these unfortunate animals had been deliberately gut shot and despicably left to wander off to die in agony in secluded parts of their range where they would pass un-noticed. Though a lengthy trial ensued and ranchers were named, in the end no charge stuck. The accused were let off on a technicality concerning the difficulty of proving which bullet belonged to which rifle. This horrible incident occurred eight years after an earlier incident involving the shooting of thirty-four wild horses by repeater rifle in the very same area. I had investigated this and taken photographs on New Year's Day, 1981, in the company of my steadfast parents, Bob and Alice, and while working for the Animal Protection Institute of America. Again, this involved the Callaghan wild horse HMA in Grass Valley.[13]

---

13 *Reno Gazette Journal* Thu., Oct. 13, 1988. "Dead mustang total rises to 450" By Doug McMillan. "Bureau of Land Management officials said that 450 wild horses have died in the mustang shootings north of Austin. They emphasized that the number could climb higher as investigators complete their field work and do more body counts on the ground. BLM public affairs officer Maxine Shane said they have counted 153 dead horses around Mt. Moses, an 8,600-foot mountain near the Lander-Pershing County line about 40 miles northwest of Austin. Working over the weekend, BLM agents also found another 100 dead horses in the Mt. Callaghan-Bald Mountain area, stretching about 20 to 40 miles north of Austin. That brought to nearly 300 the number of wild horses found slaughtered … since the first mustang massacre of 41 horses was discovered there Aug 5. The carnage spreads across 160 square miles of rugged mountains and foothills in Lander County. Shane said evidence suggests that the shootings began about two years ago and continued until late last spring or early summer. …"

I asked Ms. Karen Sussman of ISPMB about this massacre, and she remembers that the final count was around 800, though many estimated over 1,000 shot. Though considerable evidence implicating certain ranchers was gathered, no one was ever convicted. Sussman remembers that most were gut shot so that they would wander away from the site of the shooting to die agonizing, prolonged deaths, and be less probable to detect. Jacobs (1991) reveals similar illegal killings in Nevada probably by ranchers that went unpunished and suggests those that come to the light of public attention are only the tip of the iceberg.

SALT LAKE CITY

On August 23, 1980, I gave a speech with ad lib at the annual Wild Horse Forum in Salt Lake City, Utah (Appendix V: 1980 Wild Horse Forum Speech available by request from author). This forum had been initiated by Wild Horse Annie to foment wild horse/burro interest, increase wild horse/burro knowledge, and further secure their viable populations on western public lands. What I noticed at the forum, however, was a conspicuous grandstanding by adherents of the "sagebrush rebellion," a movement by ranchers and others to wrest control of public lands from the federal government. Mostly present were western state politicos seeking to promote their own greedy agendas, i.e. more and more livestock and/or big game, ecologically damaging open-pit mines disruptive to water tables, etc., at the expense of other, more general public interests, values, and presences related to leaving the natural world alone and enjoying its abundant ecological services gratis. Attendees were divided between those favoring and those hostile toward wild equids, and the latter constituted an obnoxious majority. In my case, their hostility was to reach beyond the covert or merely verbal.

My speech was scheduled right after a break that followed a tendentious diatribe by a portly Utahan sagebrush rebel. His had been a tedious repetition of the same old prejudiced remarks one could hear in many rancher bars. My talk was prepared to: (1) highlight the current status of the wild horse and many positive points justifying this returned native species; (2) counter biased claims by their enemies concerning them and reveal discrepancies in fulfilling the law; and (3) propose a plan of action involving better public education, stepped up law enforcement, and curbing exploiter monopolization of the public lands.

During the fifteen-minute break preceding my talk, I entered the restroom to freshen up. A long hall with a light switch led to the actual lavatory whose entrance was by way of another swinging door on the left. This reminded me of the chutes used to load captured wild horses and gave me an eerie feeling. The former speaker also entered this lavatory while I was at the washbasin. Casting a slanting glance in my direction, he proceeded to use the urinal, then went quickly back out. But on his way he decided to do me "a terrific favor" by dousing all the lights in both the lavatory and the hallway. This left me in total pitch-blackness in the huge bathroom.

Suddenly I lost all visual orientation, and though I cried out, no one heard me. About my sole hope of getting back in time for my speech was my sense of touch. I discovered that only by going crudely onto my hands and knees could I prevent myself from banging into the numerous bathroom fixtures. Basically, I had to form a mental model of this large lavatory much as a mouse would do in a labyrinth and grope my way past the wash basins and toilet stalls to the hall door. It took several minutes before I was able to gain the hall door. Gratefully pushing this open, I then saw a tiny beam filtering under the door to the main auditorium—which seemed like a beam from heaven!

Much relieved, I stood up and walked to this exit then back again into the world of the living. "What a dirty trick!" I ruminated, just as I was being anxiously called by the forum spokesman to address this considerable gathering of ca. four hundred. As I strode to the podium, I pondered how many sitting before me would do such tricks, and what dirtier ones they might play upon the wild horses and burros out in the sparsely populated vastnesses of the western public lands.

My speech went well and commanded the audience's fixed attention. I spoke of my organization's recent national exposé of illegal barricading of public waters in Nevada. This had prevented wild horses from drinking; so, in desperation they tried to crash through piked and barbwired barricades. One particular incident had recently surfaced near

Ely in eastern Nevada and within a legal herd area. Some of the horses discovered had became caught between the taut barbed strands and perished in a long and anguished way, as graphic photographs taken by miners John and Mary Bisoni and published by the Associate Press revealed. I also emphasized the ecological, aesthetic, and moral values of wild horses and sought to convey this in my own personal manner. I spoke with particular conviction that day, for having experienced in the flesh some hint of the dreadful persecution the wild ones have suffered for so long.

PINE NUT RANGE

While growing up in Nevada's "Garden Spot," the spectacular Carson Valley, one of my favorite activities was exploring the intriguing Pine Nut Mountains to the east. Here I would spend days discovering its multiple facets, observing its diverse plants, including thousand-year-old pinyon pines and venerable junipers, as well as animals such as the gray fox, golden eagle, and pinyon jay. In this twenty-six-mile-long, fifteen-mile-wide range, my encounters with wild horses were especially memorable and included witnessing them plunging through sparkling snowy drifts on crystalline, full-moon nights. The "Pine Nuts" would have made a wonderful national park had it not been so coveted since the days of the Comstock by ranchers, miners, hunters, timber harvesters, wood gatherers, etc. Its combination of extensive sagebrush-grasslands (or steppe) along its foothills; extensive, mid-elevation forests; and highland meadows, which covered the oft snow-capped, 9,450-foot Mount Siegel, made it a provident home range for native Washoe Indians. The latter are a stocky people some of whom still harvest pinyon nuts during the autumn as they have for centuries past. These nuts make for especially good eating in toasted form during cold winter days. These handsome, bluish-green trees could provide a much more ecologically benign and abundant source of food for us humans today when compared with the beef or mutton that we extract at such a devastating cost to the fragile desert here.

During my boyhood, the Pine Nuts provided a splendid home to, over time, an estimated two thousand wild horses who had harmoniously adapted here since their return to the land of their not-so-distant ancestors during the mid-nineteenth and early-twentieth centuries. Forming a mosaic of somewhat overlapping home ranges, which shift over the generations, they had evolved a type of natural rest rotation both in the short- and long-term. And the Pine Nut mountain ecosystem throve and was enhanced because of their presence.

It is an absolute necessity that natural rest from grazing/browsing occur in any given habitat regardless which herbivore species, including equids, are involved. But it should be recognized that these animals naturally "rest rotate" their own grazing when not overly restricted by fences and other barriers. Such rest rotation allows an area the time to regenerate. A certain period of rest should be prescribed/allowed to naturally occur in order to maintain a healthy ecosystem. Likewise recognized should be the size this system requires to properly function over long periods while sustaining a long-term-viable equid population and the niche separation among the diverse herbivore species present (Jenkins and Ashley 2003, 1155). All this should be carefully based upon objective observation and science. And this depends upon our learning to be humble observers and harmonious coexisters with the Rest of Life rather than violent imposers of arbitrary and selfish will.

The latter I have witnessed in my home region where escalating pressures from "civilization" have resulted in ever more grievous assaults upon the Pine Nut ecosystem. Hordes of livestock have over-grazed the forage, turning once grassy meadows into unpalatable sagebrush flats or eroded gullies. And timber and wood gatherers have eliminated nearly all of the ancient pinyon pines and Utah junipers—some a thousand or more years old. Large quantities of pinyon and juniper went to stoke the ore-smelting furnaces of the nineteenth century Comstock silver mining boom. Many trees were used as fence posts to corner in and possess the land, contrary to the more ecologically benign Indian tradition that valued nature's freedom. Furthermore, the federal government has waged a lethal and gruesome campaign to extirpate natural predators, e.g., puma, coyote, bear. And as though this were not enough, low-grade gold mines have created polluted Superfund sites in the southern portion of this otherwise spectacular range (Sunrise mine). Nature's delicate balance has been mangled by "progress."

Ranchers have sought to squeeze as much meat production as possible out of this "high wet desert" (Trimble 1999), but this has come at a terrible price. Though relatively wet for the Great Basin in which Nevada sits, the Pine Nut Range is still dry and desertic with only nine inches of average yearly precipitation (slightly lower at lower elevations and higher at higher elevations). Many ranchers and homesteaders have fenced or even cemented off the natural springs and rivulets in order to pipe the natural water sources for their livestock and crops in the valleys to the west (Carson and Eagle) or to the east (Mason and Smith). Alfalfa in particular, requires enormous amounts of water. Manipulating this water has come at the expense of the native plants and animals, many of which have grown alarmingly scarce, e.g., the endangered pygmy rabbit (*Sylvilagus idahoensis*). Add to this picture, all the additional roads and fences crisscrossing the range, disrupting the wholesome movements of the animals, upsetting the cycles operating throughout time, and you will get an idea of the serious disturbance that has occurred.

SIDEBAR: OVEREMPHASIS ON GAME ANIMALS: Modern culture's big emphasis on maximizing the production of game animals for annual harvest, especially mule deer (*Odocoileus hemionus*) in the West, goes along with all this brutal assault. While native, deer were never as unnaturally abundant as they have now become (Baker 1985). Much of this is due to man's vicious war against the predatory species: the wolf and its diminutive cousin, the coyote, the grizzly, the black bear, the puma, or mountain lion, the bobcat, the wolverine, and even the majestic golden and bald eagles, not to mention the prodigious California condors. And the list goes on. Most of these species continue to be ruthlessly exterminated by any conceivable means: shooting (including in reckless contests), trapping, poisoning, den raiding, including smoking and burning out, M-14 injection traps, *ad nauseam*. Many other species are incidentally victimized in the process. The repression of predators that have coevolved with their prey has upset nature's apple cart and lead to ever more extreme responses by "civilization." Again, the Pine Nut Range has been greatly victimized in this war against predators in order to satisfy the overbearing demands of both cattle and sheep ranchers and hunters.

I have identified with America's last hardy wild horse/burro survivors since my boyhood wanderings in the Pine Nut, as well as Virginia, Wassuk, Clan Alpine, Sierra Nevada, and other ranges; the gross unfairness with which these returned natives have been treated distresses me. Since the act's passage, the legally entitled equids have been increasingly removed from and marginalized on the great majority of their legal herd areas (see Figure 5 on page 53; Appendix I: Forever Wild and Free speech available by request from author). In the Pine Nut Range only 41% of the original 251,893-acre herd area (HA) remains as a designated 104,318-acre herd management area (HMA) in its northern half, excluding the once vital summering meadows on Mount Siegel. And the Pine Nut mustang population has been repeatedly reduced since the 1971 act. In the early 1980s, an appropriate management level (AML) of 385 horses in the reduced Pine Nut HMA was established. BLM authorities promised me that this would be permanent. Yet this has been repeatedly reduced so that today's AML is only 179 wild horses, far below the viable population level that is recommended by the Equid Specialist Group (see Ch. IV, 127). Outrageously, after year 2000, BLM officials have proposed even lower AMLs to accommodate the further onslaught by developers and the "whole nine yards" of "progress" bereft of any meaningful refinement in our attitudes, lifestyles, and relationship to the Rest of Life. It is ironic that some of the recent subdivisions around the Pine Nut Range bear "wild horse" in their name, yet often these same developers or their clients, when faced with having to build a fence to keep the mustangs out of golf courses or residential lawns, merely request BLM to remove them.

SOUTH PANCAKE WILD HORSE HERD AREA

One of my most memorable encounters with the wild ones involved some very energetic and diversely colored mustangs of the South Pancake Range. This labyrinthine range is located in a remote part of eastern Nevada about a dozen miles west of the small town of Currant in enormous Nye County. In the late summer of 1980, I spent the better part of a week in this enchanting region to assess the safety and well-being of the wild horses. I uncovered an illegal wild horse trap in a box canyon near Ikes Spring and noticed just how frightened the wild horses were when I approached them, whether on foot or in my vehicle. Each time I drew near a band, its horses would tense up as the lead stallion and mare, raising their heads, quickly assessed the danger. The patron would issue a high-pitched whinny and the whole band would thunder away, oft up some twisting, rocky canyon and into higher pinyon-juniper cover. Judging from their wary behavior, these animals were being seriously harassed, subject to roundups and even shootings. This was also verified by the above mentioned illegal horse trap, which I dismantled one cool evening, enjoying the bonfire.

Being a hot mid-August and given that the major water sources had been monopolized by local ranchers, the several wild horse bands of the South Pancake Range had become dependent upon one major source still available to them called Sand Springs. This was out in a valley to the west of the mountain. The BLM was taking pains to maintain this water source. My plan was to get better observations and photographs of the horses in the late afternoon and early evening just as they came into water. This turned out splendidly, and the orderly fashion with which these bands came in to drink was quite impressive. Each band took its turn and only the time necessary for its members to replenish themselves, roughly a half-hour, then, upon signal of the mare, adroitly scampered off in the direction of the band's home range as, in *legato* fashion, the next band would come into drink. Sometimes I noticed a bit of aggression by a lead stallion, as when a younger stallion from another band came to investigate one of this patron's mares.

In the first hour before the sun went down, the dusty desert air took on an enchanting, mellow glow that exquisitely revealed the rainbow colors of the wild horses. There were many chestnut bays and a number of sorrels with a ruddy golden sheen (see Figure 9). Present also were multihued roans of the blue and strawberry variety, and some palominos and buckskins as well, the latter bearing dark dorsal as well as hock stripes and often referred to as *grullos*. These stripes are considered primitive, but they would be more rightly labeled adaptive to life in the wild as they visually disrupt a horse's outline, providing protection from enemies through camouflage. I have also wondered whether the dark stripe down the spine serves to absorb heat during cold periods or to shield from harsh solar rays, i.e. for either energizing or protecting the vital spinal cord.

Figure 9. South Pancake bands with striking medicine hat stallion nicknamed "El Espanto." Photo by author, August 1980.

During this dusky hour, one vivacious young stallion caught my attention. He was a true "medicine hat," and horses with this pattern have long been revered by Amerindians. Bearing a black "helmet" on top of his head and with black ears as well, the rest of his body sported patches of orangish-brown and black against the white background. The dark mane and tail were long and flowing and lifted in the air when the stallion adroitly ran off in the company of his small band. I will never forget the sheer beauty of this scene.

In the early 1980s, several hundred wild horses roamed the South Pancake Range. But I am now saddened to report that they and their descendants have been eliminated, or zeroed-out, from this herd area due to the dirty politics. I am particularly offended by those appointed officials who are trusted with defending these animals but who favor exploitive interests over the general public. My hope is renewed, however, at the thought of restoring this legal herd area with free-spirited mustangs. But first we must dispel the dark cloud that has been hovering over our public lands for decades.

FALL 1996 NEVADA WILD HORSE TOUR

In the early Fall of 1996, I jumped into my trusty, white 1973 Volkswagen camper bus, custom crafted in Weidenbruck, Germany, and nicknamed the "Grey Ghost." Together the Ghost and I set off on a tour of Nevada's wild horse herds with some gas money afforded by Wild Horse Spirit, an NGO based in Washoe Valley and dedicated to achieving justice for the equids.

For the better part of a month, I revisited some of the distinctive herds I had earlier come to know, particularly during the 1980s when I worked as a watchdog for the wild equids. My aim was to verify BLM's claim that drought was forcing it to conduct massive helicopter round-ups for the wild horses' own good, i.e., so they wouldn't starve or perish of thirst. Figure 10 shows the loop that took me from Carson City east through Fallon, then further east to the remote, historic towns of Austin, Eureka, and finally Ely. From Ely, I headed south to the Mormon towns of Pioche and Sunnyside, thence on to the rail town of Caliente, and thence south again all the way to Ash Springs, nearing Las Vegas. I went from the "high wet/cold desert" of northern Nevada to the "hot dry/low desert" of the southern part of the state, experiencing a considerable drop in elevation and latitude. Ash Springs is situated at the eastern edge of the renowned Groom Lake, aka Area 51 of both secret military and UFO fame. This is a very "hot" desert, indeed, for the publicity it receives and for its high summer temperatures and levels of radioactivity, an aftermath of atomic testing. From Ash Meadows I went to Rachel, where I met UFO observers, who seemed sincere in their claims. Midday I struck northwest to the old mining town of Tonopah where I visited the BLM office, then, in the afternoon, I wound my way to the Marietta Wild Burro Sanctuary. The final leg of my trip brought me north again through the agricultural town of Yerington and then back to my home in picturesque Carson Valley—Nevada's "Garden Spot" sandwiched between the usually snow-capped Sierra Nevada and the Pine Nut Ranges.

Map of Nevada
"Wild Horse Tour" taken by author Sept.-Oct. 1996

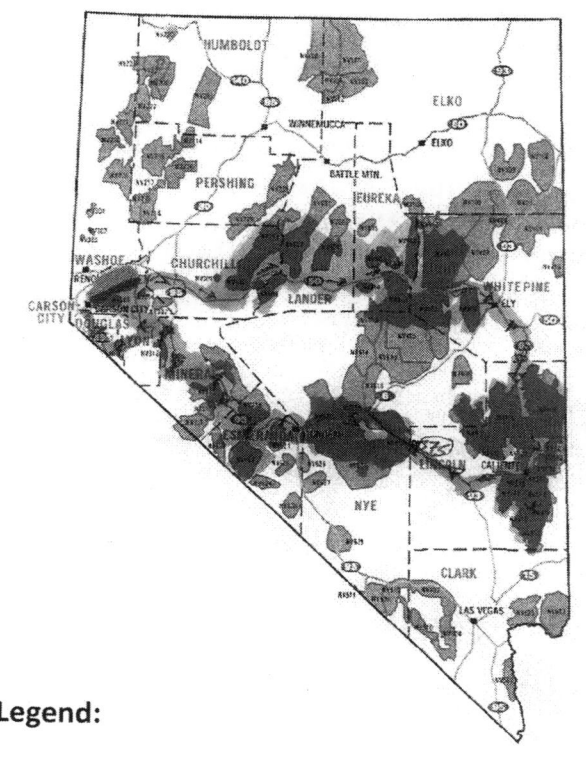

Legend:

Herds Managed by the Nevada Deptartment of Agriculture

Herds Managed by the Bureau of Land Management

Route followed by author

BLM areas visited by author September and October 1996

Figure 10. Map of wild horse/burro inspection tour in Nevada by author, September–October 1996.

I was determined to investigate the possible ruse that wild horse enemies were making of the dry season. Drought was their excuse before the public for the draconian roundups aimed at practically eliminating the wild horses and burros from their legal herd areas.

Out of Caliente I visited a helicopter roundup conducted by Dave Cattoor and his crew, the biggest of the wild horse eliminators in the West, estimates of whose government paid earnings range from 20 to 40 million-plus dollars (and still getting the big contracts in 2011). Part of the time, I was accompanied by BLM-contracted photographer Bob Goodman of Reno. After a week's efforts to locate and gather wild horses, the capture crew had concluded that their endeavor was, in their own words, "like trying to squeeze blood out of a turnip!" Goodman admitted that BLM expected him to take shots of emaciated, starving mustangs but that he had only found a scattering of wild horses, nearly all of whom were in very good shape, i.e., real hardy survivors thriving in freedom in spite of all the obstacles people were throwing their way. Of course, as in any population, a few of the very oldest horses were in decline, a normal stage in their life cycle. From their natural death, many other species would benefit, including scavenger and decomposer species: various birds, lizards, rodents, beetles, etc. Though Goodman was expected to produce photos of emaciated mustangs on their last legs, these were simply not to be found; there were, in fact, hardly any horses left in the legal herd areas around Caliente.

With my Hi-8 video camera, I began to document this horse gathering effort, which turned out quite fortunate for the few remaining wild horses. Potential exposure to public scrutiny made both the gather contractors and BLM officials very nervous. And my heart leapt in a positive direction when BLM called a halt, not only to this but all roundups in Nevada for the remainder of this fiscal year. Nevada's herds had already been drastically reduced and to further cut their numbers would have cut to the quick, i.e., into their very survival base.

Following Caliente, I toured the Delamar and Clover Peak Wild Horse herd areas to the south, which proved particularly memorable. The Delamar Range had a scattering of the statuesque Joshua trees (*Yucca brevifolia*), signaling a transition to the vast "hot" Mojave Desert. Though very wary of humans, the few remaining bands I observed were in fine condition, though BLM officials had led the public to believe they were on their last legs. These wiry mustangs seemed perfectly adapted to the austere desert, emanating a keen aliveness, sensibility, and natural attunement. With their diverse companion species of flora and fauna, they shared life and freedom. Witnessing the wild horses reminded me of the special contribution that each species—and each individual—has to make within any given community. Many of these horses were of dark coloration, camouflaging their bodies in the desert shadows or absorbing the heat of the sun on cold winter days. It is a gross miscarriage of justice that all these herds were zeroed-out in the fall of 2009 by order of BLM's Ely District officials, who were bowing to livestock, hunter and, apparently, solar power interests and in spite of vigorous protest, including legal, by thousands of wild horse advocates among the long-time officially ignored general public.

While camping at Ash Springs, I bathed in a resplendent, turquoise mineral spring bubbling up from Earth's depths, while taking in the peaceful desert pastels of twilight. Later I quickly fell asleep under the clear and blazing desert stars, though I grew cold in the predawn hours, when temperatures plummeted to near freezing, as is typical in the dry airs of the Great Basin. When I awoke because of this cold, a brilliantly glowing globe was circling over the top-secret Groom Lake Air Force Base. Whether this was just an airplane with some very bright landing lights or a genuine flying saucer I cannot say, but my peering at this object through my binoculars quickened my imagination. Later that morning, I proceeded northwest to Rachel, where I spent a few hours investigating the UFO museum and "Little A'le" cafe. Often at risk of being shot by military guards, the people I met here had observed UFOs directly, both in and around Groom Lake. Generally they seemed quite intelligent and displayed positive attitudes toward the wild horses and burros and their freedom.

Continuing northwest beyond Rachel on Nevada's Alien Highway 375, I transited vast, inhospitable stretches of Nevada desert, strewn with expansive, glaringly white alkali flats. The vegetation was very stunted here, and hordes of cattle were evident. This region is very contaminated by radioactive plutonium, an aftermath of the atomic tests of the 1950s. In the afternoon I reached the old mining town of Tonopah, from which the BLM Tonopah Field Station oversees millions of acres. When asking to speak to the wild horse specialist at this office, I raised some eyebrows as if bringing up a sore point. But I was directed to a grocery store where the specialist was picking up some grub. Asking him (John Fisher, as I recall) where I could observe wild horses, immediately I noticed his derogatory attitude toward them through the cynical tone of his voice. His pointed statement, "There are still plenty of them crawling around out there," revealed his opinion of them as worthless misfits. He grudgingly indicated where I might find some wild horses off to the northwest and was a far cry from the professional wild horse defender I had hoped to meet. (Appendix VI: Report on Wild Horse Status on Nevada BLM Lands and Recent Drought and Removals [for Wild Horse Spirit, October 12, 1996] available by request from author.)

Following his direction, I was able to spot one unusually wild band in the Monte Cristo Range to the west of Tonopah. Judging from the extreme wariness of this wiry harem of seven, they were being shot on sight by men with long-range rifles (a wariness I have also encountered among mustang bands just south of Tonopah in the vast Alkali Lake Valley to the west of US Highway 95). Late in the evening, I entered the enchanting Marietta National Wild Burro Range further to the north and enjoyed observing these remarkable, large-eared cousins of the horse (see Figure 14, p. 185) under the light of a full moon. Their social structure is different from that of horses, less hierarchal, and their breeding is more promiscuous. A jack (male burro) will defend his territory, thus gaining reproductive advantage (Klingel 1979). Burros are exquisitely adapted to the hot, dry deserts of southern Nevada where they refill an ecological niche occupied by their ancestors of a not-too-distant past, paleontologically speaking.[14]

---

14 I again remind the reader that all three major branches of the horse family Equidae originated and had their long-standing evolution in North America, including the western half where today a tiny remnant of ca. 3,500 burros barely manages to survive on public lands due to relentless persecution that is mainly government implemented and sanctioned, though basically criminal! Most of this insidious campaign stems from vested interests who are targeting the public lands for ever greater exploitation.

On the last leg of my trip home, I passed through Yerington and Smith Valley, then traversed west to the north side of Topaz Lake, a gem of a lake that is cradled at the eastern base of the Sierra Nevada. Finally I struck north to Carson Valley, passing through the officially "horse-free" southern Pine Nut Range Herd Area.

EXTREME NORTHWEST NEVADA AND THE GRANITE RANGE

The northwest quarter of Nevada is legal home to some distinctive wild horses. I have visited these wonders throughout my life and never cease to be amazed at their tenacious ability to survive in face of harsh, cold winters; hot, dry summers; and especially in face of some of their deadly human enemies who live in or around this stark region. In the spring and summer of 1980, I toured the Granite Range's wild horse herd area, proceeding from foothill sagebrush through stunted forest to the phlox-carpeted alpine meadows that pose atop this spectacularly abrupt range, which is situated just to the west of the vast Black Rock Desert.

To me the beauty of Granite Range's mustangs is unsurpassed. Some are fine-boned, large-eyed, solid grey or white colored, and bear dish-shaped foreheads—all Arabian characteristics (Figure 11). During the spring the bands spread out to take advantage of greenery made possible by winter precipitation followed by warmer temperatures. I followed steep trails to finally obtain an overview of them. Each band was well ensconced in its own particular home range, a logical part of the wild horse habitat mosaic it had claimed as its own over the generations. Fresh tracks eventually led me to the living presences themselves—but they were quick to discern this possible interloper. As the morning sun waxed, reached its glaring zenith, then waned into shades of pensive mellowness, the horses revealed their daily foraging and watering schedules, their elaborate courtship, involving deft pursuit of mare by stallion, coaching of young, among other facets of behavior[15] too numerous to list. The dramatic confrontations between stallions vying for a mare involved their rearing up, biting, and pawing at each other. These contests were thrilling to observe, as were the more tender moments between mares and their offspring. The one offset the other in a harmonious way.

Figure 11. Granite Range wild horses north of Gerlach, NV, summer 1980, by author.

Months after my spring visit, I returned to the Granite Range in August during the critical dry period of late summer, when temperatures

---

15 Horses have an eleven- to twelve-month gestation, which varies depending on climate, forage or water availability, stress, social status, and other factors. Wild horse births peak in April and May, matching warmer weather, spring green-up, and more nutritious vegetation. To observe the first tottering steps of a newborn foal is to appreciate one of nature's great marvels. The foals innately stand and walk within an hour of birth; the tender bonding moments between mare and offspring make one question the supposed differences between horses and people. A mare coaches her colt or filly in the intricacies of local survival while he or she is still all curiosity and playfulness. A foal will eat the fresh feces of its dame in order to obtain necessary intestinal micro-fauna and -flora adapted over the generations to digest the particular desert vegetation where it lives.

soar over ninety degrees Fahrenheit. I was angered that the horses I had observed in the spring were being set up by local ranchers who hold the water rights and, I hasten to add, by the BLM officials who refused to act on the wild horses' behalf to secure their access to year-round water. In the mustang's highland summering meadows, I discovered a tiny, muddy seep dug down about twenty-feet below the surface by a BLM backhoe in order to sustain a few bands trailing in. The highland meadow itself was overly restricted by fences erected by the ranchers and designed to exclude the mustangs from water and prime grazing areas. These tricks had caused a weakening of the wild horses; I was outraged to see them being marginalized within their own legal herd area. Though government authorities were in a position to exact concessions from the permittees who grazed sheep or cattle here, this was clearly not their intention, and a more just sharing of the natural water sources with the wild horses seemed a long way off.

While livestock grazing on the public lands is a privilege and not a right, wild horses do have a legal right to occupy their designated herd areas. But BLM Winnemucca District officials had chosen to dig ever deeper into a muddy seep to provide water for the bands in place of truly fending for a decent, natural source for the horses (remember Implied Federal Water Rights). The latter were experiencing severe stress because of this setup, and I noted from remains that the "angel of death" was a frequent visitor to this herd. The stunning portraits I took of these light-colored mustangs revealed them to be still valiant and alert. With heads held high, they were proud of being free, though in the face of severe persecution. The pictured horses speak for themselves (see Figure 11).

Since my visits in 1980, BLM has greatly lowered the population of the spectacular Granite Range herd area. Its current appropriate management level is only 258 in roughly one-hundred thousand acres, but my flyover here in February 2011 only revealed one band of five. With the drastic reduction of the Calico Complex of five HMAs in early 2010, I fear these horses have been reduced far below genetic viability and that their unique ecological adaptations have been devastated. Lamentably, much the same has occurred in nearly all the other legal herd areas to the north and south, east and west of the Granite

Range in Nevada and California, as elsewhere throughout the West. Outraging wild horse supporters, the Winnemucca District and the BLM as a whole announced its plans to further majorly reduce the wild horse population of the Calico Complex along with adjacent HMAs in northeastern California and southern Oregon (July 2011). This comes in spite of their having just taken nearly 2000 mustangs off in 2010. As of December 2011, these further roundups are largely done, and I witnessed these brutal affairs for four days. When coupled with tampering with mare reproduction by means of PZP injection and skewed sex ratios, this is, indeed, managing for extinction.

The Granite Range herd was studied by wildlife ecologist Joel Berger, and its singularities are described in his book *Wild Horses of the Great Basin* (Berger 1986). Though documenting many positive aspects of wild horses in the wild, including their ecological compatibility with bighorn sheep and providing valuable factual information, Berger ends his book with a sour, derogatory note against them, perhaps as a way of keeping on "OK" terms with the anti-wild-horse establishment (see also Berger quote in Fuller 2009).

FURTHER NORTH TO CALICO MOUNTAIN, HIGH ROCK, & NORTHEASTERN CALIFORNIA HERDS

Several miles north of Gerlach skirting the east side of the Granite Range, Nevada State Route 34 becomes a gravel road winding its way into the colorful Calico Mountains. With luck and a practiced eye, one may spot the equally colorful wild horses here. These intensely alert and agile desert survivors liven the landscape as one climbs north from that haunting immensity known as the Black Rock Desert. This may appear an enormous mirage, caused by reflection off its resplendent playa, which (I am told) is the world's largest "sea of mud." An eternal feeling pervades this region and its sparse, but hardy plant and animal inhabitants, which are generally a pale color like the desert itself, abounding in light silvery greens. Not surprisingly, in addition to beauty, this area hides some gruesome secrets; so it was on Saint Valentine's Day 2006, that here took place one of the most cruel and repulsive crimes against our nation's last wild horses.

SAINT VALENTINE'S DAY MASSACRE

Four light-colored, full-bodied mustangs were shot with "varmint rifles" designed to kill smaller animals. Varmint rifles emit bullets that do not explode within their victims but pierce through, so as to better preserve the hides. These once lively horses were left stretched out to agonize on the desert sagebrush slopes located along Big Hog Ranch Creek, a few hundred yards below the band's watering spring. A fur trapper named Alice Gladwill has her residence several miles to the north of this site. Accompanied by her son, she happened to be checking traps when she caught the nefarious culprits in the act. Though trappers are generally inured to animal suffering, Alice and her son were incensed by what they witnessed that day and took several color photographs (see Figure 12). A number of bullets closely shot into each of the horses left them thrashing in agony amid the sagebrush near the creek. One was a pregnant mare who aborted her fetus in her prolonged death throes. Members of the same band, four adult horses died agonizing deaths. The perpetrators of this unspeakable crime dashed off in their white, cab-and-a-half, camper-backed truck upon the approach of the trappers. The latter pursued the culprits, noting the description of their vehicle and that in it an older male driver was accompanied by a younger man. Unfortunately, with all the dust being kicked up by the truck, they were unable to discern the license plate number. Additionally they were afraid of getting too close for fear of being shot.

The suspects got away, most likely shooting south past Gerlach to Interstate 80, and, thence, either west toward Reno or east toward Winnemucca (thought they will never allude Justice in the ultimate reckoning). An intensive search was undertaken by local and federal agents, but no one was ever apprehended. An unprecedented reward was posted for fifteen thousand dollars in places like Cedarville and Gerlach, but after several months no fruitful leads resulted. In a talk with Mrs. Gladwill in October 2009, I learned that she was convinced that the Washoe County Sheriff's deputies based in Gerlach had been in on this dastardly deed.

Figure 12. Wild horses shot and left to agonize on St. Valentine's Day 2006, in Calico Mountain HMA. Photos by Alice Gladwill.

My investigation of this incident (Appendix VII: St. Valentine's Day Massacre of Wild Horses in Calico Mountains available by request from author) revealed that a major sporting store in Reno had organized a varmint hunting contest over the St. Valentine's Day weekend in question. My inspection of the crime site revealed several coyote carcasses lying around the remains of the dead horses. Only the coyotes' lower jaws had been removed, not the pelts that trappers would surely take. Very probably these jaws were presented as proof in the hunting contest to win a sports boat. Varmint hunters engaged in this contest could have killed the wild horses to attract scavenging coyotes, bobcats, mountain lions, badgers, etc., in order to shoot the latter, extract evidence of their kills, and win the contest. Though my efforts at the sporting store did not reveal the winners, such could very well be the heartless criminals responsible for this hideous atrocity (see mention of this case in Fuller 2009, 106).

It is a federal crime to kill, capture, or harass a wild horse or burro; this is punishable by a two-thousand dollar fine and/or one year of imprisonment under the Wild Free-Roaming Horses and Burros Act of 1971. Some legal experts indicate that the "destruction of federal property" clause of the U.S. legal code and the Sentencing Reform Act of 1984 authorize that wild horse killings be punishable by up to one hundred thousand dollars and/or ten years in prison. The 2006 Saint Valentine's Day mustang massacre has continued to haunt me. The blood and suffering of these highly evolved, sentient beings, present in horse form, still calls to me in clarion tones demanding justice!

MORE ATROCITIES & A ROUNDUP AT HIGH ROCK

Some ranchers shoot wild horses or burros to divert predators such as coyotes from their livestock (whose unnatural numbers augment predator populations). They also do this to shoot the predators, of course. In the late 1980s, one rancher from northeast California was charged by state and federal wildlife officials with the crime of shooting a wild horse in order to inject its remains with strychnine and, thus, poison

many predators and scavengers. This resulted in the death of a federally protected golden eagle. However, in a very suspect miscarriage of
justice, the accused was let off due to "insufficient evidence" (Jacobs
1991, 300).

I returned to the Calico area in September 2006, this time to witness a BLM-contracted roundup in the High Rock Herd Management
Area. Escorted by an armed BLM law enforcement agent, I arrived mid-
morning at the ongoing capture. A group of twenty healthy-looking
wild horses had just been helicopter driven for several miles to be
crammed tightly into tiny, six-foot-high, portable metal pens. All were
very frightened, disoriented, and traumatized. Some were choking on
the fine alkali dust that had been stirred up by the commotion, and
their deep coughs lent a somber note to the scene. In their anguished
confusion, many were kicking and biting each other (particularly right
after being penned), or pawing desperately on the hard earth under the
corrals to find a way out.

As a grayish white, full-muscled mare in her prime was separated
from the stallions into a mare pen nearer to the loading chute, suddenly her upper left leg, or radius bone, just snapped, causing her to
abruptly plummet to the ground with a dull thud. It was most pitiful
to observe her in such great despair, valiantly struggling to stand—
even the law enforcement agent shuddered and turned her face away.
Quite probably the mare had suffered one of the strong hind kicks
we had been observing among the corralled horses, and this kick had
parted her leg. Quickly one of the capture crew brought a short-
barreled rifle and shot her in the head, the loud report lending yet
another ominous note to the scene. The poor mare's mortal remains
were unceremoniously dragged off and left in a wash (Figure 13).
Off in the distance, I could hear the squealing devices of the varmint
hunters, imitating rabbits in great fear. These are surefire lures for a
variety of predators and scavengers who are shot from behind blinds
as they near the sound. I reflected that, for obvious reasons, the
dead mare would serve these varmint hunters' gruesome purposes
as well—and so too had the livestock-controlled puppets employed
by the BLM.

Figure 13. Mare with broken left radius bone resulting from violent kicking by desperate wild horses just after helicopter corralling, September 26, 2006 BLM roundups. Shot.

The helicopter roundup was difficult for me to observe. My heart was with the wild horses; I felt their removal from a life of relative freedom in the natural world to be very unjust. But I gritted my teeth and noted many details of the operation and later returned to this site to inspect more closely. My report includes observations and interviews concerning this and other nearby herd areas (Appendix VIII: Inspection of Wild Horse HMAs in NW Nevada and NE California, with observation of wild horse gather [9/2006] available by request from author).

Upon my return visit about a week later, I walked several miles upslope from the capture site (whose portable corrals were still assembled) and noticed the horses had been helicopter-driven over some very rough and rocky, steep terrain. Some of the horses had stumbled, and one horse had fallen on its side and died, either on its own or with human assistance, judging from the matted hair and blood-stained ground. From the evidence, I gathered that he had possibly broken his leg in a large ground squirrel hole just above the site. At the high end of the mountain where the wild horses and the menacing helicopter chasing them had first appeared, I came across a mangled, barbed-wire fence in which the frightened, chased horses had become entangled (see Sidebar). Of course, such unsafe hazards are supposed to be detected and eliminated by BLM personnel during site inspection before helicopter captures begin.[16]

SIDEBAR: GROSS INJUSTICE AT TRIPLE B COMPLEX: During the first week of July 2011, I uncovered loose barbed wires in the Triple B Complex (of three HMAs and one Wild Horse Territory). Here Ely/Elko Nevada BLM offices planned to excessively reduce the wild horse population from 2,198 horses on 1,682,998 legal acres to 472 horses. This signifies that while there were 766 acres per horse, BLM considered this to be an overpopulation and planned to reduce the herd to 3,566 legal acres per individual horse. – Preposterous on the face of it! Additionally, record precipitation during the past two years has resulted in a flourishing of vegetation and much more water available, yet the position of BLM is that there is not enough water for the wild horses. Though a temporary injunction had been lifted and the roundup allowed to proceed in July and August 2011, it was mercifully halted by a federal judge due to humane abuses, but not until over 1,200 wild horses had been removed. Hopefully this miscarriage of justice will result in an order to restore the captured wild horses. (I am a major plaintiff in this ongoing case and can keep those interested informed.)

---

16 In September 2011, filmmaker James Anaquat Kleinert and friends of the Spring Creek Basin wild horse herd near Telluride, Colorado, discovered similar barbed wire as well as slick muddy conditions in an area where BLM planned to immediately roundup wild horses. Because of the outrageously low numbers of wild horses left in this area, Kleinert and others have now sued to stop the roundup. Ca. 22,000 acres of HMA had been reduced from ca. 56,000 acres of the original 1971 herd area. The decidedly unfair appropriate management level for wild horses is only 65 individuals—a sure prescription for inbreeding and chance die out! Only ca. 80 wild horses remained as of September 2011. ("Saving the American Horse" 2008; www.theamericanwildhorse.com)

Additionally, my inspection verified that sufficient forage was present for the wild horses in this area. This included tall stands of giant wild rye grass (*Elymus cinereus*) along with sustaining stands of Indian rice and needle-and-thread grasses. Also revealing was the fact that hordes of cattle were present in the High Rock Herd Management Area. They were especially concentrated in the riparian habitat along a stream and around the Little High Rock Reservoir. It was obvious that the wild horses were reaching remote, often steep, rocky areas (for which their soliped hooves are so well adapted) to judiciously graze the vegetation in more widely spread fashion, not the cattle. And it is again funny how BLM personnel seem to overlook this very suitable adaptation.

I was particularly disgusted to encounter a morass of cattle manure mixed with muddy, eutrophic water in a trampled, lower stream just west of the Little High Rock Canyon and just east of Little High Rock Reservoir. This was about a mile east of the capture site. Here hundreds of cattle were clustering on a meadow and the stream that fed it. The overgrazing and hoof action by these "hoofed locusts" were devastating the plant life and soils, and their manure was contaminating the waters. The roadbed across this stream had itself become a quagmire, making it impossible for me to cross even with the half-ton, four-wheel-drive Chevrolet Silverado pickup I drove. It became obvious just who was making a mess of the Little High Rock ecosystem—and this certainly wasn't the wild horses!

SIDEBAR: THE ETHOS OF THE PLACE

While camping at the old Denio Camp cabin and corrals just west of the High Rock capture site, I wrote a poem that came to me in the dead of night. I had just been stirred from my slumber by an owl's hootings proceeding from a giant willow tree, then was kept awake by noisy disturbances proceeding from a dilapidated pioneer cabin. These came from a curious, clod-hopping cow around 2:00 AM. The poem conveys the ethos I sensed here.

The Lake of Tears—a Rubaiyat

You know, we've lived a million years,
also we've shed a million tears,
and then you multiply this by
a million, million times—Oh! Dears!

…They say there is a lake nearby,
a place where all one's sorrows lie
together with one's joys assuaged,
commingled in pursuit On High.

With tears from years gone by 'tis filled:
this wond'rous, magical lake of thrills,
that like a crystal ball foretells
the fates of one and all: instills

A ray of hope to ev'ry one
who plunges to its depths head on,
who trusting in the care of God
makes sacrifice…and all alone!

—Chill lake, in you such mystery
abides beyond our lives petty!
Do we then dare take up your quest?
Seize we your challenge to dive free?

For 'tis in diving to the depths
that we again discern concepts

of heights that then can be attained
as we must surely are upswept.

*'Tis **lake of life** I now refer,*
this lake in which we're now immersed,
this lake of give and take—and learn
again to yearn for Heav'n—EMERGE!

With waves so bright does gleam this lake!...

MORE INJUSTICE IN NORTHEASTERN CALIFORNIA

In my inspection of other legal wild horse areas to the west, including the Devil's Garden Plateau Wild Horse Territory in the Modoc National Forest north of Alturas, California, and the New Ravendale HMA on BLM land south of Alturas, I encountered very few sign of mustangs, but an almost total monopolization of the horses' legal areas by livestock and big game, or, more to the point, by the people who manipulate and "harvest" the latter. This is particularly egregious when it is realized that these legal wild horse HMAs have already been greatly reduced from their original legal herd areas established in the early 1970s. For example, the New Ravendale HMA is only 14,896 acres while the original herd area is 32,182 acres, representing a reduction of over half—yet still the wild horses are marginalized even within the reduced HMAs. This is clearly a gross miscarriage of justice, both for the wild horses and for the public who support them.

Though I explored the Devil's Garden Plateau Wild Horse Territory for three days, I was unable to lay my eyes upon a single wild horse in the flesh. I finally encountered a mound of horse droppings, or "stud pile," and an old wild horse trail. Wild horses may re-ingest this material during times of extremity, and a mound can also serve as a valuable seed bank for the restoration of the ecosystem as well as a provisioner of soil humus.[17] Hundreds of hefty cattle were observed and many fences disrupted natural horse movements within this legal territory. It became

---

17 These "dung depots" are also valuable transmitters of gut microorganisms capable of digesting local forage–so vital to all ages and especially critical for newborns.

increasingly apparent that Modoc Forest Service officials were greatly overlooking their legal duty to preserve and protect the wild horses here. Indeed, during my visit at the Forest Service office in Alturas, wild horse specialist Marty Butow urged me to vigorously protest the current plan to simply zero out all the wild horses from this territory. In addition to being a cattle pasture, this high volcanic plateau is a big waterfowl hunting area, made possible by extensive lakes and ponds, especially the 4,600-foot elevation Wood Flat Reservoir. Here I observed a variety of migratory birds including ibis both alighting and taking off while eating lunch. Clearly water was not a problem for the wild horses, being available for them on a year-round basis, but human greed and official corruption most certainly are.

About thirty miles south of Alturas, while visiting BLM's New Ravendale Wild Horse HMA, I came upon a big padlocked gate with the name of the "9-6 Madeline Ranch" emblazoned on a large, imposing arch along with a boldly capitalized **NO TRESPASSING!** sign. Thus, I was prevented from entering this legal wild horse herd from its western side. Clearly the rancher had taken it upon himself to block public access. Talking to another local rancher, I learned that almost all of the wild horses had been removed from this HMA, but that I might still find a few stragglers if I traveled twenty miles east toward the Nevada state line along a dirt road. With a disparaging tone of voice, this grandpa said I would start seeing "a lot of horse shit" with which the stallions liked to advertise. I told him this stuff builds soils and disperses the seeds of many worthy plants. Managers of a private hunting reserve had also fenced along the edge of the public road upon which I had entered, further preventing access to the western side of the HMA. The road's name is Garate; the ranch here is Rancho Garate. As was the case with the USFS and its Devil's Garden Plateau herd, New Ravendale's wild horses were "out of sight and out of mind" to their legal guardians in the BLM, as well as to all but a few of America's wild horse supporting citizens.

As I drove away from this situation, it struck me how both BLM and Forest Service officials were working year after year to accomplish the practical elimination of wild horses from the wild, even from areas that had already been substantially reduced from the original legal herd areas or territories. I returned home even more disillusioned with my government's upholding of the act than I had anticipated. And the stark hostility toward the wild horses and their freedom, operating both in private and official circles, seemed the very incarnation of deadliness.

THE TIP OF THE ICEBERG

In December 2009, just to the west of the Calico Complex, the shooting deaths of six wild horses were discovered. The scene of this dastardly crime was forty-five miles northeast of Susanville, California, in the Buckhorn HMA. Evidence gathered by assigned BLM investigators led to charges against two men from Lovelock, Nevada. Along with several other wild horse supporters, I attended the preliminary hearing for the arraigned individuals on April 27, 2010, held at Reno's Federal District Court. I was keenly disappointed, however, to learn that these two were only being charged with a single misdemeanor rather than a felony. The killing of six wild horses is a gross violation of the 1971 act and should not be so lightly considered. Both men were released on their own personal recognizance by Judge Robert A. McQuaid, pending the trial set for June 22, 2010. Section 8 of the act makes the killing of six wild horses/burros a felony, with, in this case, a maximum sentence on six counts for six years prison (one year per count) and a maximum fine of $12,000 ($2,000 per count). Another law governing the destruction of federal property (the wild horses) could also be invoked for much longer sentences and higher fines (see page xi, point 4, and page 171). Over eight thousand letters of protest were sent into the judge demanding maximum penalties for these shootings (Sonner 2010). The two charged men, Todd Davis and Joshua Keathley, pleaded guilty and were sentenced to six months prison time. Apparently, they were drunk at the time of the crime. Crimes such as theirs that actually surface represent only the proverbial tip of the iceberg.

SOLDIER MEADOWS

Another impressive wild horse-containing area I visited occurs in and around Soldier Meadows in the Black Rock Range East and the Black Rock Range West Herd Management Areas of Nevada. The latter two are located within the Black Rock Desert-High Rock Canyon Emigrant Trails National Conservation Area and are just to the east of the High Rock Wild Horse HMA at the northwest tip of the Black Rock Range. The valley of Soldier Meadows itself lies around five thousand feet of elevation while surrounding peaks rise to about eight thousand feet. Though these remote and little productive areas would seem like a perfect place for mustangs within their legal HMAs, we should not underestimate the reach of human greed and ingratitude toward horsekind.

During the fall of 1997 and as the environmental director of the Pyramid Lake Paiute Tribe, I inspected Soldier Meadows along with a team of professionals from various agencies. Our tour included the vast Black Rock desert playa, portions of the old Applegate-Lassen Emigrant Trail, with its famous Black Rock (that has acted as a guiding landmark for man and beast since centuries past), some thermal hot springs, and various mountain canyons with their stunted vegetation. Strangely, the Black Rock Range possesses neither pinyon pines nor junipers that I could see (Trimble 1999, 146), and pinyon pines seem to pretty much drop out to the north of here due to some ecological factors, such as temperature, photoperiod, soil, or a combination of factors. By late afternoon, we arrived at Soldier Meadows, which, together with their animal inhabitants, were basking in a late afternoon sun's warm, mellow rays. Over the meadows' surface trickled glistening mineral waters; seen darting furtively in these scintillating waters were minnow-sized desert dace (*Eremichthys acros*), a tiny fish of exquisite proportions found only at Soldier Meadows and considered vulnerable to extinction by state, federal, and international authorities (International Union for Conservation of Nature 1996, 72). Also present was the rare and sensitive Soldier Meadows Cinquefoil (*Potentilla basaltica*), found growing only here and in one small site in Lassen County, California. Suffice it to say that the life-restoring qualities that oozed from this delightful desert oasis were keenly sensed.

But Soldier Meadows also had a crowd of cattle being allowed to trample and over-graze this last habitat of the desert dace. Some were actually stepping right in the stream where the dace swam. To tell the truth, as in Little High Rock canyon, these bovids were making a muddy mess of the place and, in the process, jeopardizing the future of a number of uniquely adapted plant and animal populations. Alongside their diarrhetic droppings and tracks, I noticed the much neater spore of native wildlife species, including the returned native wild horses. Round rabbit droppings were scattered about in tiny mounds as were the more oval- or cylindrical-shaped droppings of the mule deer and pronghorn. The faint and unobtrusive trails of these animals stood in stark contrast to the lavish splatterings and cloven earth dissections made by the poor cattle, who, through no fault of their own, had been foisted upon this desert by ecologically careless people obeying the blind traditions they had brought with them from moister European biomes. The fact is that cattle are quite ill-suited to the desert, where they have a hard time surviving without man's considerable assistance. And their flatulence is a major factor contributing to life-threatening global climate change (de Haan et al. 2006).

The narrow trails of scampering coyotes, fox, and bobcat often overlapped those of native herbivores; occasional. large, claw-less tracks of a mountain lion could also be deciphered—a sign that all was not yet lost for this ecosystem. At watering sites, predators often lay in wait for their prey; as a consequence, most prey species are instinctively wary and do not linger along riparian sites. Like mule deer and pronghorn, the wild horses of this region did not tarry at Soldier Meadows. Like orderly spokes on some giant Indian medicine wheel, the narrow mustang trails radiated away from the watering source and back to each band's distinctive home range. Our tour of about a dozen professionals observed no wild horses right at the meadows. Only by scanning with our binoculars were we finally able to spot two bands a half-mile to one mile away. One young band had only three horses, while the other was composed of seven, including the patron and the lead mare—a typical band number for the harsh Great Basin desert.

I became particularly annoyed when the U.S. Fish and Wildlife Service (USFWS) biologist began heaping verbal abuse upon the wild horses before our small group. He blamed them for the critical riparian destruction that was here obviously being perpetrated by cattle, or, more to the point, by cattlemen. So I quickly reminded our tour that it was

cattle[18] who were camping and defecating on and devastating the meadows, as was plain to observe, not the wild horses. In reaction to my
statement, the biologist became livid, and his face flushed purple as he
vomited forth some even more choice vituperative remarks insulting
to the mustangs and their supporters. Hopefully, the majority of the
professionals on the tour let the plain facts from the world of nature
speak for themselves as concerns what species were causing Soldier
Meadows's ecological problems, for in the finer analysis this was truly
our own two-legged kind.

In the year 2000 a well-to-do land developer, Jim Kudrna from Reno,
purchased the Soldier Meadows Ranch and set up a resort and tourist
operation, emphasizing off-road-vehicle (ORV) exploration. Though
earlier and contrary to the facts, he had taken it upon himself to
declare the wild horses "exotic" and wanted them removed, now he
is negotiating for a wild horse preserve on his considerable private
lands that would hopefully include the public lands where he has grazing privileges. Ms Neda de Mayo and her Return to Freedom NGO
from Lampoc, California, is working to make this laudable idea a reality as of summer 2011, perhaps as one of the new ecosanctuaries. To
his credit, Mr. Kudrna has restored many water sources on his land
so that both cattle and wildlife, including wild horses and burros, can
drink. To prevent the animals from causing undue degradation, he has
placed large stones around the bedrock sources, or fissures. In my capacity as an ecologist and with a mind to advise on its suitability as a

---

18 In all fairness, when left to adapt in the wild, any species, including cattle, usually become more harmoniously integrated due both to phenotypic changes and to generations of *natural selection*—that great
principle Darwin, among others, hit upon a century and a half ago. But in our modern, livestock-ori-
ented, and agriculturally manipulative culture, we humans rarely permit this natural integration to occur. With the horse, *Equus caballus*, whose family, genus, and even species evolved right here in North
America, returned native *pre-adaptation* falls quickly into place within the mother ecosystem. But for
the cow (*Bos Taurus*) a species whose origin is in much moister habitats in Europe, such adaptation is
much harder to achieve, and would take a much longer time or may, indeed, simply result in cattle's
extinction in this part of the world. Given where it came from, it is no wonder that the cow camps in
and alongside the springs, streams, lakes, and meadows. These are the ecological conditions to which it
has adapted for thousands of years and for which it is best suited.

horse sanctuary, I did a thorough inspection of this area this summer (2011) and issued a report with positive recommendations to Return to Freedom. (For further information on the assault on the Soldier Meadows wild horse herd go to www.americanherds.blogspot.com and www.returntofreedom.org)

OTHER HERDS FARTHER AFIELD AND MORE INJUSTICE

I have visited many of the ca. 350 wild horse and burro herd areas/territories throughout the West. But areas actually inhabited by horses and burros have now been reduced to ca. 180 on BLM land and 37 territories on USFS lands, for ca. 217 areas in total. Of those herds not already eliminated, almost all have been reduced to non-viable populations subject to inbreeding and chance die-out—the latter occurs especially when they experience illegal shootings, poisonings, fencings, or extreme seasonal weather events. How these innocent animals have been "set up" constitutes an appalling story—a true subversion of the act and, consequently, the will of all Americans. –Now, to continue our sampling of the herds.

LITTLE BOOK CLIFFS

The Little Book Cliffs Wild Horse Range is set amidst the picturesque "book-stack" geological formation north of Palisade, Colorado. It was the first wild horse sanctuary and was officially declared in 1967 through the efforts of Wild Horse Annie. Many of its horses descend from early Ute Indian ponies of the mid-nineteenth century. This lively and colorful herd compatibly accompanies an exuberant pinyon and juniper forest, which serves it as a natural shelter and concealment. In August 1996, I was guided by local wild horse advocate Marty Felix to observe this herd and was impressed by the resplendent palominos dashing in and out of the trees. They seemed like angels delivering a special message concerning all life's essential freedom and our need to restore such.

Yet, even in this inaccessible area, the greedy hand of the oil and gas industry—that incredible blob!—has reached out to supplant the mustangs. Along with Colorado's few remaining herds, the Little Book Cliffs mustang population has been reduced to a small token level. The number BLM plans to leave in Little Book Cliffs as an appropriate management level is a low 150 horses. Yet, BLM's FY 2008 report indicates that only 100 wild horses still inhabit this 36,000-acre HMA (reduced from 52,000 acres). Again, BLM is bending over backwards to accommodate the overbearing demands of big business and blind tradition while ignoring the rights and merits of its charges: the wild horses in the wild, even in that small portion of land that has—by law—been set aside for them.

MORE ON NEVADA'S BURROS

In October 2008, I passed through Goldfield, Nevada, south of Tonopah, and caught a glimpse of three black burros. They seemed particularly harried and took off running as soon as I stopped the car to look at them through my binoculars. Such extreme skittishness indicates exposure to gunshots, as I have noted in other regions, e.g. Elko BLM District in northeast Nevada as concerns wild horses. The BLM (U.S. Department of Interior 2008) listed seven burros as still surviving in the Goldfield HMA. These must include the ones I saw. In February 2011, I again searched the area for burros for several hours, but saw none, and only one feeble trail with old tracks and droppings. Are they gone now, mere ghosts of their former presence?

I have visited the Marietta Wild Burro Range in central Nevada three times and am always enchanted by this desert burro redoubt. Surrounded by colorful mountains and fascinating desert plants and animals, here the burros have quickly regained their natural survival instincts, including their cohesive behavior (see Figure 14).

Figure 14. Marietta wild burros in their federal sanctuary in south-central Nevada, by author. October 1996.

Burros display ingenious ways of avoiding intense desert heat and will often seek the cool adiabatic breezes in the late afternoon or the partial shade of canyons and trees during midday's penetrating overhead solar radiation. Their long ears act as very efficient heat dissipaters. Like horses, they may cover many square miles in their quest for forage and do not camp on or over-graze any given area—unless people force them to do so through unwise erection of fences, the monopolization of water sources, etc. This forces them to desperation! I observed them coming out to the Marietta playa during the cool of the night. They congregated around a spring to drink and interacted socially. Varying in pitch and duration, their brayings carried far up the desert canyons and conveyed an elaborate and idiosyncratic language all their own.

In spite of the burros' perfect adaptation to the Marietta region, BLM officials have had the audacity to declare an appropriate management level of only 110 animals. This population level is not even close to long-term viability and could automatically self-destruct. Again, this is a case of "managing for extinction." It is telling that only 104 wild burros were reported as still surviving in this sanctuary as of 2005 and again in 2008 by BLM workers. Perhaps the extinction vortex is already going into effect.

SIDEBAR: DESERT TORTOISE: Though the Desert Tortoise numbers in the hundreds of thousands, it is considered endangered and its presence is used as a spurious excuse for eliminating burros (as well as horses). The campaign to save the tortoise provides a bandwagon for burro enemies, upon which some environmental groups readily jump, much to their discredit. The questionable proofs that burros are detrimental to the tortoise are full of arbitrary judgments and hardly objective. So as expected, burros have been eliminated supposedly to help the tortoise and other desert wildlife, including the trophy-hunted bighorn, but the greater truth concerning the wild burros, tortoises and the other species exists out in the desert, not in the artificial world of computers, tendentious documents, and prejudiced minds.

TWO OTHER OUTSTANDING WILD STALLIONS AND ONE OUTSTANDING WILD MARE

In August 2010, I gained the winning bid at a BLM auction for an equally impressive fifteen-year-old palomino stallion who was gathered by BLM during the winter of 2010. Complete with flaxen mane, he inspired the name of Lightning for the white zigzag bolts on his left flank (see Figure 15).

Figure 15. Wild band stallion Lightning with whom author spend the afternoon while he was still free in Calico Mountain HMA, NW Nevada. October 2009. By author.

I had come to know this paragon of horse-kind in his glorious freedom, both during October 2009, and in earlier visits dating since 2006 (see "Wild Lightning and Friends" 2010, a YouTube showing him in the wild). He remains reproductively intact and is now again free to roam on a several-thousand-acre sanctuary in California along with a venerable, older dark mare dubbed Princess Diane, upon whom I also successfully bid. She is of the rare "curly" type known for cold hardiness and longevity. Another younger *grulla* mare has joined Lightning, and this small band helps to form a herd of far-flung origins, all together numbering about three hundred. Lightning's band is from the Calico Complex in northwest Nevada, which was drastically reduced by helicopter round-ups in early 2010. Another magnificent stallion I witnessed jump over a six-foot high metal capture corral and push through a tight barbed wire fence to escape to freedom on January 2, 2010, in the Black Rock East HMA. This inspiring demonstration of true spirit, resolve, physical prowess, and love of freedom is pictured on the front cover of this book and also featured on several web pages and YouTube videos (see "a Stallion's Courage" 2010). Possessing a white diamond on his forehead, this black stallion was appropriately named Freedom, and may God protect him in freedom and grant him a peaceful life free from human harassment and interference. Than his valiant escape I have never witnessed a more inspiring event.

CHAPTER VI:

UPDATE & REFLECTIONS ON AMERICA'S WILD EQUIDS & WHAT HAS HAPPENED TO THEM, AT THE 40TH ANNIVERSARY OF THE ACT

It is a bright morning, and much water has flown under the bridge concerning America's wild horses and burros since I first took up pen to compose this book four years ago. Much has come to light due to the persistent efforts of many wild horse/burro altruists from all over our nation and world. America will no longer tolerate the continued discrediting and elimination of its national heritage species from their rightful homes. Rallies have been held in Washington, including Horses on the Hill Day, September 28–30, 2009, during which Arizona Representative Raul Grijalva expressed his outrage that the will of the general public for reform and reinstatement of the mustangs and burros was being ignored by authorities and by the Senate.

This was followed by the March for Mustangs, March 24–26, 2010, again in the nation's capitol. Here ardent speakers such as Wendie Malick (soon to star as Wild Horse Annie in a Hallmark Channel film), R.T. Fitch (of *Straight from the Horse's Heart* fame), educator Rob Pliskin, humane observer Elyse Gardner, film maker Ginger Kathrens, as well as singer Clay Canfield raised their voices to let the wild ones again be free. Many mustang supporters impinged on Lafayette Square then marched on the Department of Interior to chant their message demanding a positive change. Then again on March 10–11, 2011, a spirited press conference and protest took place in Phoenix, including a candlelight vigil for fallen wild horses and burros. Protest events have taken place at cities around the country and around the world opposing the federal bureaucracy's planned obliteration of the herds. Tens of thousands of people are demanding to be heard with their message for change. And major media such as the Associated Press and CNN are starting to break away from control by anti-wild-horse factions that would overwhelm us with their propaganda if they had their way. Americans are growing tired of these tirades and will no longer be duped.

RECENT ROUNDUPS AND LEGAL PROTEST

During October 1, 2009 to September 30, 2010 (FY2010), 10,137 wild horses and 476 wild burros were rounded up by BLM contracted helicopter pilots. PZP fertility suppressant was administered to 443 released mares. Total FY2010 program expenditure was $65 million worth of taxpayers' money. Of this, $44.6 million was spent on roundup, removal, and holding and very little on helping those wild equids who remained in the wild to so remain. Major roundups, e.g., Antelope Valley, in the Ely BLM District, stopped short, apparently for lack of horses, indicating considerable illegal capturing or killings or overblown population estimates.

Since FY2011 began on October 1, 2010, until March 1, 2011, BLM contractors eliminated 5,825 wild horses and 75 wild burros from the wild, and they PZP-treated and released 469 mares back into the wild. As of early April 2011, $4.5 million had been spent capturing and removing these wild equids, while holding costs are projected at $38.5 million.

Still planned for removal are 4,686 wild horses and 150 wild burros after July 1st. In spite of an appeal in which I was plaintiff and a temporary injunction, a massive roundup of circa 1,700 wild horses in the Triple B, Maverick-Medicine, and Antelope HMAs was proceeding in eastern Nevada until over 1,200 were gathered and the roundup was abruptly stopped for humane violations. These areas I had inspected just before the roundup commenced to find ample forage and water, but only very few, sparsely distributed wild horse bands. The latter were being closed out of the abundant water sources of this spectacular region at every possible opportunity and with the complicity of local, state, and federal agencies, including White Pine and Elko counties, Nevada Departments of Wildlife and of Agriculture, BLM, USFS, and USFWS (Ruby Lake National Wildlife Refuge). (Field trip report available upon request from author.)

PROPOSED ACTS AND ACTIONS—PAST, PRESENT, AND FUTURE

In the 111th Congress in early 2009, the Prevention of Equine Cruelty Bill, H.R. 503, was introduced to address horses' dire plight in these ultra-modern times of seemingly exclusive human focus and rampant artificiality. It gained nearly two hundred co-sponsors in the House, and its companion S. 727 bill gained twenty-eight senator co-sponsors. But it was allowed to die in December 2010, just as its predecessor had in 2008, and just as similar bills dating back to 2004 and concerning horse export to 1989 have likewise died (Valerie James-Patton, pers. comm.). Though the more substantial Democratic majority was expected to do this more justice, it was blocked in the Senate. Now in the 112th Congress, the American Horse Slaughter Prevention Act of 2011[19] will take up where the other left off to prevent exportation of horses to slaughter. Many horses have been going to Mexico "for other purposes," but in fact are being cruelly slaughtered in such places as San Barnabe near Presidio, Texas.

---

19 Please contact your senators and representatives to pass this bill, S. 1176, which has just been introduced by Senator Mary Landrieu (early 2011) to carry the noble fight for compassion onward and upward. I pray it will not meet the same dismal fate as former bills.

The Restore Our American Mustang (ROAM) bill (S. 1579 of the 111th Congress) has met a similar fate. It would have rescinded the infamous Burns Amendment to the act that has allowed wild horses to be sold to slaughter via killer buyers since 2005. This amendment to an appropriation bill was sneakily placed by Senator Conrad Burns (R-MT) and has caused horrific suffering for many horses and anguish for the people who care about them. The ROAM bill was passed by a substantial margin in the House of Representatives, but was shamelessly allowed to die in the Senate at the close of the 111th Congress (12/2010). It could have restored many of the zeroed-out herd areas and territories, opened up additional areas, and increased populations to more truly viable levels in viably sized and appropriate habitats. The western senators in the hands of public lands livestock interests again managed to kill this valiant attempt at reform. But this gives us all the more reason today to draw up and introduce a more refined version of ROAM and to see that it is passed by both Houses, then sent to the president for his signature. This would truly befit the fortieth anniversary of the Wild Free-Roaming Horses and Burros Act.

To help us on our way, here is valuable background information on ROAM: In February 2008, Congressmen Nick J. Rahall (D-WV) and Raul M. Grijalva (D-AZ) introduced it as H.R. 1018 to amend the 1971 Wild Free-Roaming Horses and Burros Act. Though it was questioned by many advocates leery of what might happen to further weaken the act, to its credit it aimed to:

> (1) allow federal agencies to find additional suitable areas for equids to freely roam,
>
> (2) require more consistency and accuracy in the protection and management of wild horse and burro herds and more public involvement with this,
>
> (3) facilitate the creation of sanctuaries for wild equid populations on public lands,
>
> (4) prohibit killing healthy wild equids and rescind the notorious Burns Amendment of December 2004,

(5) strengthen the adoption program, and

(6) rescind the massive and cruel helicopter roundups.

But there was also a heavy emphasis on promoting contraception/sterilization among the herds in the earlier ROAM. Additionally, there was a potential abandonment of original herd areas allowed by the act without a balancing provision to assure equal gain of new land of equivalent or better habitat quality and size for the wild horses and burros. This had long-time advocates worried that if made an act, it would allow a cave-in to long-time enemies of wild equids and allow them to get away scot-free in spite of many years of wild horse/burro abuse.

After receiving widespread public outcry, Secretary of Interior Kenneth Salazar withdrew his Salazar Plan, derisively know as "Salazoos," that would have created mid-western and eastern "sanctuaries." This plan would have subverted the act by domesticating the wild ones and rendering them non-reproducing, dead-end populations lodged in pastures outside the West. Thousands protested the "Salazoos" and let him know just what they thought when they marched on his Washington office in March 2010, and a year later in Phoenix. They loudly chanted: *Learn to Share Freedom and the Land with the Wild Horses and Burros!, Forever Wild and Free! Stop the Roundups Now!* and other stirring slogans. A secretary under the Secretary did finally come out to receive our letter demanding a moratorium on roundups. Someone of authority must have heard us, since several police and homeland security vehicles suddenly presented themselves as did—to our delight—four large, well-groomed horses mounted by capitol police. As we chanted, these horses stood alongside us winking in approval—there to represent the horse nation amid the constellation of beings and to stand up for their kind's right to live free.

Since April 2011, Salazar and BLM's plan is now to create "ecosanctuaries" for those forty-three thousand wild horses/burros in holding. These could be either on private or on a combination of private and public lands. One catch again is that these would all be non-reproducing herds, not vital wild herds as the act intended. And where these ecosystems involve legal herd management areas, *the number of wild horses/burros maintained on these lands would be subtracted from the appropriate/allowable management levels of the HMAs.* Thus, it would be a way of further under-mining any truly wild, vital, and reproducing wild horse/burro population.

Many see the ecosanctuaries as a response to billionaire Madeleine Pickens's offer and those of others (e.g., Neda de Mayo of the Return to Freedom sanctuary) to provide a sanctuary on private and public lands for the forty-three thousand+ wild horses that have been over-gathered off the public lands. Pickens's sanctuary would be on her two recently purchased ranches in northeast Nevada, which would possi-bly include permitted public lands grazing. However, local Elko County commissioners have stubbornly opposed her project. Many advocates perceive ecosanctuaries as a whitewash for what BLM is doing. To re-ally root out the injustice, America must deal with the failure by federal authorities to curb the excesses of public lands ranchers and other exploiters. Any serious reform must mandate "closure to livestock" in many of the legal herd areas/territories—long a legal option—as well as secure permanent water by exercising the Implied Federal Water Rights that came with the creation of herd areas/territories and similar rights that would secure complete habitats for much larger, truly long-term viable populations of wild horses and burros *in the wild*.

CALLS FOR MORATORIUM AND NAS STUDY

In mid-February 2008, U.S. Representative Raul Grijalba (D-AZ) re-quested the Government Accountability Office (GAO) to investigate possible corruption in our nation's federal wild horse and burro pro-gram, specifically naming the U.S. Bureau of Land Management for in-tensive inquiry. In July 2010, he composed a letter to President Obama that was signed by fifty-four fellow representatives and asked for an im-mediate moratorium on wild horse and burro roundups and a National Academy of Science investigation of the wild horse and burro program. Such a three-year investigation was recently solicited by the BLM it-self—perhaps in response—and approved for funding by Congress in late 2010 to the tune of $11.5 million, though if plans for future round-ups occur, precious few wild horses and burros and their functional bands and herds would remain to study. Again, in a letter of July 5, 2011, Grijalva is calling upon Secretary of the Interior Kenneth L. Salazar to reform our nation's wild horse and burro program, citing specific examples of gruesome spaying projects aimed at mares in southern Wyoming and the past over-gathering of herds (Cohen 2011). His letter cites proven self-stabilizing wild horse herds, e.g., at Montgomery Pass on the California-Nevada border, which has not had a roundup in ca. 30 years, and at Arizona's Cerbat Mountains, famous for their distinctive Spanish mustangs. Grijalva points out the customary paltry budget for wild herd and habitat monitoring compared with roundups. In general he calls for a rectification of the discrepancy between true horse conservation and actual practices of the BLM/USFS. Considering Arizona had hardly any wild equids left in its legal herd areas, it seems ironic that the past few years have been chosen to complain. Still it is not too late for these herds to be reinstated where they have both legal and moral right, and, what's more, an ecological niche fashioned by a continuous evolution that dates back many millions of years. According to wild horse reproductive expert Dr. Jay Kirkpatrick, "[m]odern horses evolved on this continent 1.6-million years ago...The two key elements for classifying an animal as a native species are where it originated and whether it co-evolved with its habitat. The horse can lay claim to doing both in North America" (Fuller 2009, 112). In this light, the proposal by former U.S. Secretary of the Interior, the late and honorable Stewart Udall to create a National Wild Horse Park is also entirely justified.

Roundup curtailment would give the National Academy of Sciences (NAS) time to evaluate the wild horse and burro program and recommend reforms. It is absurd to plunge ahead with drastic reductions from the already overly reduced herds, as this would render moot reform actions recommended by NAS. Were BLM to complete its roundup plans for fiscal years 2011 and 2012, ca. 20-thousand wild equids would be eliminated from the wild, representing nearly $223 million in total cost over the lifetime of these equids. And the total wild equid number in federally supported short-term and long-term holding facilities would soar to over 60,000. These would contain captive equids who, as the situation presently stands, would not be adequately monitored by the public. I concur with president of The Cloud Foundation Ginger Kathrens when she asserts that these considerable taxpayer dollars should be applied "to range improvements, livestock and fence removals ...

water improvements, and any number of projects that ... improve the condition of the [herd] area[s] for wild horses [and burros] and all other wildlife species" (Allen 2011).

A 2010 report by BLM's own Office of Inspector General indicates that BLM's wild horse/burro population census lacks a rigorous scientific basis, oversight, and checks, including on purported rates of increase (20% annual increase is typically applied in many HMAs). This is a major reason for the present NAS review of the program, which will include a review of natural predation as a mortality factor and, hopefully, of reserve design as a new approach to attaining naturally self-stabilizing, but long-term viable herds. –Unfortunately in mid-April 2010, Congress approved another massive budget for BLM's wild horse/burro program giving it everything it asked for as concerns roundups, which resumed on July 1, 2011. What will happen to those horses losing their freedom remains problematic, especially considering the fates of those who have gone before them.

BROKEN ARROW WILD HORSE HOLDING FACILITY & CALICO ROUNDUPS EXAMINED

During the first couple months after the Calico roundup ended on March 1st, 2010, the public was allowed to observe the mustangs three days per week, for two hours per day, at Broken Arrow. Later we were restricted to two hours on Sundays, then later public viewings were suspended—hardly a transparent situation in spite of President Obama's promise for increased transparency. Only one local veterinarian, Richard Sanford, was responsible for overseeing the health of all the Calico horses, many of whom have already died for a variety of reasons, including pulmonary infections and digestive collapse.[20]

---

20 The following indicates how callous the APHIS (Animal & Plant Health Inspection Service) veterinarian Al Kane seemed toward the wild horses when overseeing the Black Rock East HMA (part of the Calico complex) gather on December 31, 2009. When I asked him whether the wild horses ever damaged their lungs and suffered pneumonia and/or serious respiratory disease after being helicopter chased during very cold winter conditions (such as were present), he said he did not remember a case where this had been a serious problem for the horses and stressed instead how hardy they were. This was simply not believable to those several wild horse advocates present and I imagine many of the officials themselves who knew about horse's large and sensitive lungs.

After the Calico roundups, the Broken Arrow facility became crammed with over two thousand wild horses, and subsequently became similarly crammed with wild horses gathered during the Twin Peaks HMA and Ely District roundups. Many spontaneous abortions have occurred as a consequence. As of April 27, 2010, at least 126 wild horses had perished in the whole Calico roundups and holding operations, but as of October 2010, the number rose to two hundred. Though only seven deaths were reported during the actual Calico roundups, many more roundup-associated deaths undoubtedly occurred—coyotes, ravens, and other scavengers disposing of their remains – particularly tender, footsore colts and fillies – far from human view. One such death very probably happened when a Cattoor helicopter drove a mustang into a non-Wild-Horse-Annie cattle guard, i.e. one without iron rebars. This was in the northern Calico Mountain HMA, as three of us discovered in a return visit to this HMA (see the article CRAIG DOWNER'S REPORT ON THE CALICO COMPLEX IN THE HELICOPTER'S WAKE... April 10, 2010 http://humaneobserver. blogspot.com/search?updated-max=2010-05-23T08%3A56%3A00max-result=7&reverse-paginate=true).

By April 24, 2010, 225 foals had been born of the Calico horses at the Broken Arrow facility as the wild horse foaling season went into full swing.[21] The foaling season had brought a temporary halt to wild equid helicopter gathers from March though June. By April 24, 115 males four years of age and younger had been castrated at the facility. Many of these were in obvious and extreme pain and some could hardly get to their feet (see CASTRATION BLUES: JUST DEAL WITH IT and other BLM Classics. April 27, 2010. http://humaneobserver.blogspot. com/2010_04_01_archives.html). On April 27, 2010, a three-year-old mare was euthanized after being unable to deliver her foal.

---

21 It was pitiful to witness these newborns lying or standing alongside their caring mares and looking out brightly to the world. It was also very upsetting to realize how these innocents had been deprived of their natural homes and lives because of an unwillingness to share freedom on the part of humans. By law these wonderful animals belong to all Americans; government employees and contractors have the public trust to care for them. Their plea presents an urgent challenge to live in harmony with such exemplars of freedom through prescriptions for coexistence such as reserve design.

The hold on the Calico horses for possible return to the range did not apply to stallions four years of age or younger, hundreds of whom were castrated by BLM workers at Broken Arrow in order to be put up for adoption in June (see http://www.animallawcoalition.com/wild-horse-and-burros/article/1119). Yet this was contrary to an agreement by BLM with plaintiffs to hold off until the judge's final decision that was due by May 26, 2010 (Novak 2010). Had Judge Friedman ruled in favor of the wild horses, ordering their return to the Calico Complex of HMAs or perhaps to some of the already zeroed-out or under-populated HMAs, his ruling would have called into question many other excessive wild equid reductions that ensued from July through September 2010, and subsequently. These have either entirely eliminated wild horses and/or burros from their legal herd areas or reduced them to cripplingly low levels, compromised in their ability to reproduce. All of this, of course, is part of the blatant subversion of the Wild Free-Roaming Horse and Burro Act that wild horse/burro advocates are desperately fighting. We adamantly remind Americans and those in positions of public trust that this act was unanimously passed, and we should now be celebrating its fortieth anniversary by restoring, not continuing to undo, its true intent.

It has been observed in many herd areas that after the helicopter roundups and their disruption of the wild horses' social units, immature mares will be bred who otherwise would not have been, and that many of these die agonizing deaths trying to give birth to fetuses that are too large for their birth canals. To such incidents attested members of America's Wild Horse Advocates concerning the Spring Mountain mustangs of southern Nevada. Madames Rhea Little, Melissa Ohlson, and Darcy Grizzle were three of the compassionate ladies who tried to save some of the above described mares and their offspring in what was surely a labor of love (pers. comm., August 2011).

During one of my regular visits to the Broken Arrow holding facility on April 11, 2010, strong winds were kicking up large quantities of sand and dust. In spite of the boarded panels around the feeding troughs, the sand was mixing in with the half-grass and half-alfalfa hay being fed to the horses. In the pens, many morose horses stood around with their backs to the wind. Their manure piles and occasional forays of playfulness attested their efforts to establish some semblance of a normal life. Hope springs eternal, indeed.

For two months, an increasing decline in morale among the horses had been noted at Broken Arrow. Frequently I encountered very depressed horses who, in spite of having plenty of food and water, seemed without the will to live. Many times, I observed fights breaking out between stallions and also between mares (the sexes are kept in separate pens). The forceful kicks and bites that resulted accounted for many limping horses, pronounced contusions, and open flesh wounds (all well documented by photos/videos).

What appeared to be "pigeon fever" had manifested itself, especially among young adult horses two to four years of age. Though according to BLM, biopsies failed to confirm active cases of this disease at the site. But whether the malady was pigeon fever or some other infection, it was a real hardship on the horses, contributing to their decline. Such ailments are obviously exacerbated by overcrowding. Pus sacks on the chests of the horses may also have been caused, as BLM officials claimed, by metal bars separating the individual feeding slots along the access corridors, and some improvements to this situation have been made, including placing rubber tubing around certain horizontal bars. Horses often push each other from behind during the feeding hours, causing chest abrasions. BLM estimates that, of the 1,922 horses captured in the Calico Complex roundup, about forty horses had suffered from pigeon fever, as indicated by bare chest patches. So I remain perplexed as to how the outward manifestations I saw could look so like pigeon fever and how some low incidence of the disease was known to occur, yet still no pigeon fever was officially reported as being active among these demoralized, overcrowded, and often bickering horses (see PIGEON FEVER, BUSINESS AS USUAL (?) and HAPPY BLACKOUT EASTER WEEK? March 30, 2010. http://humaneobserver.blogspot.com/2010-03-01-archive.html).

On a tour of Broken Arrow on April 18, 2010, BLM guide Dean Bolstad stated that the Calico horses were in declining condition before they were gathered, even claiming that as many as 30% were emaciated before roundup. This was a gross exaggeration, however, since nearly all horses captured were actually quite fit, as attest many observers who witnessed them coming off the range. Several, including myself, were familiar with these horses shortly before in their wild state, e.g., Lightning the striking palomino stallion (see Figure 15 on p. 187 and CALICO HAS LOST ITS LIGHTNING – LIGHTNING LOSES ALL. February 26, 2010. http://humaneobswerver.blogspot.com/2010/03/26-february-2010-calico-has-lost-its.html). And besides, wild horses should not be judged by standards used for domestic horses. If there were a few in declining health due to age or accidents, it is certain that the health of many more of these animals is now seriously deteriorating and that many more have died precisely because they have been violently jerked out of their rightful homes,[22] where the horses should be born, live out their natural lives, and die. The harsh and excessive helicopter roundups that continue to be carried out in order to accommodate the outrageous demands of wild horse enemies in human form are a disgrace to America and to humanity today. These are chiefly public lands ranchers but include other resource exploiters including trophy hunters (e.g. Safari International, Bighorns Unlimited) who regard the horses as merely "in the way" of their version of progress.

POSSIBLE HORSE CLONING

It appears that contractors operating at Broken Arrow may be involved with the cloning of horses, as this was featured on the web site of Bovance company for its cloning of "N Bar Primrose 2424." This unnatural horse offspring was sold at an auction with the chief Broken Arrow contractor listed as seller. Bovance is owned by two cloning companies: ViaGen and Trans Ova Genetics. In turn ViaGen is owned by the pharmaceutical company Geron. We should find it highly disturbing that the care of America's wild horses is being entrusted to someone involved in genetic manipulation. Also disturbing is the fact that this holding facility is now almost entirely off-limits to public viewing, with only a rare public tour day or two being offered every few months. Many of the Calico Complex wild horses still languish here, their numbers growing

---

22 In his candid article, veterinarian Bruce Nock, Ph.D. pointed out that stress caused by the helicopter roundups has been the primary cause of the captive wild horses' present woes (Nock 2010).

ever smaller due to broken necks, disease, confinement, fighting, and an equivalent of Post Traumatic Stress Disorder—the stress of the helicopter roundups, of being enslaved and overcrowded, of having been torn from their families. The result is that an overwhelming disanimation and moroseness comes over them like a pall. This I painfully sense, and it is one mortality factor not mentioned in BLM's official reports.

THE CALICO CASE REVISITED AND WHAT CAME OUT OF IT

Our suit before the D.C. court asked that the Calico wild horses in holding be returned to their largely empty HMAs where, if six hundred remained as BLM asserted, there would be almost one thousand acres per horse. One acre is approximately the size of a football field, and one hundred acres per horse in this semi-arid area would still not be overpopulated, provided the wild horses get their fair share of the water present. A thousand acres per horse is hardly a fair proportioning of resources, considering the thousands of domesticated cattle and sheep permitted to graze on these same lands and this in spite of the "principally" wild horse presence clause of the act (section 2 c). In the Calico Complex, only one-quarter of forage is allocated to wild horses, and nearly all the remainder goes to livestock. In the 1.2-million-acre Triple B complex in BLM's Ely District, only 6% to 10% of the forage has been allocated to the wild horses.[23] Our appeal (Cloud Foundation et al vs. Salazar et al) is to be heard again later in 2011 or early 2012. Hopefully the 1,200+ wild horses already gathered can be returned to their rightful areas.

Public vigilance and protest is placing BLM's wild horse and burro program under ever more intense pressure. Along with many, I have been present during the sporadic public observation days, both of the roundups and of the holding facilities, particularly Broken Arrow (a name, by the way, that symbolizes White repression of Native Americans).

---

23 And if you think this is extreme, try the 2% to 3% total wild horse forage allocation in BLM Wyoming's White Mountain/Little Colorado HMAs (Edwards 2011).

As a consequence of our Calico suit before Judge Friedman, among the 1,922 wild horses who were gathered in the dead of the 2010 winter[24], all horses older than four years were ordered to remain at the Broken Arrow facility un-castrated until the case was decided. Unfortunately the judge again let these horses down by declaring a "lack of standing" of the professional, long-time-Calico-wild-horse-observing Nevadan plaintiffs, i.e., author Terri Farley and myself. In my opinion, this was a way of avoiding justice, most probably due to political pressure from well-heeled and connected public land grazers. And also involved here was a failure by counsel to emphasize the plaintiffs' chief declaratory complaints during court proceedings.

On the bright side, Friedman did rule against the Secretary of Interior's proposal to create seven wild horse reserves in the Midwest and East, five to be privately and two, federally owned. In these reserves, those wild horses deemed overpopulated, or "in excess," were to be put out to pasture for the rest of their lives, here to become non-reproducing, dead-end populations with sexes separated and stallions castrated. Thus obliterated would have been the distinctive lineages that have become especially adapted over generations through natural selection to the various ecosystems from which they were drawn, as accords with the pure and unadulterated intent of the act. In spite of all this, Interior Secretary Salazar, a Colorado cattle rancher, had the audacity to claim that these reserves would be a fulfillment of the 1971 act, vaunting them as places where the public could view wild horses, though in fact they would be viewing prisoner horses squeezed off of their legal herd areas in the West to a truly excessive degree. Wisely—or so it appears—BLM's recently released Strategic Plan for wild horses and burros has scraped this preserve concept, but we should remain ever on guard. Reminding me of the forty years of Biblical tribulation, I consider it auspicious that 2011 is the fortieth anniversary of the Wild Free-Roaming Horses and Burros Act of 1971, for this year must surely be the year when we begin to turn things around for wild horses and burros in the wild by revitalizing the act's true intent—and by this I mean by restoring the herds to their rightful land and freedom!

---

24 Although Friedman had requested a postponement of roundups until his final decision due on May 26, 2010, his timid request was rudely ignored by BLM officials.

SIGNIFICANT MEDIA ATTENTION

Mounting public outrage has resulted from our wild horse efforts, and various media are further exposing the anti-wild-horse prejudice that has long existed. Gradually the wild horses' and burros' greater story is being revealed, which promises to reverse an intolerable situation. On Sunday March 27, 2011, I attended the premiere of Katia Louise's fine film *Saving America's Horses: A Nation Betrayed* at the Laemmle's Sunset 5 theater in West Hollywood. This dramatic and thoroughgoing film brought much to light, including the insidious conspiracy by certain vested interests to undo wild horses and burros in the West as well as the many positive ecological and social contributions these beautiful animals make.

On Sunday, March 21, 2010, my local paper the *Reno Gazette-Journal* did a full-spread, front-page story calling into question BLM's negative policies toward the wild horses and burros in the wild and making a strong case against their disproportionate numbers and resource allocations (Mullen 2010). Later that week, CNN TV's popular "ISSUES" program covered our rally, coming out strongly on the side of wild horses, with host Jane Velez-Mitchell personally denouncing the roundups as cruel and unjustified. In October 2010, a major French TV program aired, as had earlier ones in Germany, where major coverage in *Der Spiegel* magazine also resulted. Most recently *The Atlantic* has published a poignant critique of the grossly unfair wild horse reductions and massive stallion castrations that BLM had planned for herds in Wyoming as well as the national program as a whole (Cohen, A. 2011).

MONITORING OF ROUNDUPS, HMAS VIA OVER-FLIGHTS

More Roundups and Holding Aftermaths Gone Awry for the Horses

As attest vigorous activities by The Cloud Foundation, American Wild Horse Preservation Campaign, In Defense of Animals, Wild Horse Education, HSUS, Animals' Angels, Grass Roots Horse, Respect for Horses, America's Wild Horse Advocates, etc., the wild horse and burro movement is conscientiously monitoring helicopter roundups and the fates of wild horses and burros who have lost their freedom and languish in glorified concentration camps, whether public or private. These include the Palomino holding facility north of Reno, Ridgeview in southeast California, and Litchfield east of Susanville (CA), as well as at the private Broken Arrow holding facility several miles north of Fallon (NV) that has already been discussed.

One egregious case involves the Elko Nevada BLM District's Tuscarora wild horse roundup conducted by Cattoor Livestock Gathers out of Nephi, Utah. Here many wild horses were pushed to collapse by helicopter stampeding during the searing heat of mid-summer 2010 just as the wild horses of eastern Nevada's Triple B Complex have now been overtaxed, overheated, and killed (Deniz Bolbol, pers. comm., 8/2011). Later some of the Tuscarora horses died because of water intoxication when they were thoughtlessly allowed to rapidly drink their fill after being chased by helicopter in high temperatures. Another case I witnessed on January 5, 2011, concerns the Eagle HMA wild horse "gather". This day saw frigid temperatures of minus twelve degrees Fahrenheit at dawn and reached a high of about twelve degrees above zero in and around Pioche, Lincoln Co., NV. Though observers including "Meet America" TV host Ann Griffith and I requested the roundup be halted under such hazardous conditions, the Ely BLM official in charge, Chris Hanefeld, allowed it to proceed and at least seven pneumonia-related horse deaths resulted as a consequence (www.ustreamtv.com click videos, pets & animals, type in Strongest Horses on Earth; www.artandhorseslauraleigh.wordpress. com & www.wildhorseeducation.com).

Yet another "gather" plan that went woefully awry took place in January 2011, in the Winnemucca District's Augusta Mountain HMA. Though the AML for this herd is 185 to 308 wild horses and the herd was at 294, not even the upper limit, according to roundup observer Laura Leigh a total of 103 wild horses were removed by helicopter and taken to Broken Arrow. The announced plan of November 22, 2010 by BLM was that ca. 275 wild horses were to be gathered, including about forty from outside the HMA in the Fish Creek Mountains and that all but forty were to be returned to the wild and the mares given PZP-22 to inhibit their reproduction for a few years. The upshot is that over two-and-a-half times the announced number were permanently removed. Another important point not mentioned by BLM officials is the fact that the Fish Creek Mountains were part of the larger original herd area established in 1971 and a vital part of wild horse year-round habitat. As is the case with so many of America's herds, the Augusta Mountain wild horses are being plainly victimized. This compels me to ask where their caring defenders—especially those in authority—are and what they are doing about it.

OBSERVER FLIGHTS OVER HERDS

On May 3, 2010, I flew over and transected the entire width of the Calico Complex of five wild horse HMAs, but was only able to observe thirty-one wild horses—but 350 cattle! The wild horses were far from the water sources, but almost all of the cattle were camped on and damaging these considerably. Though I presented my findings to the BLM, their chief response was to try to discredit my findings rather than to responsibly own up and rectify what was so plainly wrong.

Again, during my flight over Twin Peaks HMA on September 24, 2010, I observed only seven wild horses but 186 cattle in a 133.3-mile straight-line transect. Many advocates have joined me in calling for the restoration of two hundred wild horses and all of the score or so of gathered wild burros in this 798,000-acre HMA. In its April 20, 2011 decision, Sacramento Federal District Court refused to declare a suit brought by wild horse advocates against this roundup as moot, which is a positive sign that justice for the wild horses might still be served.

On March 9, 2011, I realized another reconnoiter flight in northwest Nevada and parts of northeast California and southern Oregon. This flight buzzed around the Sheldon National Wildlife Refuge (NWR), and parts of the High Rock and Calico Mountain complexes of wild horse HMAs. Both the forty-year-veteran pilot familiar with the region (Bill Drake) and I were alarmed to find a near total absence of wild horses in this vast and clearly visible region. We found only one band of five in the Granite Peak HMA, sunning themselves at the western base of some rocky cliffs. Alarmingly, we found wild horses to be absent in the traditionally wild-horse-inhabited Fish Creek area. Due to the past history of illegal killings in this vast and stark region and the decision to eliminate all wild horses from the Sheldon refuge in spite of earlier studies and agreements affirming the wild horses' ecological compatibility (Meeker 1979), I am now urging a renewed effort to save what is left of this historic herd. Still, I must contend with the fact that on August 15, 2011 the final elimination by helicopter roundup of Sheldon's historic wild horse herd commenced—in total betrayal of this refuge's earlier agreement to allow the wild horses to stay on as naturally integrated components of the refuge and in perpetuity (Velma Bronn Johnston, 1976, pers. comm.). Because of observable construction activities, during the flight I was reminded of another enormously invasive project that was used to pseudo-justify the massive reduction of the Calico wild horses: the Ruby Valley natural gas pipeline, whose construction is now passing through the HMAs of the northern portions of both the Calico Mountain and High Rock HMA complexes. Referring to them as mere "nuisances," this project's justifying document, or EIS, urged a drastic reduction in wild horses and failed to consider accommodations for coexistence (aka NEPA's *mitigating measures*).

A RAY OF HOPE

A ray of sunshine appeared in the form of a major court victory by the Colorado Wild Horse Coalition and The Cloud Foundation, legally represented by Valerie J. Stanley of Maryland. The ruling by D.C. Federal District Judge Rosemary Collyer ordered BLM not to zero out the West Douglas wild horse herd, since it had failed to prove the population to be "in excess." Though some observers believe this was a technical slip on the part of the BLM, much of the wording of the Collyer judgment impugned BLM's justification for arbitrarily declaring an overpopulation of wild horse herds throughout the West. In spite of this strong ruling, BLM officials obstinately persisted in keeping the West Douglas HMA on its FY2010 schedule for zeroing out (www.horsetalk.co.nz/news/2009/08/054.shtml). Indeed, Colorado BLM has prepared another environmental assessment with somewhat different wording and approach, but that again plans to eliminate all the wild horses from this HMA, rendering it an oxymoronic wild-horse-less herd area. Thankfully, again wild horse advocates legally protested this before a New York federal court in October 2010.

THE GREEN HORSE AND IMPRESSIVE FILMS, AND MORE FERMENT

Around the world, wild horses and burros are coming to be more appreciated in their own right rather than as mere pawns of man. This includes their role in ecological restoration projects, as is increasingly recognized in projects from UK's Kent County to Siberia, from southern France to Mongolia (Zimov 2005; http://www.getxnews.com/2010/02/wild-horses-to-help-white-cliffs-wildlife-thrive/; http://www.bbc.uk/insideout/southeast/series1/wildhorses.shtml). And the "green horse" is well depicted in the recently premiered award-winning *Saving America's Horses: A Nation Betrayed*. Other films to watch in this regard are Mara LeGrand's *Horses in the Winds of Change*, James Kleinert's *Disappointment Valley* and his newest award-winning *Wild Horses and Renegades*. Both Louise' and Kleinert's films were shown at the Missoula's International Wildlife Film Festival in May, 2011, where I was present to monitor a lively panel discussion that included Michael Blake, academy award-winning director of *Dances with Wolves* and long-time, ardent defender of wild horses.

ADOPT-A-HERD/HERD WATCH

In a wise and far-seeing effort to make each herd in America as publicly valued as the Pryor Mountain herd, an adopt-a-herd/herd watch program is being promoted by ordinary citizens, including Ellen-Cathryn Nash, whose Internet radio program *Howling Ridge* has sparked interest across the nation (www.blogtalkradio.com/howling_ridge_radio). Also the Equine Welfare Alliance (EWA), led by Vicki Tobin of Chicago and John Holland of Pennsylvania, continues to campaign effectively to prevent the ongoing slaughter of horses, including wild, and to restore equids in their rightful areas in the West. EWA organized the International Equine Conference that was held in Alexandria, Virginia, from September 26-28, 2011. Here prominent wild horse activists and horse defenders spoke, including myself, representing the wild horses and burros.

Though originally launched under the auspices of The Cloud Foundation, the program known as Herd Watch was the instigation of Laura Leigh, who has now formed her own organization Wild Horse Education. It is envisioned to be a volunteer program that will monitor wild horses and burros and their habitat as well as roundups and holding facilities across the West. It aims to create a central database concerning each of America's herds and to draw attention to many of the herds that are little known though equally as valuable.

According to BLM, in 1971, 339 wild herds were designated for protection, though, as earlier indicated, the original number is well over 350 due to the many irregularities that occurred in the incipient years of the act. Since 1971, BLM and U.S. Forest Service have zeroed out at least 159 herds, including the twelve Caliente Complex herds. The idea is that through Herd Watch, volunteer teams will assemble and analyze data, photographs, and information following their visits to diverse herd areas/territories. This will include a thorough literature review pertaining to each herd area/territory. This will permit us to effectively pressure government agencies as well as communities to treat wild equids fairly and restore them to their rightful habitats. Big Blend Internet Radio's enthusiastic, inquiring and genial hosts Lisa Smith and Nancy Reid have also done much to rally support for wild horses and burros in their *Nature Connection* and other programs (see http://bigblendradioshows.com/March25NatureConnection.html and past shows).

PROMISING DEVELOPMENTS

Two other developments, this time on the official side, potentially augur well for the reform of our nation's wild horse program. One concerns BLM's contracting of an independent outside firm to conduct a Conflict Resolution mediation between BLM and wild horse and burro advocates. I had the honor to share my ideas with the mediator along with several others, including both traditional friends and enemies of wild horses and burros. I urged the implementation of reserve design (Chapter IV) as a way to attain self-stabilizing wild equid populations, and stressed that livestock grazing within the legal HAs should be curtailed to allow for higher equid numbers. As I indicated, natural barriers, predators, and buffer zones are key elements of reserve design, as are educational outreach programs aimed at teaching the positives associated with wild horses and burros. As a nation, America, and as a species, humans, should recognize the merits of wild-horse-or burro-containing ecosystems. The final report from this mediation needed to go further in recognizing the true merits of reserve design and calling for its implementation, but at least some of my points were heeded. The recommendations overemphasized invasive reproductive interference through PZP drugs and skewed sex ratios while only minorly recognizing restoring natural balances and fairer proportions for wild horses and burros on public lands.

Another promising development already discussed is BLM's September 2010 request to the National Academy of Sciences (NAS) to do an objective and independent review of its wild horse/burro program. Hopefully this truly will be independent and objective and yield information that will justify restoring the herds. The sum appropriated from Congress for this was $11.5 million—enough in my estimation to take down many illegal fences, secure many water sources, buy out many key grazing leases, and seriously begin a reserve design implementation for viable and naturally self-stabilizing herds. If NAS' recommendations are to help restore the wild horse/burro herds, an immediate moratorium should be placed on all further roundups, for these are cutting the herds to the very quick.

Reserve design would initially define the habitat needs for a viable wild horse/burro population in each legally designated region, then work out a plan with all parties concerned to allow for its harmonious thriving. It remains to be seen whether officials will truly listen, but I have great hopes. Speaking positively, a well-conceived strategy will allow for the harmonious coexistence of a great variety of species within healthy wild-horse/burro-containing ecosystems. Here man's chief role will be that of ecosystem protector and appreciator, rather than imposer of blind traditions that discriminate against wild horses and burros in the wild. Unfortunately, the minimum grazing fee of $1.35 per animal unit month (AUM) has again been authorized on BLM and USFS lands under provision of the Taylor Grazing Act of 1934, continuing what is basically a give-away to public land grazers, including many of the very wealthiest individuals and corporations in America and making it harder for responsible authorities to cut back on the excessive livestock on BLM and USFS lands. This latter is imperative in order to reinstate and revive our wild horse and burro herds, even according to a January 31, 2011 news release from the U.S. Department of the Interior itself. With a will and a vision, the current unacceptable situation can be changed.

CALL FOR MORATORIUM AND CHANGE IN POLICY, PERSONNEL

President Barack Obama should order an immediate moratorium on all roundups. This would permit a fairer plan in place of the current negative prescription for America's last wild horses and burros. The latter is nothing more than a cynical plot to subvert the true intent of the act. A new and more positive attitude and policy toward our wild equids would confound those who fail to value wild horses and burros in the wild and work persistently against them. Present policies are extremely hypocritical in claiming to uphold *multiple uses* upon the public lands, while doing just the opposite. Among reforms most obviously needed, personnel currently running the program must be changed—or even charged—and a new and positive approach both within the Department of Interior (Bureau of Land Management) and the Department of Agriculture (U.S. Forest Service) must be rapidly instituted. A clear directive must come out of Washington to reinstate the Wild Free-Roaming Horses and Burros Act in policy and in practice in order to restore the herd areas and territories together with other appropriate and/or conjoining equid habitats throughout the West. This would be a fitting celebration of the fortieth anniversary of the Act, one of action and not just of complaining or of hype.

VARIOUS FIGURES – WHICH TO BELIEVE?

Around 88 million acres of land would have originally qualified under the act for wild horse/burro presence on BLM and USFS lands, but these legally justified areas have been reduced to 53.5 million through various political subterfuges during the four decades since the act's passage (sources: United States Geological Survey publication prior to 2008 referred to in MacDonald, 2008 [November 24] and in Animal Welfare Institute 2007, 8; and http://www.8newsnow.com/story/11285225/i-team-special-stampede-to-oblivion [added interview with retired BLM biologist J. Phillips re: early years of wild horse/burro program], 11/2009; John Phillips, pers. comm. 8/11/2011).

In more recent years, those portions of the various herd areas that are to be actually designated for occupation by wild equids (herd management areas) have plummeted to 26.6 million acres. Though on February 28, 2009, BLM claimed there were 36,940 wild equids (33,102 wild horses and 3,838 wild burros) on its lands in 180 HMAs and though on February 28, 2010, BLM again claimed there were 38,365 wild equids (33,692 wild horses and 4,673 wild burros), independent researchers, such as Cindy McDonald of Las Vegas, have put the numbers at less than twenty thousand (sources: http://www.blm.gov/public_land_statistics.htm [select year] and MacDonald, C.R. 2008 [July]). Researchers such as MacDonald have signaled various fudge factors—especially rate of population increase—that BLM employs to overly magnify population numbers as well as the ignoring of significant mortality factors, including illegal killings, fencing off of public waters, over-fencing within legal herd areas, non-Wild-Horse-Annie cattle guards that cause gruesome deaths in panicked horses (photos available by request from author), etc. Also entering into the picture here are—of course—over allocations of forage to livestock as well as double counting during censusing flights, especially since planes scare horses to move to other areas to which the planes then proceed to fly. Also there needs to occur individual recognition of the horses, rather than treating them only as so many ciphers. (See Figures 16, 17, & 18)

In spite of a preponderance of livestock and big game animals in relation to wild horses and burros upon the public lands and the pervasive

The Numbers

- 38,500: BLM reported total of WH&B population (as of 2/28/11, not validated)
- 26,600: BLM high AML (appropriate management level) for WH&B population
- 16,000-18,000 BLM actual current targeted low AML for WH&B population
- 21,354: WH&B population as of 2/28/11 using BLM's own data & 20% growth model (independent analysis)
- 240,000-480,000: Approximate head of livestock on WH&B management areas
- Up to 3M livestock on BLM lands
- Up to 1.5M livestock on USFS lands
- 20 million mule deer, 1 million elk, 700,000+ pronghorns, 70,000 bighorns (considered a "species of concern") on Federal, state & private lands

- 245 million: Number of acres BLM currently manages
- 160 million: Number of BLM acres allocated to livestock use
- 53.8 million: Number of BLM & private acres originally designated for WH&B in 1971
- 31.6 million: Number of BLM & private acres currently managed for WH&B
- 22.2 million: Number of acres WH&B have lost since 1971
- 27 million: Number of BLM acres currently allocated to WH&B use (with livestock)
- 11%: Amount of BLM land currently designated for WH&B use

- 83%: Amount of forage allocated to livestock in BLM WH&B areas
- 17%: Amount of forage allocated to WH&B in BLM WH&B areas
- 339: Number of BLM original Herd Areas designated for WH&B in 1971
- 179: Number of BLM reduced-size Herd Management Areas currently designated for WH&B
- 160: Number of WH&B Herd Areas BLM has zeroed-out

- 193 million: Number of acres USFS currently manages
- 91 million: Number of USFS acres allocated to livestock use
- 2 million: Number of USFS acres allocated to WH&B use (with livestock)
- 1.04%: Amount of USFS land currently designated for WH&B use
- 650 million: Number of Federal land acres
- 4.5%: Amount of Federal land acres (BLM/USFS) designated for WH&B use (with livestock)

Costs to Taxpayers:
- $75.7 million: FY2011 total cost of BLM's WH&B Program
- $11.4 million: FY2011 cost of roundups, including fertility control
- $48.2 million: FY2011 cost of BLM warehousing WH&B
- $766,164: FY2010 cost of BLM WH&B census & range monitoring (3.3% of budget)
- $144-500 million: FY2011 cost of livestock grazing program
- $13 million: FY2011 cost of predator control program to benefit livestock

Compiled by Carla Bowers, 10/26/11, Revised 11/6/11
For NAS/NRC Study Panel of BLM Wild Horse & Burro Program
All numbers above are verifiable

Figures 16, 17, & 18: The Cloud Foundation fliers of November 2011 presented to congressmen and public. These reveal gross unfairness and inconsistencies. (Continued)

Over-Inflated Population Estimate as of 2/28/11 Used for Funding: 38,497

CHART 1 - BLM WILD HORSE & BURRO PROGRAM

PUBLISHED ANNUAL POPULATION ESTIMATES USED BY BLM TO ACQUIRE FUNDING & CORRESPONDING ANNUAL GROWTH RATES

Numbers Are Over-Inflated & Non-Credible As Compared To BLM's Claimed 20%/Year Growth Model (See Chart 2)

Conclusion: Halt Roundups/Removals; Conduct Independent, State-Of-The-Art Census

Numbers Based on BLM Publications 'Public Land Statistics; Wild Free-Roaming Horse & Burro Populations, Removals & Adoptions' 1999 - 2010*

YEAR END DATE	BLM PRE-REMOVAL POPULATION ESTIMATE	MINUS ANIMALS REMOVED [1]	POST-REMOVAL POPULATION ESTIMATE WITHOUT FOALS ADDED	NEXT YEAR END DATE	BLM PRE-REMOVAL POPULATION ESTIMATE WITH FOALS ADDED	POPULATION INCREASE (Column 6 minus Column 4)	GROWTH RATE % (Column 7 divided by Column 2)
9/30/99	47,376	(8,631)	38,745	9/30/00	48,624	9,879	20.85%
9/30/00	48,624	(3,210) [2]	45,414 (2/28/01)	[Transition from fiscal years, 10/1-9/30, to 3/1-2/28 years]			
2/28/01	45,414	(16,082) [3]	29,332	2/28/02	38,815	9,483	20.88%
2/28/02	38,815	(11,056) [4]	27,759	2/28/03	37,196	9,427	24.29%
2/28/03	37,186	(9,991) [4]	27,195	2/28/04	37,135	9,940	26.73% [6]
2/28/04	37,135	(10,073) [4]	27,062	2/28/05	31,760	4,698	12.65%
2/28/05	31,760	(9,964) [4]	21,796	2/28/06	31,206	9,410	29.63% [6]
2/28/06	31,206	(8,336) [4]	22,870	2/28/07	28,563	5,693	18.24%
2/28/07	28,563	(6,066) [4]	22,497	2/28/08	33,105	10,608	37.14% [6]
2/28/08	33,105	(5,733) [4]	27,372	2/28/09	36,940	9,568	28.90% [6]
2/28/09	36,940	(8,221) [4]	28,719	2/28/10	38,365	9,646	26.11%
2/28/10	38,365	(9,272) [4]	29,093	2/28/11	38,497 [5]	9,404	24.51%
					Average Annual Growth Rate 2000-2011:		24.54%
					5-Year Average Annual Growth Rate 2007-2011:		26.98% [6]

* Available at: http://www.blm.gov/wo/st/en/prog/whbprogram/herd_management/Data.html

[1] Not including USFS removals from 2005-2010 (777 FY05; 245 FY06; 737 FY07; 133 FY08; 90 FY09; 137 FY10 totaling 2,119 animals).

[2] 3,210 animals removed 10/1/00-2/28/01 out of a total of 13,277 removed in FY01 to attain BLMs estimated population of 45,414 as of 2/28/01.

[3] Remaining animals removed 3/1/01-9/30/01 (FY01) totaling 10,067 plus 6,015 animals removed 10/1/01-2/28/02 (50% of FY02 removals).

[4] Fiscal year removals synchronized 50/50 with 2/28 years per Dean Bolstad recommendation 10/27/11, Reno.

[5] From BLM Herd Area Statistics as of 2/28/11.

[6] Quite above the BLM claimed 20%/year growth rate model.

By Lisa LeBlanc 11/28/10, Updated by Carla Bowers 11/4/11

20%/Year Growth Model Population Estimate as of 2/28/11: 21,354

CHART 2 - BLM WILD HORSE & BURRO PROGRAM

MORE REALISTIC ESTIMATED POPULATIONS & PROJECTIONS USING BLM'S CLAIMED 20%/YEAR GROWTH MODEL 2007-2012

Numbers below are based on applying BLM's claimed 20%/year growth model[1] to reported, estimated national populations as of February 28, 2007, and subtracting BLM's reported removals as per BLM Public Land Statistics for FY2007-FY2010, National Preliminary Final Gather Schedule for FY2011 & projected removals for FY2012. Estimated population numbers on the range may be well under BLM's targeted 26,600 high AML, thus negating the need for funding for additional roundups/removals. Long-term genetic viability of the herds is threatened at these potential low numbers.

Conclusion: Halt Roundups/Removals; Conduct Independent, State-Of-The-Art Census

FISCAL YEAR*	WINTER REMOVALS**	EST. POPULATION AS OF 2/28	PLUS 20% GROWTH RATE	EST. POPULATION AS OF 7/1	SUMMER REMOVALS**	EST. POPULATION AS OF 9/30
2007	-3,495	28,563 [2]	5,713	34,276	-3,495	30,781
2008	-2,571	28,210	5,642	33,852	-2,571	31,281
2009	-3,162	28,119	5,624	33,743	-3,162	30,581
2010	-5,059	25,522	5,104	30,626	-5,059	25,567
2011 [3]	-4,213	21,354	4,271	25,625	-4,213	21,412
2012 [4]	-3,800	17,612	3,522	21,134	-3,800	17,334

* Fiscal year is 10/1 through 9/30.

** Winter removal months 10/1 through 2/28. Summer removal months 3/1 through 9/30 (Note, BLM removes only burros between 3/1 & 6/30 of each fiscal year.)

Total removal numbers for FY2007-FY2010 from Public Land Statistics, available at: http://www.blm.gov/wo/st/en/prog/whbprogram/herd_management/Data.html

Fiscal year removal numbers divided 50/50 between winter & summer roundups per Dean Bolstad recommendation 10/27/11, Reno.

Above removal numbers do not include USFS removals FY2007-FY2010 (737 FY07; 133 FY08: 90 FY09; 137 FY10, totaling 1,097 animals), available from link above.

[1] "... Herds grow at an average rate of 20 percent and can double in size every four years", available at:
http://www.blm.gov/wo/st/en/prog/whbprogram/history_and_facts/quick_facts.html

[2] Estimated population as of 2/28/07 reported in BLM Public Land Statistics, available at:
http://www.blm.gov/wo/st/en/prog/whbprogram/herd_management/Data.html

[3] FY2011 preliminary removals of 8,426 total available at: http://www.blm.gov/wo/st/en/prog/whbprogram/herd_management/Data/completed_fy_11_gathers.html

[4] FY2012 projected removals of 7,600 total extracted from BLM News Release dated 2/24/11, "BLM Accelerates Fundamental Reforms . . . " & quote from Dir. Abbey, available
at: http://www.blm.gov/wo/st/en/info/newsroom/2011/february/NR_0223_2011.html

By C.R. MacDonald 11/20/10, Updated by Carla Bowers 11/4/11

marginalizing of wild equids even within their legal areas, BLM plans on reducing the nationwide population to an appropriate management level (AML) of only 26,600 wild horses and burros, or ca. 12,000 less than what it still claims live on the public lands today, in spite of several massive roundups that have already occurred this year as of December, 2011. The national AML closely approximates one remaining wild horse or burro for every thousand HMA acres still to be designated for these animals according to BLM's plan. Surely this begs the question: what other users besides livestock, hunters, etc., are displacing the wild horses/burros? Much of this has to do with misplaced alternative energy projects. To wit: we should be installing solar energy captors on our rooftops, not out on the public lands! To continue business as usual would prove devastating to soils, air, and watersheds throughout the West (Debbie Coffey 2010 a & b, pers. comm.; for various articles conduct an Internet search for "Debbie Coffey, independent researcher"). Wild horse/burro activists must keep up the pressure to expose official betrayal of the wild equids. We should perfect and increase our democratic participation in the public review process concerning BLM and USFS plans for the wild equids. In particular, this concerns the periodically reviewed Resource Management Plans, or RMPs, for each BLM district, and the equivalent for US National Forests that bear a legal duty to preserve and to protect as well as to manage wild horses and burros. And we must not shrink from both thinking and acting "outside the box" in order to bring much needed change.

"FAMOUS LAST WORDS"

Though BLM spokesman Tom Gorey claims that his agency does not remove wild horses/burros to make room for livestock, in effect, precisely this is happening. And this applies even more to the Forest Service. The latter had only 3,620 wild horses and burros on its 37 remaining, active territories as of September 30, 2008. Over half of the USFS's original 1971 legal wild horse/burro territories have already been zeroed out; and livestock are pervasive in these still nominally legal wild horse/burro territories. Regardless the exact figures, however, it is clear that both BLM and US Forest Service must restore our national heritage horses and burros within the many million acres of legal herd areas and territories from which they have been almost or totally eliminated.

In his February 24, 2011 press release, BLM director Bob Abbey announced other components of the reforms to include the NAS study, reducing annual removals to 7,600 thus maintaining current numbers (according to BLM), enhancing humane animal care and handling, promoting volunteer monitoring and ecotourism, as well as improving transparency and openness. The promise to limit roundups to 7,600 is proving false (present chapter, 190-191). Nonetheless, it is the wild horse advocates' fervent hope that serious and much needed reforms, not in word only but in deed, will soon be adopted and result in a true restoration of wild horses and burros as long-term viable populations throughout the West. It is our prayer that the pall of negativity toward these animals and their natural freedom will be dispelled. Our dream is that a new dawn will now break for the free life of the wild horses and burros in America and for a nobler, more generous spirit within the very heart of man.

Wild horses and burros must no longer be in the hands of officials who view them more as semi-domesticated livestock than as naturally integrating, returned native wildlife on public lands, not longer in the hands of such officials as recently retired national director Don Glenn, who would hardly ever seriously consider anything any wild horse advocate had to say. Fairer minded individuals must be installed, those who have taken to heart their responsibility to re-infuse the program with a positiveness toward their charges. These persons will possess a new vision for our public lands, one that truly values wild horses and burros and the ecosystems they both inhabit and benefit. They will implement ways to benignly and profitably live with the wild ones. Their greater vision will guide our steps to restore these remarkable animals—and the Earth as a whole. And if it takes the creation of a new government wild equid agency with this mandate, then so be it.

Horses and burros were born of a wedding of power and of beauty, and all past history has now joined—shall we say "conspired" in the positive sense—in order to again grant them a piece of freedom here in their ancient cradle of evolution, the North American continent. Here they contribute so much that is of true and lasting value. Here they have a greater relationship and a greater story still to fulfill.

CHAPTER VII:

HIGHER THOUGHTS

PREAMBLE – THE HEAVENLY VIEW OF LIFE

Perceived from a higher plane, evolution is a marvelous attunement of life's spirit, or consciousness. This is physically expressed in all diverse organisms, but most importantly it is experienced by many individually unique beings enrolled in this school. Throughout the ages of this ever greater unfolding, we regain our true nobility in logical stages that continually open up to greater perfectionings. Philosophers call this the Eternal Return, and this perennial philosophy forms the backbone of many of the world's great religions. I believe that a "deep ecology" (Devall and Sessions 1985) is today again awakening us human souls to our kinship with all the Rest of Life and thereby to God. In essence, this realization of our greater relationship rekindles the universal love that unites all individual members of our great family both on Earth and throughout the universe.

This Universal Love is re-quickened due to our true comprehension of ourselves, both individually and collectively. It is inextricably bound to true self identification and results in a true valuing of each individual and of each family and of all further groupings both on Earth and throughout the universe. It is made possible when we humble our worldly ego to rightly perceive life's essence and thereby the relationship of all living creatures or beings to God – the perfect and whole one, the source. Universal Love results in a true valuing of each individual's great freedom to follow its own unique path, fulfill its own unique role, and prove its own indispensability to the whole. This valuing is also for each collection of individuals, be this a species or a community, etc., as it unfolds freely throughout time and moves as a collective step by step to fulfill its appointed role as a group within the cosmic scheme and for its appointed time.

True identity resides in the individual being, who commands respect even reverence no matter what his/her/its external form, temporal condition, or circumstance. For each one is the essence, pure consciousness. No mere "thing" can compare, for the being is the divine spark, ever united to God, no matter how seemingly confined, limited, or compromised in a physical body in a physical world, for the soul of all manifest life ever exists transcendentally to all that is merely external—created rather than creator.

What kind of a world have we humans created for the noble horses and burros? For what kind of an experience have we set them up? Surely they deserve better, as do all species whose individuals have each uniquely evolved here on Earth over the vast eons of time. These spiritual presences are not merely the repressed slaves of humanity. The great liberating truth concerning life is that we all go forth together in inter-complementary fashion. And the sooner we acquire the wisdom to appreciate and respect the amazingly diverse presences who share planet Earth as home, their natural place and freedom, role and reason, the better for all concerned. We must acquire a naturally and even supernaturally attuned wisdom that will permit us to integrate harmoniously with the Rest of Life. This will be true progress, and it will open all life up to brighter dawnings for the common good. Praise God!

LESSON TO BE LEARNED

We humans must overcome our own egotism, our tendency to value the Rest of Life only inasmuch as this can be possessed and controlled to become a mere appendage of ourselves. The intense resentment expressed by some people, particularly ranchers, against wild, free-living horses and burros in the West has deep roots in human history. Several thousand years ago, people first began catching, taming, and manipulating horses. It is believed that at first they captured wild foals or colts, usually after killing or driving off their mothers (Trippett 1974). But in so doing, they committed a serious transgression against these creatures. By depriving them of their natural liberty and seeking to mold them into mere servants, they disrespected their higher reason in our shared world. They imposed their own egocentric designs upon the horse, just as they had earlier done with domesticated cattle and sheep. From here on, humans increasingly transgressed against these animals' basic integrity, natural fitting, and indispensable freedom. Of course, this situation has been exacerbating for many centuries, and the psychological patterns that support this animal slavery have become ingrained. Consequently, there is a fierce resistance to owning up that involves blind instinct and knee-jerk reaction. Some people upon seeing wild horses can only think of enslaving or killing them, as is true in relation to many other species. But a higher perception of wild horses as fellow beings wearing slightly different forms, and being true to their own nature, dictates a very different relation not only with wild horses but with all of horse-kind, whether slave or free.

ANGELS AMONG US

Today the pervasive conflict between human ego-centeredness and an altruistic identification with life's larger family has become ever more difficult to ignore. This struggle goes on in each of us and in all of us together. When people of compassion such as Velma B. Johnston ("Wild Horse Annie") or Henry Bergh ("the Great Meddler" who founded of the ASPCA [Pace 1942]) took notice of the grossly cruel treatment of horses, wild or domestic, they took valiant and intelligent steps to stop this. And they met with fierce resistance from the perpetrators, often the old guard. Once in the New York of the late 1800s, Bergh resorted to fisticuffs to rescue a fallen horse of burden. Annie also had her scrapes, including with those threatening to kill her, just as they had the mustangs. The latter "came a calling" late one night at the home she shared with her gentle mother Trudie Bronn and which overlooked the sparkling lights of Reno (Henry 1966; Downer 2008). But she was prepared with a loyal dog and a loaded rifle—both quite competent and valuable companions in critical times.

Anyone who reprimands his/her fellow humans even ever so gently by pointing out a better way of relating to fellow beings manifest in slightly different forms but the same in essence, may expect a similar reaction. Yet, the consequences of our failing to act according to the dictates of higher conscience are much worse, especially when taken in the long term, including future generations. This concerns our self-respect, our respect as a species, and, as we should well realize by now, the very future of life on planet Earth. Merely to decry some existing condition of life as wrong without looking to its root cause and indication for needed change, including in one own life, is the epitome of smug hubris and callow irresponsibility.

TRAGIC FATE OF WILD HORSES BEING ROUNDED UP—THE HELL ON EARTH

We would do well to follow the courageous examples of Bergh and Johnston when dealing with the terrible inhumanity to wild equids that is occurring today. One example of this inhumanity occurred at BLM's Salt Lake Wild Horse and Burro Center located near Herriman, Utah. Here hundreds of wild horses were filmed knee-deep in mud and with abscessed shoulder wounds. Some had simply lain down in the ooze and lacked either the will or the strength to get up again. Though national attention was brought to their plight by Lisa Friday of The Cloud Foundation in mid-April 2011, BLM was very slow to relieve the terrible suffering of these horses and finally reacted nearly a week later by removing over one hundred from this pit of despond.

From a humanitarian point of view, most tragic is the large portion of gathered wild horses that go to slaughter in Mexico and Canada. According to the U.S. Department of Agriculture, as of December 22, 2007, year-to-date horse numbers sent to slaughter via New Mexico to Mexico was 16,965, compared to 7,920 horses that had been sent to slaughter via same in 2006. Graphic videos document the terrible suffering of these animals during the slaughter process (www.wildmustangcoalition.org). Some taken at Mexican slaughter plants, or *camales*, show the metal-panel-squeezed horses agonizing during their last struggle for freedom, for very life itself, as a strong arm squeezing a dagger stabs them repeatedly in the neck, a cruel act rarely immediate. Many of BLM's unadoptable wild horses are also going to slaughter plants in Canada, where their mortal remains have become part of a lucrative trade in horse meat to Europe, Asia, especially Japan, etc. Many of these are also wild horses that were adopted but which the owners after having gained title after one year are able to sell to slaughter, even though they signed an agreement that they would not do this. Hopefully a popular bill introduced in August 2010 to the Canadian Parliament to ban commercial import or export of horses for the purposes of slaughter in Canada will soon be passed (see "Health of Animals Act, Bill C-544" 2010). Also encouraging is the European Union's imminent ban on the import of such cruelly slaughtered horse flesh from the Americas and abroad.

PRESENT PLIGHT OF WILD HORSES: CRUELTY, SUFFERING, AND DEATH

There is no greater tragedy today than that which concerns the wild horses and burros who have been removed from the public lands. More wild horses languish today in government holding facilities than are left in their legal BLM and USFS areas throughout the West. Fluctuating according to scale of roundups, as of April 2011, Cindy MacDonald reported (www.americanherds.blogspot.com) over forty-three thousand mainly horses but considerable burros removed from freedom and about sixteen thousand horses/burros still on the public lands. This would make the September 2011 number now in holding around 50,000. As just indicated, a large percentage of these wild equids are being surreptitiously shipped over the borders into Mexico or Canada where they are inhumanely slaughtered and their bodies shipped abroad for human consumption or eaten right in Mexico or Canada. Yet in section 8(4), the act clearly states that no commerce or profit making

as concerns these animals shall be allowed! Whether in Canada or in
Mexico, the methods used frequently do not kill the horses outright;
the horrible result is that far too many are skinned and butchered alive
and in excruciating pain, though I pray that the Biblical verse concerning
God's not giving anyone more pain than he can bear is true. Given their
betrayal by man, when death finally comes it must come as a merciful
liberation to these poor spirits in horse/burro form—and some say
that through suffering a spirit is purified and enabled to rise to higher
spiritual planes. Many of the excessively gathered wild horses who have
been shipped to Canada are slaughtered through the inhumane captive bolt method.[25] Again, I pray that Canadian Bill C-544 will soon be
passed. And we owe a helping hand to the Member of Parliament who
introduced it: Mr. Alex Atamanenko.

Many wild horses are given over to Mexican rodeos, or *charreados*,
where an entertainment known as "horse tripping" occurs. This counts
among the most cruel and sadistic sports ever devised. Though outlawed in most U.S. states, this barbarism is given free reign in Mexico
and elsewhere in Latin America. The Redwings Horse Sanctuary (1995)
of Lockwood, California, has rescued some of the horses destined for
this abysmal sport. Here is how this NGO's officials describe the cruel
practice: "... 'cowboys' get the horses running then throw their lassos
to grab hold of the...innocent horse's legs. The horse crashes to the
ground—often breaking the...animal's legs and/or neck." [After this sadistic treatment, broken, crippled and suffering terribly, the wild horses
are unceremoniously] "dumped at a livestock auction and sold to a
killer buyer." This cruel mockery of horses and the humane laws that
protect them—as well as all human decency—must soon become a
thing of the past.

---

25 The captive bolt method forcefully shoots a steel bolt at the head of the horse with the intent of pen-
    etrating the brain and instant killing the horse. However, the horse's brain is encased in a very solid
    bony structure and is well in the rear of its cranium, making captive bolt killing difficult. Also, the horse
    moves his head around at many different and wide angles because of his long, marvelously designed
    ophistocoelous neck. This makes it very hard for a direct blow and killing. Many blows are glancing.
    And besides this, who has ever asked a horse what he feels? (Grandin 2011)

SLAUGHTER AS A SOLUTION?

Slaughter is such a sad ending for the earthly life of the horse! And for wild horses it would be far better that they be allowed to pass on out in the great and vast wide-open spaces of the West where they were born and lived out their lives. But those perpetrating horse abuse only mock such sentiments. For them it seems that all life—except their own of course—reduces to "bottom line," for their mentalities are definitely at bottom rung. Do horse flesh eaters/promoters, including U.S. Representative Susan Wallis of Wyoming, consider all of the gross injustice, loss of natural freedom, and cruel and prolonged deaths they cause when promoting/ buying/consuming this meat? Perhaps they are dimly aware of this and of much of humanity's strenuous objection to this, as film exposes have been aired in Europe, America, and throughout the world (see www.theamericanwildhorse.com and films: *Saving America's Horse: A Nation Betrayed* by Katia Louise, 2011; *Saving the American Wild Horse* by James Kleinert, 2008; and *El Caballo* by High Plains Film, 2001). Also the Equine Welfare Alliance (www.equinewelfarealliance.org) spearheaded by John Holland and Vicki Tobin has been very active in exposing and confronting the evils of horse slaughter as well as in defending wild horses. Other organizations include the very well informed Animal Law Coalition, as well as Simone Netherland's Respect 4 Horses, which in the fall of 2010 valiantly saved Nevada's beautiful Walker Lake mustang herd from removal by BLM, with help from ardent wild horse advocates such as Carla Bowers and Kudo of ARM.

Local grassroots movements to shut down horse slaughter plants in Metcalf, Illinois and in Bedford, Texas have been successful, but transport of a large portion of America's wild as well as domestic horses through portals in New Mexico and Texas to slaughter plants in Mexico and through portals to Canada, e.g., in Idaho and Montana, continues apace.[26] Unfortunately in November 2011, the U.S. Congress decided to renew funding of federal inspection at U.S. horse slaughter plants, thus permitting their renewed operation after several years of closing.

---

26 Detailed 2007 and 2010 reports by Californian wild horse advocate Valerie James-Patton and John Holland expose this cruel treatment (Google Equine Welfare Alliance) as do the reports of the dedicated Animals' Angels organization.

The inequalities and inequities that so called "civilization" perpetuates have become monstrous. They are, in fact, iniquities! Whether in the U.S, Mexico or in Canada, the vast majority of horses are slaughtered in cruel ways, some even being skinned alive while their blood drains from their slit jugular veins. These are hellish acts to witness, but the hell they are to experience, perhaps only the spirits of the horses know. The resultant "products"—for this is about all horse exploiters seem to regard them as—are packaged and exported for human or animal consumption.[27]

BACK FROM HELL—A WAY FORTH

The greatest laws governing life, including our own, involve morality and abide in the pure consciousness of each one of us, yet are reflected in the external world. Through progressive reawakening to our higher natures, we both can and will rectify our relationships including to soul groups of other kinds in slightly different forms such as horses and burros.

There is a way forth from our present dilemma. The Earth has reached a critical state due to humanity's near exclusive absorption in humanity alone. The proof is to be found in global climate change involving increasingly violent and widespread storms and droughts and in the general ecological breakdown that involves mass species' extinctions, the disappearance of coral reefs, tropical rainforests, wetlands, and polar ice caps. And the desertification that has and continues to result from domestic hordes of ruminant grazers is a plague that threatens nearly half of the terrestrial globe (Downer 1987). Blindly accepted tradition along with thoughtless ecological tinkering is producing the unbridled rape of natural resources of every conceivable type. This includes open-pit mining of micro-grade metal ore bodies that involve consuming entire mountains to obtain a relatively few pounds of gold, etc.; "fracking"

---

27 One encouraging development is that the European Union is placing restrictions on the imports of horse meat, including from Mexico and Canada. This long overdue action is due to a strong campaign to stop such cruel slaughter that reveals both the inhumanity involved here and the toxicity of horse meat including carcinogenic anti-inflammatory "bute" (phenylbutazone) and de-worming chemicals (*Saving the American Wild Horse* 2008).

to extract natural gas from bedrock; and massive processing of oil tar sands—all three of which are massively devastating to Earth's remaining ecosystems! So much of what is killing our planet relates to the gross pollution and contamination of Earth's air, water, soil, and even very living tissues and genomes that our modern lifestyle entails. Indeed, we are reminded every day that while we are the problem, by the same token we are the solution to the problem and that what must be changed does, indeed, concern how we live and what we do every day; and that this depends upon our values in and for life and, so, our very conception of what life basically is, where it has been and where it is going. In all humility, we humans must reconsider our relation with the Rest of Life and its great right to live free in the world of nature and how we ourselves can respectfully restore and harmoniously live at a modest level therewith. If we really do believe in a *Hereafter* and a *"Herebefore"* relating to the spiritual realm, then just why on God's Green Earth are we humans so hellfire bent on cramming this once so beautiful and free planet to overflowing with too many incarnate souls in human form, now exceeding seven billion?!

An elevated state of consciousness is now resulting due to the very crisis we are experiencing. Though it may not seem so from life's mere external view, a great inner awakening is now taking place among all of humanity and among all sentient creatures, and this heralds the long-promised Golden Age, a time when the lamb shall lie down with the lion and all beings shall realize that we are all in this great ship of life together. With this great dawning, our lifestyles shall be transformed. Our relationships with other individuals and kinds will be transformed, as will our relationships even with the so-called "inanimate" world.

When the sun comes up with each new day, I again affirm that a special restoration of freedom is occurring on our shared home planet Earth, and that this freedom is not the freedom for mankind to torture and destroy the Rest of Life, but rather that true freedom for All of Life to realize its true self and place both here and in the universe, both in this time and in all time. This restoration is a further evolvement, and it is not only for humanity but for All of Life together. The words found in the perennial philosophy concerning "the many in the one: the one in the many" (Devall and Sessions 1985) are becoming *living words* indeed, for awakening our hearts, quickening our minds, and being put into practice by dint of an all-uniting inspiration and sacred intent.

We humans must learn to let bygones be bygones as far as our in fact quite tiny and superficial differences go. These are really great nothings that will vanish into non-existence with the Great Rising of the Sun! For God's sake, much, much more unites than divides us, and even in our so-called differences are to be found those indispensable keys by which we complement one another. Similarly, so many possibilities exist for us to unite in achieving a greater harmony with the Rest of Life, including the horses and burros. This greater consideration will meet our inmost needs, if we just recognize a few guiding principles. One I call Life's Precious Freedom. This concerns the basic and inalienable right of each individual and of each kind to pursue and fulfill its own unique course amid the panoply of all fellow beings, of all fellow kinds. To reinstate this freedom, we must sacrifice our unwholesome desire to control and manipulate the Earth and her creatures for narrow, selfish ends that are for humanity or subsets of humanity alone. We must realize that our own true fulfillment cannot be obtained at the expense of the Rest of Life but must be incorporated into a noble holistic vision and motivation that steers forth toward our shared Goal.

HIGHER THOUGHTS INDEED

As concerns this Goal, a spiritual perception of life is essential. By seeing beyond the physical life from birth to death to the greater life before birth and beyond death, we gain the essential perspective that permits us to behave nobly. By realizing physical life's greater source and purpose in the transcendent realm of spirit, our appreciation of life is enhanced and we identify with the "whole of life." We act for life's "common good." We perceive in other life forms not mere appendages of man, but heavenly ordained beings and groups of beings fulfilling their own special yet indispensably interrelated roles. Recognizing life in this higher context, we do not demand all in one short lifetime, but appreciate its grander cyclings and, along with these, its more subtle satisfactions, those born of the higher mind and refined emotion, of a more universal view and identification. And, as with all progressive steps upon Jacob's ladder, each one of us must make sacrifice of the lesser in order to attain the greater. Stepping from a lower to a higher rung, still one realizes that one could not have risen this high without each and every lower tier that supports him. Also remember that the so-called lesser is never lost but only incorporated into the greater whole within our emerging consciousness, our more perfected relationship with *all*.

How do we realize our honorable goals in relation to wild horses and burros and their natural freedom? Each one must answer this question according to one's unique perspective in order to responsibly fulfill one's own special role. This is both possible and necessary. Our inborn conceptions of and ideals for life are not planted in our minds and hearts in vain. Without an awareness of these, our merely going through the mechanics of living seems worthless, but with these, a noble purpose and meaning for life is re-instilled, one that transcends mere externalities, one that is born and reborn and borne within. Our blossoming ideals truly energize us to a higher vibrational plane, increasingly attuning us to a great universal symphony. They overthrow profane idols. They vanquish failure in any as in all lives together.

Life's safety net is composed of interwoven biodiversity, i.e., a great number of harmoniously, mutually related life forms. When people thoughtlessly wipe out vast numbers of individual plants, animals, and decomposers, whole populations and even entire species — as is occurring today — they tear at this mutually sustaining safety net and jeopardize life's long term survival. Here I am reminded of a quote from the German philosopher Friedrich Nietzche in his novel *Thus Spoke Zarathustra*, "I am become destroyer of worlds," for how prophetic this statement has become in relation to humanity today. For these reasons, we must wake up before it is too late! We must learn to identify with life's greater whole, including all plants, animals, and decomposer recyclers, creatures of land and air and sea. We must not remain so exclusively focused on our own kind.

An inherent right to live free and naturally in our shared world belongs to every unique individual and to its kind. Each individual being, whatever its outward form or expression, innately knows how it uniquely fits into the ultimately benign, age-old evolutionary process and how to uniquely act at each successive time. This process sums us all up like the threads that together weave some vast tapestry whose design grows increasingly clear with all succeeding days, years, lives, generations, evolutionary epochs, and very ages. Its conception permits a true vision for all of life together, *not man apart*, for all times past, present, and future—and each instant is all three of these in one, in our shared experience of such.

What are some solutions to our present ecological dilemma? First, let us wisely and compassionately identify with the Rest of Life, including horses and burros and the plants and animals with whom they have coevolved and belong in freedom. Let us respect all creatures, all kinds, and their right – in fact their necessity – to live in natural liberty. Let us more greatly understand and respect the natural home, or habitat, of each particular species and, so, of all species together. Let us recognize and reign in our thoughtless excesses, including our most critical of issues: human overpopulation and over-consumption of nature's bounty. And let us do this out of consideration for the Rest of Life, for by extending our circle of compassion for and our expanded identification with the Rest of Life, we will permit the Whole of Life to recover on planet Earth (Wynne-Tyson 1989).

Let us keep our public servants in the BLM and USFS as well as the President, Congressmen and judges in our prayers that they receive the necessary wisdom and willpower to stand firm in protecting and restoring the horses' and burros' rights to continue along the anciently trodden trails of their ancestors in their evolutionary stomping grounds made sacred by time and the experience of such. May these trails lead us all to a blessed surprise.

Here in the West wild horses are truly reintegrating with the land of their origin on this planet. People should listen to the spiritual song that emanates from this land and its life community, for it is a true rejoicing at the return of America's native sons and daughters, the horses. All the diverse but interrelated plants and animals remember, celebrate and welcome them, for their return to the wild fulfills a promise that has been whispered in the winds of intervening centuries since their brief departure, if in regions where they departed at all (see Chapter 1).

ONE FINAL WORD

We have so much to learn from America's wild horses and burros in the wild. Their lessons concern life's inherent need to live free in a shared world, a world in which each individual and each kind is able to exercise its right to choose its own special path assigned by the Great Spirit and to work out its own special relationship to all. Thank God there are still unfenced places where this is possible! Indeed, this is the very sacred intent of the Wild Free-Roaming Horses and Burros Act of 1971. But Wild Horse Annie would turn over in her grave to learn how the act's intention to restore viable equid populations has been subverted since her departure in 1977. This progressive, ecologically balanced law was passed unanimously, but has been thwarted by possessive people with seared consciences, by people who are, indeed, possessed by their worldly possessions and positions. When we humans only deem our own species to be important, we lose sight of our own true reason for being here, for this has to do with our relation with all the Rest of Life.

But let us not say that all is now and forever lost concerning the wild horses and burros and their freedom in their natural home. The good news is that we can undo past injustices, overcome past shortcomings. The challenge is one of volition! We can learn a better way forth precisely because of the lessons learned from our past mistakes and imperfections, when our vision for life is brought to a higher plane, sparking our will to take the next true step forward.

THE END

ADDITIONAL PHOTOGRAPHS

Figure 19. Two curious, bay-colored brothers with mare grazing in background. Virginia Range, western Nevada. Spring 2007.

Figure 20. Portrait of black band stallion, or "patron." Virginia Range. Spring 2007.

Figure 21. Clapping display toward band stallion. Virginia Range. Spring 2007.

Figure 22. Pregnant sorrel mare with foal amid juniper trees and sagebrush. Flowery Range. 2009.

Figure 23. Bright young foal following mare amid junipers. Flowery Range. W. Nevada. Spring 2007.

Figure 24. Black stallion resting on hillside. Flowery Range. Photo shows typical rocky terrain of mustang habitat. This keeps hooves in fine shape. 2007.

Figure 25. Full of bright expectations, newborn foal with mother and father. Flowery Range near settlement. Note tick-removing bird on back. Spring 2007.

Figure 26. Spry young colt on trail. Flowery Range. 2007.

Figure 27. Hardy wild mustang stallion gives us the eye amid Spanish Bayonet plants. Spring Range, s. Nevada. Spring 2009. Very few mustangs still inhabit this vast legal area, which includes both BLM & USFS lands.

Figure 28. "Friend or Foe?" this dapper stallion & mare pair seem to ask. BLM claimed the horses here were starving! Applewhite HMA near Caliente, Nevada. Area now zeroed out by BLM. Early August 2009.

Figure 29. Colorful pinto band running. S. Steens Mountain, southeastern Oregon. June 2009. In summer 2011, most of this small remnant of Spanish mustangs was removed by BLM helicopter roundups.

Figure 30. Distinctive coloration of Kiger mustang with striping on legs. S. Steens Mountain HMA, southeastern Oregon. June 2009.

Figure 31. Capture of Freedom's band of 12 from Black Rock East HMA. Dave Cattoor with Judas horse being released in background. January 2, 2010.

Figure 32. Panic-stricken horses await an uncertain future. Freedom's corralled band. Many suffer a form of Post Traumatic Stress Disorder for the rest of their lives after the violent roundups that ruthlessly jerk them out of their natural homes and break up their families and herds, which ironically count among the most important factors in stabilizing populations. Black Rock East HMA. Elephant Mountain in background. January 2, 2010.

Figure 33. Charging Freedom summons courage to leap 6' metal capture corral. Black Rock East HMA helicopter roundup. January 2, 2010.

Figure 34. With supernatural acumen and power, Freedom springs up for the final victorious leap to freedom. Is not this the true spirit of America? Black Rock East HMA. Paiute Meadows Ranch in background. January 2, 2010.

Figure 35. After soaring over the 6' metal capture corral, Freedom busts through a tightly strung, three-strand barbed wire fence, from whose nasty wires he deftly disentangled himself in an instant. Black Rock East HMA. January 2, 2010.

Figure 36. Exalting in his valiantly won freedom but incensed by this mean attempt to deprive him of it, Freedom flies back to his rightful home, but not without a sharp pang at having to leave his beloved family in the clutches of the wild horses' worst enemies. Surely they will be restored together in freedom someday. Black Rock East HMA. January 2, 2010. 11:31 AM.

Figure 37. Young Kiger mustang band of three. N. Steens Mountain HMA. This sparse and under-populated herd was gutted by a helicopter roundup in the summer of 2011. Early September 2009.

Figure 38. Bright buckskin Kiger stallion courageously faces a human intruder. N. Steens Mountain HMA. Early September 2009.

Figure 39. Two colorful mustangs frolic in the last rays of day near a spring. Mt. Airy HMA, central Nevada west of Austin. April 11, 2011. 6:40 PM.

Figure 40. Pathetic final repose in death of grayish white mare captured during High Rock helicopter roundup. She broke her upper left leg right after a violent kicking bout after being penned with other bands. May she now find peace and freedom, sanctuary away from all enemies. September 26, 2006. Northwest Nevada. (See pages 172-173 for fuller story.)

Figure 41. Handsome mustang band on last run, fleeing from helicopter. High Rock HMA roundup. From this photo, one can appreciate why they are called "wind drinkers." September 26, 2006.

Figure 42. Young mustang band on rocky knoll. Deer brush on right. Flowery Range, w. Nevada. July 17, 2006.

Figure 43. Bright young filly looks out hopefully on life followed by her protective, loving parent. Note profuse grassy feed. Flowery Range. July 17, 2006.

Figure 44. Strong and confident band mare amid deer brush, juniper and pinyon trees. Flowery Range. Summer 2006. (Rare purplish brown coat of mare.)

Figure 45. Magnificent black stallion with blaze, resting by pinyon pine. Flowery Range. Summer 2006.

Figure 46. Huddled, fearful wild horses who have just been helicopter chased and trucked over dusty, bumpy roads to BLM's Litchfield holding facility, northeastern California. Note exhausted look of bay colt, pinned back ears and presenting of rears by adults. High Rock HMA roundup. September 26, 2006. Dusk.

Figure 47. Same place and time as Figure 46. Note bleeding from left nostril and cut above this on palomino mare. Note also white iris.

Figure 48. High Rock helicopter roundup. Photo shows commotion of just penned, desperate wild horse band breathing hazardous, thick alkali dust. All this horror is perpetrated to maintain a non-profitable and ecologically harmful livestock monopoly on the public lands, and even within the horses legal areas! Sept. 26, 2006.

Figure 49. Offspring of horses in Figures 44 & 45, robust yearling male with friendly outlook. Flowery Range. Summer 2006.

Figure 50. Wild horse band. Eastern Pine Nut HMA. W. Nevada. Stallion on left. Early 1980s.

Figure 51. Sweeping panorama from east Pine Nut Range with hardy wild horse band at dusk. Smith Valley and Sweetwater Range in background, dwarf sagebrush in foreground. Taken during winter, 1970s.

Figure 52. Ready to defend his band, buckskin stallion looks apprehensively our way. Pinyon-juniper wood in n. Pine Nut Range, w. Nevada. 1980.

Figure 53. Famous "Phantom" stallion in his vast and beautiful domain. N. Pine Nut Range Herd Area. 1980.

Figure 54. Agile wild horse band retreats adeptly in burn area. S. Pine Nut Range. 1970s.

Figure 55. With mane flying, pulchritudinous bachelor stallion in prime of life strikes a noble, inquiring pose. S. Pine Nut Range. 1970s.

Figure 56. Vigorous and colorful bachelor band at full attention. S. Pine Nut Range in burn area. 1970s.

Figure 57. Famous "Twosocks" stallion fends off intruding stallion at dusk at Mark Twain, just south of Flowery Range, w. Nevada. 2002.

Figure 58. Young band of colorful horses in central Pine Nut Range meadow surrounded by exuberant pinyon-juniper forest & grass. Spring 1976.

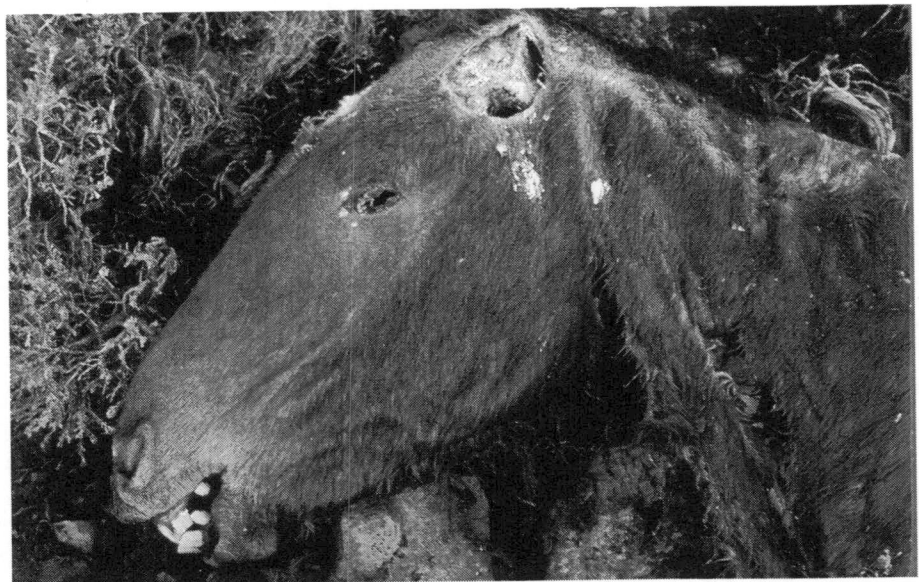

Figure 59. Wild horse illegally shot and left ear taken for illegal bounty. Grass Valley, Callaghan HMA. Toiyabe Range, central Nevada. January 1, 1980.

Figure 60. Violent commotion of penned wild horses during Little Owyhee HMA roundup, north central Nevada. Note thick and hazardous alkali dust and rearing stallion in pen with mixed sexes and ages. August 1991.

Figure 61. Ghostly cowboy figure presents himself at BLM's Palomino wild horse and burro holding facility north of Sparks, Nevada. I did not see this apparition, but the color slide did. WHOA's Dawn Lappin on right of ghost, then BLM's wild horse specialist Andy Anderson further on right. In background is a captive wild burro and Tom Owen, BLM's Carson City District Director. 1981.

Figure 62. Coordinated Resource Management Planning meeting. Central Nevada. 1980.

Figure 63. Fenced off water trough deriving from mountain spring in a wild horse herd area on Nevada BLM land. 1980. This is a typical situation throughout the West.

Figure 64. Cemented off spring source (by rancher). Sunrise Pass Road. Pine Nut wild horse Herd Area near Mineral Peak. 1980. Another typical situation.

Figure 65. Father of author and civil engineer Robert C. Downer on Como Road, n. Pine Nut Herd Area. 1980s.

Figure 66. Elegant light-colored Granite Range wild horse band. Northwest Nevada. August 1981.

Figure 67. Striking young band stallion & "medicine hat," "El Espanto" leads his band away from the human intruder. S. Pancake Range Herd Area, near Sand Springs. E. Nevada. August 1980. Dusk.

Figure 68. Same as Figure 67.

Figure 69. Burnished coopery mustang followed by his dark mare return from watering at spring. Central Flowery Range at midday. Spring 2006. Each one knows his/her special path in life and when to lead and when to follow. We are all indispensably related and here for a noble reason.

Bibliography Including Cited Works with Comments

A

"a Stallion's Courage." 2010 (June 12). http://wildhorsesneedyour. com/?p=1. A magnificent depiction of a wild black stallion and his escape to freedom, leaping out of a six-foot BLM capture corral and crashing through a barbed wire fence in Black Rock East HMA on January 2, 2010, parts of which are verbally described by Craig C. Downer. Video footage by wild horse advocate Bob Bauer of Indiana. Freedom's escape is also the subject of this present book's cover.

Abel, Carrol. Google her wild horse articles published in LA Equine Policy Examiner.

Alison, Robert M. August 19, 2000. "Canada's Last Wild Horses." http://members.shaw.ca/save-wild-horses/Research%20Paper%20 -%20R.%20Alison.htm. Substantiates the fitting place of wild horses in North America through use of evolutionary evidence and declaims against their insensitive and rash elimination in Canada.

Allen, Laura. 2011 (April 2). Call on Congress Now to De-Fund the Wild Horse Roundups. http://rtfitch.wordpress.com/2011/04/02.

American Herds. various years. **http://www.americanherds. blogspot.com**. Well-researched exposes on unfair treatment of wild equids in the United States, especially Nevada and California. Work is primarily by Cindy MacDonald.

Animal Welfare Institute. 2007. *Managing For Extinction: Shortcomings of the Bureau of Land Management's National Wild Horse and Burro Program.* Washington, D.C.: Animal Welfare

Institute. Excellent expose of unfair treatment of wild horses and burros in America with intelligent analysis of the history of the act and facts associated therewith.

———. 2008. Response to the Government Accountability Office's Report, "Bureau of Land Management: Effective Long-Term Options Needed to Manage Unadoptable Wild Horses." Document received from Chris Hyde, November 2008.

B

Baker, Ron. 1985. The American Hunting Myth. New York: Vantage Press.

Barber, Phil. 1989 (Jan. 28). Says Boss Wanted to Rid the Range of Wild Horses. *Reno Gazette Journal.* Article names ranchers and cowboys implicated in massacre of wild horses in central Nevada. Last names of implicated parties include Moorehead, Claypool, Hage, Brennon, and Thacher.

BBC. http://www.bbc.uk/insideout/southeast/series1/wildhorses. shtml. Explains how Konig wild horses are being used to restore Kent county's ecosystem, UK.

Bell, R.H.V. 1970. The use of the herb layer by grazing ungulates in the Serengeti. In *Animal Populations in Relation to Their Food Source.* British Ecological Society Symposium. Ed. Adam Watson. Oxford, U.K.: Blackwell Science Publications. This elaborate study shows how another equid, the zebra (*Equus burchelli*), complements a variety of grazers, including the Thomson's gazelle and the wildebeest by eating coarser, drier grasses. The removal of these allows other types of vegetation to grow. The study describes the seasonally timed movement patterns of the zebras and how these complement those of the other herbivores and relates to an elaborate, mutually supporting system that has evolved over thousands of generations in Africa. Undoubtedly, a similar system existed between equids in North America and other sympatric species of herbivores. Many of the observations of this elegant study apply to the wild horses and burros in North America, including the West, for the horse, far from being a misfit, restores and enhances the native North American ecosystem, and given the right setting, much the same can be said of the burro.

Bennett, D.K. 1980. Stripes do not a zebra make. Part I: A Cladistic Analysis of *Equus*. Syst. Zool. 29: 272-288.

Benton, Michael. 1991. *The Rise of the Mammals*. New York: Crescent Books.

Berger, Joel. 1986. *Wild Horses of the Great Basin: Social Competition and Population Size*. Chicago: University of Chicago Press.

Bergeron, Dick. 2003 (April). Coyote Canyon Horses Gone. *High Country Journal*. Aguanga, California.

Brungardt, Kurt. 2006. Galloping Scared. *Vanity Fair*, November: 224–234. This lively article exposes many irregularities in America's wild horse and burro program through interviews with some of the key players.

C

Cabrera, A. and J. **Yepes**. 1940. Mamiferos Sud-Americanos. Casa Argentina de Editores, Buenos Aires, Argentina.

Carson, Rachel. 1962. *Silent Spring*. Boston, MA: Houghton-Mifflin Co.

Center for Biological Diversity. 2002. Assessing the Full Cost of the Federal Grazing Program. Tucson, AZ: Center for Biological Diversity.

Clotten, Peter. 2009. *Der letzte Mustang*. Muller Ruschlikon Verlag. Stutgart, Germany. Photos by Tony Stomberg. A superbly written (in German) and color-photograph- illustrated book based on personal experience of several western herds by the author and photographer. Kiger herd is described among others.

Cloud Foundation, The. http://www.thecloudfoundation.org/index. php/news-events-a-media/news/wild-horse-issues/454-position-paper-on-pzp-22-contraceptive-drug. Kathrens, Ginger. 2010 (August 17). Position Paper on PZP-22 Contraceptive Drug.

Coffey, Debbie. 2010 a. The BLM's Snow Job About Water on the Twin Peaks Herd Management Area. *The PPJ Gazette.* June 21, 2010. http://ppjg.wordpress.com/2010/06/21/the-blm%E2%80%99s-snow-job-about-water-on-the-twin-peaks-herd-mangement-area/

_____. 2010 b. The Mining of Our Aquifers: As Long as BLM Can Make a Buck Who Cares if the Water is Gone? *The PPJ Gazette.* July 28, 2010. http://ppjg.wordpress.com/2010/07/28/the-mining-of-our-aquifers/.

Cohen, Andrew. 2011 (August). The Quiet War Against Wyoming's Wild Horses. *The Atlantic.* http://www.theatlantic.com/national/print/2001/08/the-quiet-war-against-wyomings-wild-horses/243286/#. Excellent expose of conspiracy against wild ones.

Cohen, Michael P. 1998. *A Garden of Bristlecones: Tales of Change in the Great Basin.* Reno, NV: University of Nevada Press.

Cothran, E. C. and F. J. **Singer.** 2000. Analysis of genetic variation in the Pryor Mountain wild horse herd. In *Managers Summary—Ecological Studies of the Pryor Mountain Wild Horse Range, 1992–1997.* Eds. F. J. Singer and K. A. Schoenecker, 91–104. Fort Collins, CO: U.S. Geological Survey, Midcontinent Ecological Science Center.

Curtin, S., J. **Eastcott** and Y. **Momatiuk.** 1996. *Mustang.* Bearsville, NY: Rufus Publications. Dramatic and intimate account of the day-to-day life of mustangs personally visited, studied and stunningly photographed by the authors.

D

deHaan, C., H. **Steinfeld,** M. **Rosales,** P. **Gerber,** T. **Wassenaar,** and V. **Castel.** 2006. *Livestock's Long Shadow: Environmental Issues and Options.* Rome: Food and Agriculture Organization of the United Nations.

Denhardt, Robert. 1937. Horses in the Americas. Translated from Bernal Dias by Genro Garcia, 1904, In "The Truth About Cortez' Horses." *Hispanic American Review* 17:525–32.

Devall, Bill and George **Sessions**. 1985. *Deep Ecology*. Salt Lake City, Utah: Peregrine Smith Books.

Donlow, J. et al. 2005. Rewilding North America. *Nature* 436(7053):913–14.

Downer, Craig C. 1977. *Wild Horses: Living Symbols of Freedom.* Sparks, NV: Western Printers and Publishers. Illustrated account by author based on studies undertaken while earning M.S. in Biology, specialization Wildlife Ecology at University of Nevada-Reno and including many firsthand observations in the Pine Nut Range of western Nevada. Photos by Wally Ravven, author, and others. Later reprinted in 2007 with some new digital photos of wild horses from western Nevada. Forward by Wild Horse Annie, aka Velma Bronn Johnston.

_____. 1987. Overgrazing is by Humankind. *Bulletin of the Theosophy Science Study Group*, India. 25 (5 & 6): 57-60.

_____. 2001. Observations on the diet and habitat of the mountain tapir (*Tapirus pinchaque*). *Journal of Zoology (London)* 254: 279-291.

———. 2005. Wild and Free-Roaming Horses and Burros of North America: Factual and Sensitive Statement—How They Help the Ecosystem. *Natural Horse* (December) 7(3):10–11.

———. 2008. Conservationist with a Heart: A Brief Sketch of the True Lady Wild Horse Annie, Velma B. Johnston. *Natural Horse* (July-August) 10(4):22–24. Also presented at convention of Nevada Women's History Project in Carson City, NV and presented in altered version on their website: http://www.nevadawomen.org.

_____ 2010. Proposal for Wild Horse/Burro Reserve Design as a Solution to Present Crisis. Presented at BLM Wild Horse and Burro Workshop (6/14/2010) and National Wild Horse and Burro Advisory Board Meeting (6/15/2010).

Denver Colorado. Also published in *Natural Horse*, 2010, Vol. 12, Issue 5, pages 26-27, September-October, under same title.

Duncan, Patrick. 1992. Zebras, Asses, and Horses: An Action Plan for the Conservation of Wild Equids. IUCN Species Survival Commission, Equid Specialist Group. Gland, Switzerland: International Union for Conservation of Nature.

E

Edwards, Robert. 2011. Rangeland Resource Report for American Wild Horse Preservation Campaign. Field review by range manager that provides a scientific basis discrediting wild horse removal plans for White Mountain and Little Colorado wild horse HMAs in BLM Wyoming's Rock Springs Field Office area. (August 4)

El Caballo: Wild Horses of North America. Film. Directed by Doug Hawes-Davis. High Plains Films, 2001. Excellent expose of wild horses' unfair treatment.

F

Fahnestock, Jace T. and James K. **Detling**. 1999. Plant responses to defoliation and resource supplementation in the Pryor Mountains. *J. Range Manage.* 52:263-270. (May)

_____. 1999. The influence of herbivory on plant cover and species composition in the Pryor Mountain Wild Horse Range, USA. *Plant Ecology* 144: 145-157.

Comment: The above two studies indicate that abiotic factors particularly precipitation is more likely than grazing to affect abundance of key plant species and ecosystem dynamics in the Pryor Mountains and that the effects of herbivory are more localized and prevalent in lowland grasses than in other plant groups.

Farley, Gloria. 1994. *In Plain Light: Old World Records in Ancient America.* Golden, CO: Gloria Farley Publications Incorporated.

Fazio, Patricia Mabee. 1995. The Fight to Save a Memory: Creation of the Pryor Mountain Wild Horse Range (1968) and Evolving Federal Wild Horse Protection through 1971. Ph.D. diss., Texas A & M University. Excellent and thorough-going treatment of the wild horse preservation/restoration movement, factually based.

————. 2003. Pers. comm.

Ferguson, D. and N. **Ferguson**. 1983. *Sacred Cows at the Public Trough*. Bend, Oregon: Maverick Publications. Excellent documentation and discussion of livestock monopolization of public lands.

Fite, Katie. 2010 (January 29). Katie on Calico. http://americanherds. blogspot.com/2010/01/katie-on-calico.html. Excellent dissection of a flagrant case of Winnemucca BLM's conspiracy to deprive wild horses within their legal herd area of Black Rock East, northwest Nevada.

Forsten, Ann. 1992. Mitochondrial-DNA timetable and the evolution of *Equus*: comparison of molecular and paleontological evidence. *Ann. Zool. Fennici* 28:301–309.

Fuller, Alexandra. 2009. Spirit of the Shrinking West: Mustangs. *National Geographic*, February: 100–117. Reveals many discrepancies between the law and the actual treatment of returned native wild horses in North America.

G

Germain, Jyoti Annette. 2009. Wild Horses: Wild Innocents, A Report on Federal Government Management of America's Wild Mustangs and Burros, & The Grassroots Campaign to Restore Them to Their Original Habitat & Ecological Niche. Unpublished manuscript. A thoroughgoing and erudite treatise on America's wild horses and burros by a college graduate in equine science, Santa Rosa College, California. 44 pages with bibliography; equinedeliverance@aol.com for $15 copy.

Get X News. http://www.getxnews.com/2010/02/wild-horses-to-help-white-cliffs-wildlife-thrive/. Excellent article explaining how horses restore wildlife and their ecosystem in southeast England with photos of introduced Konig wild horses.

Grandin, Temple. 2011 (Jan. 4). Speech given at Horse Summit, South Point Casino, Las Vegas, Nevada.

Groff, A. L. 2008. America's Wild Horses Will Roam Free Under New Legislation. Press release of House Natural Resource Committee (February 12). U.S. House of Representatives. See also http://resourcescommittee.house.gov.

Groves, Colin P. 1974. *Horses, asses and zebras in the wild.* London: Newton Abbot Publishers.

Grzimek, Bernhard. 2004. *Grzimek's Animal Life Encyclopedia.* 2nd ed. Farmington Mills, MI: Gale. See sections on horse feeding ecology on pages 141, 220, 228 and surrounding pages. To quote from page 141: "The ruminant is faced with being more selective in its feeding. In contrast, the hindgut fermentors, such as some perissodactyls (e.g., modern horses) are able to increase the rate that food passes through their gut, so they extract only the most readily digestible fraction of the food and excrete the indigestible material. As a result, although they must feed almost continuously, they can be much less selective in what they eat. This allows horses to survive on poorer-quality food than artiodactyls are able to do" [i.e., dry flammable vegetation]. To quote from page 228, Feeding Ecology and Diet: "Equids are primarily grazers and have dental adaptation for feeding on grasses. Their high-crowned molars with complex ridges allow them to effectively grind grasses with higher-fiber content. Though individuals will select the most nutritious and low-fiber forage, they can process senescent [dying] and higher fiber grasses. Equids also have a single stomach and hindgut fermentation. This allows them to digest and assimilate larger amounts of forage during a 24-hour period. By contrast, ruminants with a four-chambered stomach are limited in the volume of forage that can be digested in a 24-hour period. Equids are more effective in assimilating forage and can tolerate and survive on a greater breadth of diet in terms of relative forage qualities/nutrition."

H

Hague, Holland. 2007. On the Report of a 1,000-2,000 Year-old Horse Find In Winnemucca Flats, Nevada. Unpublished report of Hague. (February 27)

Haile, J. et al. 2009. Ancient DNA reveals late survival of mammoth and horse in interior Alaska. *Proceedings of the National Academy of Sciences* (December 29) 106. no. 52:22352–22357. See also http://www.pnas.org/cgi/doi/10.1073/pnas.0912510106.

Handwerg, Katherine. 1980. Grazing Fees and Fair Market Value. Eugene, OR: Cascade Holistic Economic Consultants. Very penetrating analysis.

Harmonay, Maureen. Google her articles on wild horses published in LA Equine Policy Examiner.

Harris Rees, Charlotte. 2011. Chinese Sailed to America Before Columbus. www.asiaticfathers.com

"Health of Animals Act" Bill C-544. 2010. http://www.parl.gc.ca/HousePublications.aspx?DocId=4633655&File=30&Language=E&Mode=1. Bill before the Canadian Parliament to forbid both the import and the export of horses for slaughter for human consumption. This would stop import of both wild and domestic horses into Canada from the US.

Henderson, Claire. 1991. Statement of Claire Henderson in Support of Senate Bill 2278 (North Dakota). Anthropologist brings out little recognized facts concerning already present horses in America when Columbus arrived in 1492.

Henry, Marguerite. 1966. *Mustang: Wild Spirit of the West.* San Francisco: Rand McNally & Co. Somewhat embellished account of Wild Horse Annie's life, but true to its spirit. Well illustrated by drawings.

Holland, John. 2010. Research Paper: Horse Slaughter Trends from 2006 to 2009. Chicago: Equine Welfare Alliance. February.

Holland, John and Vicki **Tobin**. 2010 (July 27). How do you make 2000 horses disappear? Let BLM manage them. Equine Welfare Alliance. http://equinewelfarealliance.org/uploads/Missing-Horses-Final.pdf.

Horsetalk. "Judge prevents removal of entire wild horse herd." Accessed April 5, 2009, http://www.horsetalk.co.nz/news/2009/08/054.shtml. News item regarding BLM's obstinate stance on zeroing out of West Douglas wild horse herd.

Hubert, Marie-Luce. 2007. *Mustangs: Wild Horses of the West*. Buffalo, NY: Firefly Books. Excellent photos and description of day-to-day life of wild horses based on first hand observations over all seasons of the year.

Hudak, Mike. 2007. *Western Turf Wars: The Politics of Public Lands Ranching*. Binghamton, NY: Biome Books. A very timely expose of the livestock industry's monopoly of the U.S. public lands. Especially see interview with Bobbi Royle of Wild Horse Spirit, pages 297-307.

I

Illinois State Museum. 2004. FaunMap. Springfield, IL.

International Union for Conservation of Nature Species Survival Commission. 1996. IUCN Red List of Threatened Species. Gland, Switzerland: IUCN.

J

Jacobs, Lynn. 1991. *Waste of the West: Public Lands Ranching*. Tucson, AZ: Arizona Lithographers

James-Patton, Valerie. 2010 (July 29). A Slick In The Night. Equine Welfare Alliance. http://equinewelfarealliance.org/uploads/A_Slick_in_the_night_VJP.pdf.

Janis, C.M. 1976. The evolutionary strategy of the Equidae and the origins of rumen and cecal digestion. *Evolution* 30:757–74. This explains in eloquent terms how equids are capable of thriving in what would be to other herbivores very marginal ecosystems, such as the desert valleys and ranges of Nevada, especially compared with ruminants evolved in moister, more lush and verdant biomes, such as Hereford or Black Angus cattle.

Jenkins, S.H. and M.C. **Ashley**. 2003. Wild Horse, *Equus caballus* and Allies. Ch.53 In Wild Mammals of North America: Biology, Management and Conservation. 2nd Ed. Eds. G.A. Feldhamer, B.C. Thompson, & J.A. Chapman. Baltimore and London: The John Hopkins Univ. Press. See pages 1148-1163. Contains a discussion of density dependent population limiting factors as well as many other aspects of wild horse biology, including evolution and ecology. Quoting from page 1159: "[Wild] horses and burros are intensively and expensively managed by federal agencies in the United States ... [m]uch of this management, however, rests on assumptions about impacts of equids on plant communities and on other herbivores that have not been tested experimentally." From page 1158: "... the National Research Council (1982) concluded that sociopolitical as well as ecological factors influenced decisions about appropriate management levels ... and this still appears to be true ... many populations of [wild] horses ... are well below ecological carrying capacity ..."

Joseph, Frank. 1999. Giants of the California Desert. *Ancient American* 4(27): 11-13. April-May.

K

Kathrens, Ginger. 2009. Cloud: Challenge of the Stallions. Another very fine and personable account by award-winning filmmaker of the Cloud series of PBS *Nature* series of films. A real treasure that takes the reader inside Montana's Pryor Mountain Wild Horse Sanctuary.

Kesper, R. R. and M.A. **Keenan**. 1980. Nocturnal activity patterns of feral horses. *Journal of Mammalogy* 61:116–18.

Kirkpatrick, J. F. and P. M. **Fazio**. 2005. Wild Horses as Native North American Wildlife: Statement for the 109th Congress (1st Session) in Support of H.R. 297: A Bill in the House of Representatives. January 25. http://www.wildhorsepreservation.com/pdf/Wild_ Horses_as_Native_North_American_Wildlife.pdf

————. 2008. Ecce Equus. *Natural History*, May: 30.

Kleinert, James Anaquat. Wild horse filmer. See "Saving The American Wild Horse."

Klingel, Hans. 1979. A Comparison of the Social Organization of the Equids. In Symposium on the Ecology and Behavior of Wild and Feral Equids. Proceedings: University of Wyoming. Laramie. September 6–8, 1979 (*op. cit.* University of Wyoming).

Knapp, George. 2007. Pers. comm.
[see under "Stampede to Oblivion" and "Wildfire Burns …"]

Kuchinsky, Yuri. 2005. Frank Gilbert Roe on Very Early Indian Horses. http://www.globalserve.net/~yuku/tran/9h0.htm

Kunzig, Robert. 2008. Drying of the West. *National Geographic*, February: 90–113.

L

Landrieu, Mary. 2010 (July 28). Wild horses symbolize U.S. freedom. Speech before U.S. Senate by Democratic senator from Louisana in opposition to cruel and massive roundups.

Lindsay, E. H., N. D. **Opdyke**, and N. **Johnson**. 1980. Pliocene dispersal of the horse *Equus* and late Cenozoic mammalian dispersal events. *Nature* 287:135–38.

Lococo, Andrea. 2005. Fact, fiction on West's wild horses. *Denver Post*. Excellent debunking of BLM's myths against wild horses and burros. http://www.denverpost.com/opinion/ci_2776716. June 5.

Long, Steven. 2011. Federal Probe Raises Questions About 47 Seized BLM Horses Going Out of Holding Pens to Alleged Slaughter Ring. *Horseback Magazine*, Texas. http://horsebackmagazine.com/hb/archives/10582. (August 1)

Looking Horse, Arvole. 2008. Pers. comm. At Wild Horse Summit, Las Vegas, NV, morning of Monday October 13, 2008. Reachable through International Society for the Protection of Mustangs and Burros (ISPBM), P.O. Box 55, Lantry, SD 57636.

Luis, C., C. **Bastos-Silveira**, E. G. **Cothran**, and M. **Do Mer Oom**. 2006. Iberian Origins of New World Horse Breeds. *Journal of Heredity* 97(2):107–113.

M

MacDonald, Cindy R. 2007. "Wild Burros of the American West: A Critical Analysis of the National Status of Wild Burros on Public Lands 2006." February. http://www.americanherdsxtras,blogspot.com/2008/01/burros.html

———. 2008. "America's Mustangs & Burros: What's Left, The High Costs of Miscalculating, and Will They Survive. July http://americanherdsxtras.blogspot.com/2008/07/americas-mustangs-burros-whats-left.html.

———. 2008. "88 Million Acres?" November 24. http://americanherds.blogspot.com/2008/11/88-million-acres.html.

MacDonald, David. 2001. *The New Encyclopedia of Mammals*. New York, NY: Oxford University Press. See pages 456–458 and 471–472. To quote: "Food is fermented after passing through the stomach, so the passage rate of vegetation is not as limited as it is in the ruminant grazers, enabling equids to consume large quantities of low-quality forage and to sustain themselves on more marginal habitats and on diets of lower quality than ruminants. Even when vegetation grows rapidly, equids forage for about 60% of the day and up to 80% when conditions worsen."

MacFadden, Bruce J. 1992. *Fossil horses: systematics, paleobiology, and evolution of the family Equidae*. Cambridge, U.K.: Cambridge University Press. Valuable compendium and analysis of information. Among other sections, be sure to check out Chapter 12: Population Dynamics, Behavioral Ecology, and "Paleoethology" and also page 112.

Martin, P. S. 2005. *Twilight of the mammoths: ice age extinctions and the rewilding of America.* Berkeley, CA: University of California Press.

Martin, P. S. and H. E **Wright**. 1967. *Pleistocene Extinctions.* New Haven, CT: Yale University Press.

Meeker, Jo O. 1979. "Interactions Between Pronghorn Antelope and Feral Horses in Northwestern Nevada." Master's of Science Wildlife Management thesis, University of Nevada-Reno.

Milkweed, The. 2011. Japanese Trading Sushi for U.S. Horsey? April. Page 3. Publication of a milk producers' association in U.S.

Mitchell, Jim. 1986. "Nature may be limiting wild horse population." *Reno Gazette Journal*, page 34. (July 6)

Morrison, J. C., W. **Sechrest**, E. **Dinerstein**, D. S. **Wilcove**, and J. F. **Lamoreux**. 2007. Persistence of Large Mammal Fauna as Indicators of Global Human Impacts. *Journal of Mammalogy* 88(6):1363–80.

Mullen, F. X., Jr. 2010. Wild horses: Managed wisely or to extinction? *Reno-Gazette Journal*, 21 March. Page 1 and following pages. Illustrated. Brings up unfairness issue of relative resource allocations, zeroed out herd areas, favoritism to ranchers, low population numbers, etc.

N

National Research Council (U.S.). 1980. Wild and Free-Roaming Horses and Burros: Current Knowledge and Recommended Research. Phase I: Final Report of the Committee on Wild and Free-Roaming Horses and Burros. Washington, D.C.: National Technical Information Service.

——————————————————. 1982. Wild and free-roaming horses and burros/ Final report. National Academy Press. Washington, D.C.

Neff, J. C. et al. 2008. "Increasing eolian dust deposition in the Western United States linked to human activity." http://www.nature.com/ngeo/journal/v1/n3/full/ngeo133.html

Nevada Cooperative Extension. A homeowner's guide to cheatgrass. #29-W65/99. Reno, NV: Nevada Cooperative Extension. (Date unavailable.)

Nock, Bruce. 2010. "Wild Horses—the Stress of Captivity." In BLM Calico Complex Roundup: A Case Study of a Broken System for Horses and Taxpayers. http://www.wildhorsepreservation. com/pdf/death-report.pdf. Erudite account of suffering, harm and death incurred due to helicopter chase roundups of wild horses by a veterinarian and professor.

Novak, Anne. 2010. Breaking News: Public Outrages—BLM Castrates Captured Mustangs in Secrecy. http://<u>www.thecloudfoundation. org</u>/index.php/news-events-a-media/press-release/335-public-alarm-grows-as-blm-castrates-captured-mustangs-behind-closed-doors. News release.

O

Oelke, Hardy. 1997. Born Survivors on the Eve of Extinction: Can Iberia's Wild Horse Survive Among America's Mustangs. Wipperfurth, Germany.

Oxley, Ralph and Craig **Downer**. 1994. "Deserts" In *Nature Worlds*, Tony Hare, ed. London: MacMillan Reference. See especially page 116.

P

Pace, Mildred Mastin. 1942. *Friend of Animals: The Story of Henry Bergh*. New York: C. Scribners's Sons. Excellent portrayal of the brave fight of this man for better treatment of horses and other animals.

Peck, Sheila. 1998. Chapter 5. Reserve Design. In: *Planning for Biodiversity: Issues and Examples*. Washington, DC: Island Press. Pages 89-114.

Pelligrini, Steven W. 1971. "Home range, territoriality and movement patterns of wild horses in the Wassuk Range of Western Nevada." Master's thesis, University of Nevada-Reno. Explains how wild horses naturally establish individual band home ranges and even defended territories in some seasons. The latter space their groups within the mountains and adjacent valleys they inhabit.

Pittman, J. 2008. Funds for wild horse lands and care strained. *Santa Cruz Sentinel,* 25 February.

Public Employees for Environmental Responsibility (PEER). 1997. "Horses to Slaughter—Anatomy of a Coverup within the BLM (1997-04-01)." http://www.peer.org/pubs/whitepapersid. php?row_id=14

R

Redwings Horse Sanctuary. 1995. Published Newsletter. Lockwood, CA. (as per Barbara Clarke, former director, 8/18/2011). (Title unavailable.)

Ricklefs, R. E. 1979. *Ecology*, 2nd ed. New York: Chiron Press. See pages 51-65; 382-384.

Rifkin, Jeremy. 1992. *Beyond Beef: The Rise and Fall of the Cattle Culture.* New York: Dutton. Excellent and thorough-going expose of humanity's blind promotion of livestock as a way of life and the devastating consequences this is having for life on Earth.

Roe, Frank Gilbert. 1955. *The Indian and the Horse*. Norman, OK: University of Oklahoma Press.

Rogers, P., and J. **LaFleur**. 1999. Cash Cows: Taxes support a Wild West holdover that enriches ranchers and degrades the land. *San Jose Mercury News,* 7 November. Another excellent expose with many facts and figures.

Rogovin, K.A. and M.P. **Moshkin**. 2007. [Autoregulation in mammalian populations and stress: an old theme revisited]. Zhurnal obshchei biologii 2007; 68(4):244-67. (In Russian)

Ryden, Hope. 1999. *America's Last Wild Horses*. 30th Anniversary Edition. New York: The Lyons Press. Excellent discussion of wild horses. This is the book that helped pass the Wild Horse Act in 1971. A must read.

S

Salter, R. E., and R. J. **Hudson**. 1979. Feeding ecology of feral horses in Western Alberta. *Journal of Range Management* 32:221–225.

Saving the American Wild Horse. Film. Directed by James Kleinert. Teluride, CO: Moving Cloud Productions, 2008. For more information see http://www.theamericanwildhorse.com

Simonds, Mary Ann. Pers. comm. At the Wild Horse Summit in Las Vegas, NV, in October, 2008.

Simpson, George Gaylord. 1951. *The story of the horse family in the modern world and through sixty million years of history.* Oxford, U.K.: Oxford University Press.

———. 1965. The Geography of Evolution: Collected Essays. Chilton: Philadelphia, PA. See Figure 24.

Sonner, Scott. 2010 (April 27). 2 NV men plead not guilty to killing 5 mustangs. Associated Press, Reno.

South Dakota Historical Society. 1938. Archives. Prince Frederick Wilhelm of Wurtemberg. First Journey to North America in the years 1822 to 1823.

Spirit: Stallion of the Cimarron. Animated film. Directed by Kelly Asbury and Lorna Cook. Universal City, CA: DreamWorks Productions, 2002.

"Stampede to Oblivion." KLAS-TV. November 2009. Excellent expose on mistreatment of America's last wild horses by award-winning producer George Knapp. Aired on CBS Channel 8 TV, Las Vegas. Recognized as Edward R. Murrow top award for region. See statement by Robbie Frank and others about tall flammable grass and increased fire after BLM helicopter roundups of wild equids.

Steelman, Claude. 2008. Colorado's Wild Horses. Durango, CO: Wildshots, Inc. A beautiful photo-illustrated book on Colorado's herds told by one who knows them all. Wonderful photos of the horses and their setting.

Steinfeld, H. and T. **Wassenaar**. 2007. The Role of Livestock Production in Carbon and Nitrogen Cycles. *Annual Review of Environment and Resources* 32:271–292.

Stillman, Deanne. 2008. *Mustang: the Saga of the Wild Horse in the American West.* Boston: Houghton Mifflin Co. See part III: Last Stand. Excellent research on history of wild horses in America.

Stolzenburg, William. 2006. Where the Wild Things Were. *Conservation in Practice* (January-March) 7(1):28–34.

Sussman, Karen. 2008. Various articles. *Journal of the International Society for the Protection of Mustangs and Burros.* 48(1):4–8.

T

Thompson, Gunnar. 2006. *Secret Voyages.* Seattle, WA: Misty Isles Press.

Trimble, Stephen. 1999. *The Sagebrush Ocean: A Natural History of the Great Basin.* Reno, NV: University of Nevada Press.

Trippett, Frank. 1974. *The First Horsemen.* The Emergence of Man Series. New York: Time-Life Books.

U

United Press International (UPI). 1981. Wild Horse Roundup 'Fouled Up' Research. *Casper Star-Tribune,* 26 September.

University of Cincinnati. 2008. "Exploding Asteroid Theory Strengthened by New Evidence Located in Ohio." Indiana Science Daily, 3 July. http://www.sciencedaily.com/releases/2008/07/080702160950.htm

University of Wyoming. 1979. Proceedings of the Symposium on the Ecology and Behavior of Wild and Feral Equids. Laramie, WY, September 6–8, 1974. Laramie, WY: University of Wyoming.

Important note: for all years of the *Public Land Statistics*
including below go to http://www.blm.gov/public land
statistics/index.htm Click on year.

U.S. Department of the Interior. Bureau of Land Management.
2002. *Public Land Statistics 2002.* Washington, D.C.: USDI.

U.S. Department of the Interior. Bureau of Land Management.
2007. *Public Land Statistics 2006 (April 2007).* Vol. 191.
BLM/BC/ST-07/001+1165. And later volumes. Washington, D.C.:
USDI.

U.S. Department of the Interior. Bureau of Land Management.
2008. *Public Land Statistics 2008.* Washington, D.C.: USDI. For
more information, conduct an Internet search for "BLM wild
horse and burro."

U.S. Department of the Interior. Bureau of Land Management.
2010. *Public Land Statistics 2010.* Washington, D.C.: USDI.

U.S. Department of the Interior. 2010 (June 21). The
Department of Interior's Economic Contributions. Washington,
D.C.: USDI.

U.S. Forest Service. 2000. *Statistical Summary Fiscal Year 2000.*
Washington, D.C.: USDA-FS.

U. S. General Accounting Office. 1990. Rangeland Management:
Improvements Needed in Federal Wild Horse Program. Doc.
#RCED-90-110 (August). Washington, D.C.: GAO.

U. S. Government Accountability Office. 2005. Livestock Grazing:
Federal Expenditures and Receipts Vary Depending on the
Agency and the Purpose of the Fee Charged. Doc. #GAO-05-
869 (September). Washington, D.C.: GAO.

U. S. Government Accountability Office. 2008. Bureau of Land
Management: Effective Long-Term Options Needed to Manage
Unadoptable Wild Horses. Washington, D.C.: GAO.

V

Vaughn, Terry A. 1972. *Mammalogy*. Philadelphia: W.B. Saunders Co.

Vila, Carles *et al.* 2001. Widespread origins of domestic horse lineages. *Science* 291:474–477. Confirms Forsten's findings regarding origin of modern horse in North America.

Vincent, Carol Hardy. 2009 (Dec.1). Wild Horses and Burros: Current Issues and Proposals. Washington, DC: Congressional Research Service. 7-5700. www.crs.gov.

W

Walker, Carol. 2008. Wild Hoofbeats: America's Vanishing Wild Horses, 2nd Ed. Longmont, CO: Painted Hills Publishing. Another beautifully photo-illustrated and verbally described book about Americans last wild horses, concentrating especially on Wyoming's magnificent but vanishing herds.

Walker, Ernest P. 1999. *Walker's Mammals of the World*. 6th Edition. Vol. II. Baltimore, MD: John Hopkins University Press.

Watson, Carol Knight. 2011. Is the BLM Living Up to Its Announced Reforms of 'new normal' for Doing Business? Leary, GA: *Newsletter of Amberwood Sanctuary*. July 14.

Watt, Terry. 2008. Pers. comm. by email. Ms. Watt can be reached for photos and evidence at blazingsaddles@npgcable.com.

Webpages, various. Including references for Chapter IV regarding bills, etc., concerning wild horses: www.thecloudfoundation. org, www.wildhorsespirit.org, www.wildhorsepreservation. org, www.wildmustangcoalition.org, ww.horsefund.org, http:// www.americanherds.blogspot.com, www.theamericanwildhorse. com, http://homepage.mac.com/john.brian/wild Horses/Wild Horse Ecology.html, www.humaneobserver.blogspot.com, www. savingamericashorses.org, www.stophorseroundups.org, http:// wildhorsesneedyou.com/?p=1, www.saveourwildhorses.org, www.ahdf.org.

Wheat, Margaret M. 1967. *Survival Arts of the Primitive Paiutes*. Reno, NV: University of Nevada Press.

Whitaker, Nancy. 1999. Wild Horses: the Feral Animal Label. *The Southeast Horse Report Wild and Free*. Vol. III No. 11. November. Very insightful article from wild horse advocate concerning the psychological warfare used against wild equids.

White Randall. 2003. *Prehistoric Art: The Symbolic Journey of Humankind*. New York: Abrams.

"Wildfire Burns 2,000 Acres at Red Rock Canyon." KLAS-TV. 2007. Report by George Knapp. http://www.8newsnow.com/ story/5374510/wildfire-burns-2000-acres-at-red-rock-canyon.

Wild Horses of the Nevada Desert. Film. Directed by Peter Dallas. Sacramento, CA: Wavelength Productions, 1987. Author guided filmmaker and wrote narrative for much of this film produced for Nevada Commission for the Preservation of Wild Horses.

"Wild Lightning and Friends." 2010 YouTube Created by Elyse Gardner, Humane Observer. http://www.youtube.com/ watch?v=D_Np5WxNAEU. Shows film footage by Bob Bauer and stills by Craig Downer of Lightning and his band taken in October 2009, when they were still free in the Calico Mountains, northwestern Nevada. April 4.

Williams, Jim. 1978. Mustangs Doing Just Fine. *Reno Evening Gazette*. Letter to Editor. October 14.

Wuerthner, George and Mollie **Matteson**, eds. 2002. *Welfare Ranching: The Subsidized Destruction of the American West*. Washington, D.C.: Island Press. Excellent documentation and illustrations proving livestock's very damaging effect in many ways and places.

Wynne-Tyson, Jon. 1989. *The Extended Circle: A Commonplace Book of Animal Rights*. New York: Paragon House.

Z

Zimov, S.A. 2005. Pleistocene park: return of the mammoths' ecosystem. *Science* 308:796–98. Indicates great importance of horses to establishing and maintaining tundra grassland that has a cooling effect on the earth's atmosphere. Their reintroduction in parts of Siberia is proposed as a way of preventing further global warming, especially given accelerating melting of the permafrost. This would also apply to northern North America.

INDEX

F

G

Made in the USA
Lexington, KY
08 April 2012